Toxic Demography

Toxic Demography

Ideology and the Politics of Population

JENNIFER D. SCIUBBA
MICHAEL S. TEITELBAUM
AND
JAY WINTER

OXFORD
UNIVERSITY PRESS

Oxford University Press is a department of the University of Oxford. It furthers the University's objective of excellence in research, scholarship, and education by publishing worldwide. Oxford is a registered trade mark of Oxford University Press in the UK and in certain other countries.

Published in the United States of America by Oxford University Press
198 Madison Avenue, New York, NY 10016, United States of America.

CIP data is on file at the Library of Congress.

ISBN 9780197745045
ISBN 9780197745038 (hbk.)

DOI: 10.1093/oso/9780197745038.001.0001

Paperback printed by Integrated Books International, United States of America
Hardback printed by Lightning Source, Inc., United States of America

The manufacturer's authorized representative in the EU for product safety is Oxford University Press España S.A. of Parque Empresarial San Fernando de Henares, Avenida de Castilla, 2 – 28830 Madrid (www.oup.es/en or product.safety@oup.com). OUP España S.A. also acts as importer into Spain of products made by the manufacturer.

Contents

List of Figures

List of Tables

Acknowledgments

Jennifer Sciubba thanks the Woodrow Wilson International Center for Scholars for research support for the chapters on Asia provided during her fellowship.

List of Abbreviations

AfD	*Alternative für Deutschland*/Alternative for Germany
AFL–CIO	American Federation of Labor–Congress of Industrial Organizations
AIAN	American Indian and Alaskan Native people
CCP	Communist Party of China
CDC	Centers for Disease Control and Prevention (USA)
CMIO	China, Malay, Indian, Other (Singaporean classification)
EEC	European Economic Community
EIP	Ethnic Integrated Housing Policy (Singapore)
EPL	Eugenic Protection Law (Japan)
ERA	Equal Rights Amendment
EU	European Union
FIS	Islamic Salvation Front (Algerian)
FRED	Federal Reserve economic data
GDP	gross domestic product
IMF	International Monetary Fund
IUD	intrauterine device
JACL	Japanese-American Citizens' League
KFF	Kaiser Family Foundation
LGBTQ	lesbian, gay, bi, trans, and queer people
MPI	Migration Policy Institute
NAFTA	North American Free Trade Agreement
NATO	North Atlantic Treaty Organization
NGO	nongovernmental organization
OECD	Organization of Economic Cooperation and Development
PAP	People's Action Party (Singapore)
SCAP	Supreme Commander for the Allied Powers (in Japan)
SCNR	Supreme Council for National Reconstruction (Korea)
SEIU	Service Employees International Union
SGD	Singapore dollar
TPS	temporary protected status
UAW	United Auto Workers
USAMGIK	United States Military Government in Korea
USSR	Union of Soviet Socialist Republics

Introduction

Between mid-2022 and mid-2023, four unprecedented global population milestones captured international news headlines. First, in July 2022, the United Nations posted a summary of its most recent population estimates, which announced that for the first time ever, two of every three people worldwide lived in a country with below-replacement fertility rates (the number required to keep the population size steady over time).[1] That November they announced that world population had officially reached 8 billion. Then, in January 2023, Chinese officials announced that the country had experienced its first population decline since the Great Leap Forward.[2] In April 2023, the UN announced that India had overtaken China as the world's most populous country.[3]

Each of these monumental demographic milestones triggered a rainbow of reactions among political elites (a group that includes policymakers, political figures, business leaders, media, and academics), but none so varied as the shift from high to low global fertility rates. Some expressed relief and saw the decline in global fertility rates as a victory in a decades-long quest to curb population growth on a crowded planet. In fact, neo-Malthusian environmentalists continued to advocate vocally for birth rates to go even lower. Others saw the same numbers and panicked, worried about labor shortages and strained national budgets with underfinanced pension and other entitlement programs. A click to the headlines would have shown global leaders, from Japan's prime minister to billionaire Elon Musk, warning that depopulation was nothing short of the collapse of civilization.[4]

Demographers often measure current fertility rates using the "total fertility rate"—a technical calculation that seeks to summarize the number of children that would be born to the average woman over her reproductive lifetime if current fertility and mortality rates by age were to continue. By this measure, global fertility rates have declined to about 2.25, about 7 percent above the notional "replacement" rate of 2.1. One might think that such estimates would be viewed as relatively benign and value-neutral, so it is appropriate to ask why they are seen in apocalyptic terms by some prominent world figures. In large part such concerns relate to national and regional fertility rates that are far lower than the global average. In Europe the total fertility rate is 1.4. It is 1.6 in Northern America and 1.03 in East Asia.

Toxic Demography. Jennifer D. Sciubba, Michael S. Teitelbaum, and Jay Winter, Oxford University Press.

DOI: 10.1093/oso/9780197745038.003.0001

Of course, these low rates become of particular concern to some when compared to persistently high rates in regions like Middle Africa, where the total fertility rate is 5.45, and Central Asia, where the rate is 3.2 children per woman on average.[5]

Explanations of fertility declines to low levels have long been a topic of contention. While there is consensus among researchers that the past two centuries have seen a powerful "transition" in demographic regimes from one of high-mortality and high-fertility to low-mortality and low-fertility, there is far less agreement about the social and economic drivers that underlie this transition. Moreover, few researchers projected fertility rates to decline as far below replacement level as has occurred in some countries and regions.

As might be expected, efforts to explain such low fertility and to anticipate the implications of such phenomena in political terms vary even more widely, sometimes even wildly. Fertility decisions are complicated and sensitive, and are made by millions of couples or individuals. Governments usually have only indirect impacts on such decisions. If governments believe that high costs of housing or childcare or healthcare are important factors, they can choose to subsidize such costs, or offer other incentives. But financial incentives may have little effect if cultural or other reasons are strong fertility drivers. More people are valuing independence and leisure time over raising a family; some women see marriage and family life as "patriarchal" social institutions that limit their freedom.[6] Those reasons are far from politically neutral. In fact, they go to the heart of some of the most explosive ideological debates in low-fertility countries around the world, with some expressing alarm that nothing short of the future of their societies—or of what they term "civilization"—is at stake.

That reproduction and population dynamics are so politicized and evoke such anxieties is nothing new. If this book were being written in the late 1960s or early 1970s it would certainly need to describe the then-common alarms of a catastrophic "population explosion." Different times call for different kinds of alarm, so it seems. None of us views demographic data neutrally—the consumer of demographic data always brings his or her own lens to view the data, and so any time we discuss demographic data in the public sphere, these discussions become political. It is from this experience and understanding of the way population and politics combine that we have written this book.

Ideological Distortions

This book is about how population issues are always entangled with issues of identity, modernization, nationalism, and populism. How should we understand the diverse meanings of seemingly simple concepts such as "family" and "nation"? How important is the idea of a family for the continued existence of a nation? And what are the boundaries of a "nation"?

Political conflict among and within nations has often included a strong demographic component, and population politics has historically taken many forms. These range from political leaders' overt interventions intended to change demographic trends, to political parties' attempts to hijack demographic data to facilitate electoral victory, to multitudes of interest groups (economic, ethnic, religious, racial, etc.) intent on protecting or strengthening their political influence.

When we narrow our focus to the last 80 years, we see how population politics has been a constant of contemporary affairs. Political leaders from both democracies and nondemocracies have tried to manipulate fertility, mortality, and migration in their own countries and abroad. Confrontations between the Axis and Allied powers in World War II, communist and noncommunist blocs during the Cold War, and interactions between the Global North and South have included policies to limit or promote births, to promote the health and fitness of demographic groups central to their military power, to encourage or coerce the departure of certain demographic groups into the territories of antagonistic neighbors, and even to mobilize civilians to "populate" contested territories.

On the domestic front, politicians have defined demographic groups as political categories ("demographics"), and in some cases created wholly new demographic categories. It has been common to see political leaders in a variety of countries draw population issues into the center of their political programs, to stimulate public alarm over changing demographic distributions, and in some cases to manipulate demographic data to gain electoral advantage or arouse fearful responses among supporters to shifting cultural identities and values.

The past decades have seen a flowering of high-quality demographic research, yet scientific understanding often has been drowned out by loud and emotional claims—increasingly amplified by social media—that are driven by political and economic interests, ideological commitments, and outright confusion. While the bulk of our analysis focuses on recent population politics, today's debates and divisions have deep—and often unsavory—roots in history. Indeed, in many cases demographic change over time has been the drum that politicians beat to rally support for their side and to magnify antagonism against their competitors.

That history is both national and global, for as much as national and subnational demographic trends are the focus of this book, they often reflect patterns and reactions to them that are shaped by global events. The end of the Second World War was marked by high fertility and rapid economic growth compared to the interwar years. By the late 1960s and 1970s, those economic and demographic trends had moderated, but slowing economic growth and increasing inequality produced more unstable outlooks in many parts of the world. That instability continued until the end of the Cold War and was marked by the emergence of a new set of fears, no longer focused on the "population explosion," but on the prospect of population decline.

The robust economic growth in the 1990s and early 21st century, driven by new technologies and expanding trade, was followed by periods of increasing economic and political instability that fueled new forms of identity politics and nationalism. Some of these movements weaponized population issues to spread alarm about the future of nation, race, region, and religion. Those dynamics continued into the mid-2010s, while fears of population decline have taken on new forms and have drawn from old ones. The result has been to inject into virtually all discussions of demographic issues a sense of crisis, menace, danger, and looming disaster, a crescendo over time. Since then, the emotive has tended to eclipse the scientific, whether with respect to immigration, mortality, fertility, pandemic, or inequalities in health and in access to medical care.

This book is about the persistent distortion of population issues and trends whenever they enter the political arena. Over these decades, and all over the world, politics has acted as a prism, refracting and often distorting discussions of fertility, mortality and migration. No nation is immune from this warping of knowledge about population trends, particularly evident in recent discussions of the COVID-19 epidemic and sustained very low fertility rates in some countries, most notably Japan, Russia, China, South Korea, Singapore, Germany, and other countries in Europe. Throughout the book, we show that such ideological hijacking of demographic events has been a constant feature of political life across very different countries. At certain times, different demographic issues become overloaded with tendentious political interpretations, or "ideologies." What we term "ideologies" can take many forms, but several rise to the top and require a bit of context-setting before the chapters to follow.

Ideologies around identity—who belongs to the "nation," "people," or polity—are one example. Unlike states in the other regional sections of this book, three of the four Asian states covered—Japan, South Korea, and, to a great extent, China—consider themselves to be relatively ethnically homogeneous. Historian Eric Hobsbawm, in one of the most well-known articulations of nationalism, *Nations and Nationalism since 1780*, refers to China, Japan, and South Korea as rare examples of states that are almost or entirely ethnically homogeneous.[7] But ethnonational boundaries are fluid, and a closer examination of even these three cases shows how various structural and other forces have propelled a redefinition of those boundaries over time.[8] Identity politics distort discussions of demography, but are not siloed from the other forces of distortion. In the case of South Korea, the experience of Japanese colonization motivated adherence to an unambiguously Korean identity. This focus on Korean ethnic homogeneity was a facet of resistance to Japanese colonialism, a way of constructing and reinforcing the Korean nation as distinct from that of its Japanese colonial rulers. Well beyond this region, we see how political elites mobilize collective identities in order to legitimize their regimes and their actions, and to motivate support among the populace for collective action.[9]

We must also recognize that identities are not monolithic; an individual can have multiple identities, layered and overlapping. Some scholars have argued that acceptance of these multiple identities and rejection of a monolithic collective identity are essential to a just democracy.[10] Identities are mutable and malleable; particular aspects may be highlighted by certain actors and downplayed by others. Anthony D. Smith sees ethnic identity as relational and national identity as institutionalized—people with different ethnic identities can also belong to the same national community.[11] As states become less ethnically homogeneous, national unity can be enhanced if ethnic identity is paired with a civic national identity. The former is exclusionist, the latter more inclusive. Maintaining ethnic homogeneity in a globalized era of low fertility is difficult for any state, but if the state's domestic politics allow, it can in principle maintain ultimate control over both its physical borders and the boundaries of its citizenship. Promoting a common national identity among diverse ethnic populations has proven a useful tool for the states seeking to mobilize heterogeneous groups of its citizens toward a common goal.

In each of the parts of the book, readers will see that there are different conceptions and usage of "race" versus "ethnicity." In the US context, "race" is more likely to be employed, although the "race" category in the US census actually is derived from categories of national origin more than that of race as such. Ethnicity in the European context is more often employed as referring to regional identity, such as Bretons or Catalans, and within those regions there can be different races. Clearly, the terms "race" and "ethnicity" are not consistently used globally, but there is a universality to ideologies of identity at work around the world. In this book, we use "race" and "ethnicity" according to the way they are employed in each country context (noting that sometimes they are used interchangeably even within countries, as in Singapore), but we use them to mean generally the same thing. While most scholars try to be careful about their usage of such terms, definitional issues are of less importance to people in everyday usage.

Ideologies of identity—race, ethnicity, religion, nationality—have and continue to drive party politics, perhaps most notably these days in liberal democracies, which have experienced significant demographic shifts over the last few decades. The political consequences of European integration through the Schengen system that has abolished most internal borders within the European Union have been high, spurring backlash against newcomers. These conflicts over identity are interwoven with national security concerns, as the legal arrangement of the Schengen system makes internal borders more porous while (in theory at least) enforcing the external European borders as a means to protect openness across internal ones.

Demographic change is salient because for many in the political arena, demographic shifts can be seen as existential threats, as in cases of declines in population size relative to antagonistic neighbors, shifts in age composition toward older ages, or rapid changes in ethnic composition, especially if national or regional majority groups fear being outnumbered by incoming groups. Japan's Prime Minister Fumio Kishida said in January 2023 that Japan was "on the brink of not being able to maintain social functions" due to low birth rates.[12] Vladimir Putin has on numerous occasions used his State of the Union address to call for strengthening the family in Russia as a means of addressing what he has called the nation's "most acute problem," population decline.[13] Long-standing tensions between majority and minority groups can be found around the world, often provoking political mobilizations that sometimes turn violent and even genocidal.

We also note that eugenic themes arise throughout the book. In some instances, this has taken the form of "racial hygiene," a term that has unfortunate continued relevance. In 2010 a prominent figure in the German Social Democratic Party and former board member of the German Bundesbank, Thilo Sarrazin, published a best-selling book titled *Germany Abolishes Itself: How We Are Putting Our Country at Risk*. It warned of Turkish immigrants' "innate mental deficiencies" and called for safeguarding the German *Volk* from "genetic contamination."[14] At other times such eugenic ideas present more as class preferences, efforts to improve population "quality" by restricting births of "lower classes" and promoting births among the more highly educated.

As citizens and leaders debate these core issues, population appears again and again as a means to a larger end. Throughout our review of the last eighty years, we see how modernization and state-building efforts led to increased government attention to the body—whether sex, reproduction, or health—across the globe.[15] Even as individual rights regarding the body, such as abortion rights or gay marriage, have been liberalized in many countries, their liberalization is still contested and incomplete. What has been given can still be taken away. Ideologies of identity are often highly gendered, with the female body most frequently the site of political contestation, in terms of both how many offspring women produce and who they are, ethnically or racially. China is the most obvious example. When China's leaders needed to confront how China could "endure in a rapidly changing world," they looked for the answer in the population itself.[16] Thus, population became one of many factors the Chinese state sought to control, part of its grand experiment.

China has not been the only country grappling with such questions as: What should a modern nation look like, and when should the government intervene? What should women's roles be? What is the best path to improve the health and productivity of the population? Efforts to constitute and manage demographic characteristics of "the nation" can take many forms. Whether cleverly obscured or clearly stated, it is more common than not for governments to try and shape the characteristics of their populations. Sometimes, puppet strings take the form of a series of complex tax or citizenship policies. At other times, these efforts may be stated outright as vilifications of trends deemed unsatisfactory, such as very low fertility rates, or measures designed to increase the reported size of nonmajority ethnic groups.

All these concerns are entangled with ideologies of the family, or views about who constitutes a family. The chapters that follow this Introduction include numerous examples of handwringing over declining marriage rates, for example, and exhortations of marriage and childbearing as a patriotic duty. Finally, ideas about how to modernize the nation-state also present as ideologies. These include how a government prioritizes national security and economic growth against other social or cultural goals.

Regional Dynamics

To illustrate the ideologies at play we highlight national cases in three regions that have led the way with the demographic transition from high-mortality/high-fertility to low-mortality/low-fertility: Europe, North America, and East Asia. In the European sphere we trace population politics in the first region of the world to experience widespread population aging, long life expectancy, and robust immigration. In France, Germany, and Italy politicians often have elevated demographic issues to the center of their platforms by focusing on immigration, pensions, and incentives favoring increased childbearing. The European story includes a discussion of the complex population politics in Russia. The breakdown of the USSR was driven in part by large fertility differentials between its governing European Slavic regions and those of its Central Asian republics. More recently the Russian invasion of Ukraine is but one example of the violence that can arise from different visions of demographic categories embodying ethnicity, language, and national identity.

The North American section focuses on the United States as a complex case study whose treatment over two chapters allows space to see the politics of demographic distortion in detail. Home to the world's largest stock of international migrants, alongside dynamic fertility and mortality trends, the United States shows the different ways population has been a theater of political conflict and contestation, characterized by endemic distortion and confusion.

In the East Asian sphere, Japan and South Korea are examples of two low-fertility countries with limited immigration and long life expectancy. Both continue to grapple with the place of immigration in mediating the population aging they are experiencing due to their low fertility. This section of the book also looks at population dynamics in China, where decades of low fertility and antinatalist policy have yielded one of the most rapidly aging countries in the world. Singapore, known for its strict maintenance of ethnic diversity and its official efforts at matchmaking marriage and family-building on the part of its most highly educated citizens, rounds out the section.

This review, of course, only covers a small part of the globe, privileging depth over breadth. Latin America and the Caribbean region are areas of below-replacement fertility and, in many cases, tremendous emigration for some countries and immigration into others. That region, alone, would make a fascinating volume of rich case studies. As low fertility has become the global norm, new sets of countries are beginning to experience rapid shifts in age composition and will provide another fruitful set of comparative case studies in the future. India, for example, still has a primarily young and growing population, but with a fertility rate just below replacement level, India is charting an approach to demographic issues similar to those we discuss in our three sections. Even Africa, a continent with high fertility on average, includes Tunisia with a total fertility rate of 1.82 and South Africa with a rate of 2.21. As more and more populations follow the low-fertility/low-mortality path the countries in this book have followed, we will gain a greater understanding of the ways in which ideologies shape discussions of demography.

While population politics is ubiquitous, we focus on these three regions because, in spite of their many cultural, political, and economic differences, they all have grappled over time with low fertility, shifts in mortality and age composition, and questions of national identity. Together, they increase our understanding of population politics in different regimes. Each case shows how quickly reports on, surveys of, and studies of population trends can become cannon fodder in explosive political conflicts, and touch on fundamental questions of life, death, and national identity. Our book is a warning: population politics are always volatile, and sometimes dangerous. They need to be labeled: handle with extreme care.

There is another reason that caution is essential in linking population questions with politics. The best way to understand the interaction between demographic and political or economic forces is to see them as reciprocal. Changes in the key demographic components of fertility, mortality, migration, and composition often have powerful impacts on political and economic developments. These developments, in turn, may strongly influence subsequent demographic changes. More dramatic or erratic changes in one—for example a deadly pandemic or migratory surge on the demographic side, or a war, political disorder, or economic crisis on the political/economic side—can provoke similarly dramatic or erratic shifts in the other. For this reason alone, no one interested in understanding population change can afford to leave out the political dimension, and no one analyzing political upheavals can ignore their demographic consequences.

Big Data, Big Distortions

Confronting ideological distortions around population is perhaps even more important in this era of big data. Public and private entities now can collect more information on us as individuals, and more efficiently, than ever before. A historical look at the science of demography puts today's "information revolution" in context.

While there are historical records of censuses back to ancient times, the origins of modern population data collection are more accurately located in the late 18th century, as governments began to gather demographic information to periodically reallocate political representation (initiated in the Constitution of the nascent United States, ratified in 1788); to track demographic, economic, and geographical change; and later for numerous other purposes such as configuration of constituency boundaries for elections, counting those potentially available for military service, estimating government revenues, anticipating demand for government programs, and allocating funds for local distribution. Outside of such governmental functions, the idea that society could and should be dissected and studied, analogous to a biological organism, took hold as the broad field of "social science."[17] Today, population data are still used for those purposes, but over time population data have also been collected and employed by private companies to discover causes and cures for diseases or to market products and services.

How we think about recent trends in collection and use of population data is important because our relationship with data is undergoing monumental change. Going forward, we will be able to more easily and frequently collect and use data on entire populations, rather than settle for statistical samples between larger collection efforts (such as a decennial census) as we have done in the past. We have already seen vast improvements in how we collect, store, and analyze data since the large-scale adoption of the internet at the turn of this millennium. India, the world's most populous country, has been conducting a full census for over 130 years, first taking place under the British, but with partial counts well before that. Now, the Indian government is pushing for biometric identification cards for all of its 1.4 billion Indians, and is moving toward a digital census, which Indians will be able to complete using their mobile phones.

There are still tremendous obstacles along the path toward collecting such information electronically, including lack of access to technology by some groups within every society, but the rapid pace at which such access is improving suggests we should expect real advances in data collection in the near future. As it becomes cheaper and easier to cast a wide net with data collection, a "big data" model is emerging in which as much data as possible are collected and subsequently used for multiple public and private purposes, leaving behind the old model of collecting a narrow amount of data for a specific purpose. Still, there is much room for improvement in the accuracy and reach of population data various actors collect. Collection is imprecise; we often cannot or do not trust data that are demonstrably incomplete or are collected by public or private entities that lack credibility.

Yet, improvements in accuracy perhaps bring greater risks. How will such data be employed? We are not optimistic. What we see from our study of the past in the United States, East Asia, and Europe is that demographic data are always distorted by the ideologies of those who harvest them. Population researchers generally celebrate such improvements in data collection, and eagerly dig in to learn more. As citizens, however, and students of history, we are aware of the likelihood such data will become distorted, and possibly used for self-interested or even nefarious purposes. This book serves as a warning and entreats us to be vigilant in monitoring, cataloging, and reporting on the hijacking of demographic data by political movements that seek to sow disorder or even threaten basic human rights relating to population issues.

As our exploration of ideological distortions in the United States shows, Democratic and Republican advisors have for decades been applying demographic projection methods to argue that policies affecting demographic change can lead their party to permanent electoral majorities. As is true of all projections, the predictive value of such claims is only as strong as the validity of the assumptions built into the projection model, which in this case includes assumptions about the degree to which past political orientations among voting "demographics" (ethnic, racial, linguistic, national origin, etc.) will continue into the medium-to-long-range future. Not only are those orientations dynamic, so too are identities themselves, as the major shifts among Americans who identify as Hispanic or Latino show. Over a third did not identify with any of the racial categories in the 2020 US census.[18]

Data governance is poor, and privacy-enhancing technologies, which provide individuals protection against sensitive information being collected, are still nascent and unevenly employed. In 2016, US Census Bureau researchers discovered that their census outputs could be combined with commercially available data to identify respondents and tried to implement differential privacy safeguards for some of the 2020 census data they released.[19] As we increasingly turn to technology to improve health and longevity, privacy becomes even more at risk. We may benefit from knowing more about ourselves collectively and individually, but when we cannot control what happens to the information that is collected, or how it will be used, then the risk may outweigh the reward.

We should welcome pending improvements in demographic data, but the point of this book is that actual demographic data—the Who, What, Where—is often rendered irrelevant or opaque when brought into the political arena. Rather, it is the *perception* of demographic data that matters more. Now, "population" is a story than can be and is massaged and manipulated by political actors to suit their purposes. Even if demographic data tell you that nonnatives are but a small proportion of your community, if you *perceive* them to be larger, that matters more for your political action than do the actual data. Still, we should continue to invest in trustworthy sources of demographic data and analysis to ensure that the loudest voices are not the most alarmist ones. Demographic truth matters.

Conclusion

Population politics, like medical politics, or environmental politics, is an amalgam of scientific knowledge and its uses in public debate on subjects of significance to a community. Demographers, like physicians or scientists, study phenomena and produce data and analyses about a wide array of vital issues. However, they cannot control the way political actors and those who put them in power use these data and analyses in attempts to affect future trends. When the specialists' findings enter the public arena, their scientific language is translated into political language. The gap between the two is always significant, and the outcome of the translation of science into politics is always imperfect.

There is an Italian adage that says "Traduttore, traditore": to engage in translation is inevitably to betray the meaning of the original text. This "translation" problem creates a massive space for the distortion of scientific knowledge for political advantage. Some distortion is innocent misunderstanding; other distortions are intentional. Both are endemic and both are crippling.

This book shows how in very different parts of the world, the distortion of demographic issues in public debate is both normal and alarming. There is no reason to accept this state of affairs. We do not advocate scientific purity or promote expert aloofness. Demographers, like other scientists, are citizens too, and participate in political life. It is in no one's interest to try to wall off scientists in a pristine space untouched by politics. It is equally in no one's interest to wall off politics from addressing demographic issues; ignorance and disaster have been blood brothers for centuries.

This book's primary aim is to help take the venom out of discussions of issues that matter to us all. We need a nontoxic environment in which to talk about population trends and the demographic processes that lie behind them. Every government needs to have accurate information on birth rates, death rates, ethnic composition, and migration, and an informed electorate needs to make decisions on policy proposals that bear on them.

The antitoxicity project we advocate aims to reduce or (if possible) eliminate alarmism and to replace it with informed public conversations about demographic change. Above all we need to inform citizens that there is a momentum in population movements, which in many cases is so strong that governments cannot reverse them.

Knowing the limits to what can be done in the public sphere is both chastening and essential. Humility is a rarity in politics, but more valued in science. Rigorous research and publications matter, but so does an understanding of the constraints on what governments can do when they face a future in which below-replacement fertility and volatile migratory movements seem here to stay. We show this to be the case in very varied environments in Europe, North America, and East Asia. Extending our remit to other parts of the world, such as Africa and Latin America, would only reinforce our interpretation.

The following chapters are filled with examples of how explosive are the issues raised in debates over demographic change. One way of understanding what we mean by population politics is to see it as an engagement in two tasks. The first is the provision of professionally informed studies of demographic change and the processes underlying it. The second is the critical analysis of the ways societies adapt to these powerful trends. Demographers and those in other relevant fields have an essential role to play in both these tasks. Both require a commitment to lowering the temperature of debates on these vital issues. Population politics, honestly conducted, can be a crucial antidote to fear.

Or, as the following chapters show, it can be a dangerous accelerant of violence and social conflict. The choice, at the end of the day, is ours.

PART I
EUROPE

1

Rebuilding the House of Europe, 1945–1990

Part 1: Postwar: Rebuilding Europe, 1945–1970

Introduction

The political history, the economic history, and the population history of postwar Europe followed roughly similar trajectories. Between 1945 and 1965, there was a period of recovery, marked by the political stabilization of the two blocs of East and West, by economic growth, much more rapid in the West than in the East of Europe, and by a population growth rate of between 0.75 percent and 1.0 percent per year in Europe as a whole. In the second subperiod, between 1965–1970 and 1990, there was much more instability on the level of European political and economic life, matched by a slowdown in rates of population growth and a return in both Western and Eastern Europe to the prewar trend of fertility decline.

Figure 1.1 charts the movement in annual population growth rates in Europe as a whole over the 72-year period between 1950 and 2022. A glance at this graph helps break down the entire period into two subperiods, 1945–1990, and after 1990. And within the first subperiod, we can observe contrasts between the years 1945 to (roughly) 1965 and from 1965 to 1990.

In Fig. 1.1, we see that in the two postwar decades population growth was robust, hovering around 1 percent per year, and that after 1965, the rate of growth declined, but still remained positive until the end of the century. Negative growth rates, or shrinking populations, are 21st-century phenomena in Europe as a whole, though there was a long prehistory of the fear of population decline that anticipated it. When people spoke of population decline before 2000, they usually meant declining rates of growth, projections of future declines in population size, or unfavorable comparisons between one country and another. After 2000, a decline in absolute numbers

Toxic Demography. Jennifer D. Sciubba, Michael S. Teitelbaum, and Jay Winter, Oxford University Press.

DOI: 10.1093/oso/9780197745038.003.0002

Fig. 1.1 Annual population growth in Europe, 1950–2022.
Source: UN *World Population Prospects, 2024 Revision.*

became a reality, though as Fig. 1.1 shows, European growth generally rates remained positive until very recently.

In the second half of the 20th century, population growth and economic growth went hand in hand. In Fig. 1.1, European population growth rates remain positive until the mid-1990s. So do measures of gross domestic product, reflecting technological innovation and globalization. Leading the way were "Western Offshoots"—countries of European settlement, the United States, Canada, Australia, New Zealand—and Western Europe. Both groups of countries registered economic growth trajectories, with some reverses, through the period 1945–2020. Eastern Europe showed more modest, though still positive, growth until 1990, when the Warsaw Pact and the Soviet Union collapsed. A period of decline followed, and the Eastern European region as a whole returned to 1989 levels of GDP per capita only in 2015.

Rebuilding Families, Rebuilding Nations, 1945–1965

Now that we have a clear idea of breaks in the overall period under review, let us turn to the first two decades after the end of the Second World War. In the summer of 1945, after the defeat of Nazi Germany, the order of the day in Europe was the reconstruction of shattered families. There were tens of millions of displaced persons stranded throughout the continent. Some had been victims of the Nazi regime, and had managed to survive the war. Others had lost their homes, swept away by invading armies or demolished by aerial bombardment. Still others were former soldiers or agents of the Nazis and their allies. Many of them did not want to be found, but sought with some success to disappear into new names and new lives, either in Europe or elsewhere, for a fee and through what came to be called "rat lines." South America was a preferred destination, though there were others that served the same purpose.

The vast majority of displaced persons in 1945 were those who had nothing to hide. In newspapers and notice boards all over Europe, they posted appeals for information. Have you seen my brother, photographed here? Have you any information on my husband, last seen at a particular place on a particular date? National and international organizations, churches and charities, armies and navies were all besieged by those seeking a clue, a nod, a smile, reinforcing a hope that someone could say yes, he or she is alive, and I know where you can find him or her. Those who returned from imprisonment were accosted by desperate seekers, hoping that they could help them end their vigil.

Orphans formed a class apart. Some estimates number them as totaling 15 million in 1945.[1] Many were taken from their parents, resettled in other countries, given new names. Others never entered new homes, with many abandoned in orphanages and other charitable institutions. The German Red Cross received over 300,000 requests to trace missing children between 1945 and 1958;[2] the military occupation of Germany created the conditions that led to more abandoned children, most of mixed nationality and some of mixed race.

Aerial warfare had destroyed a substantial part of Europe's housing stock. In 1945 over 14 million Germans had nowhere to live. Many had been thrown out of their homes in Central and Eastern Europe, approximately 800,000 in Czechoslovakia alone. Their forced migration was agreed by the victorious Allies at the Potsdam conference of July 1945. Another 350,000 ethnic Germans were expelled from Hungary, and perhaps 10 times that number were evicted from Poland, whose borders were changed to suit Stalin.[3] These episodes of ethnic cleansing were a shameful part of the reckoning that followed the Second World War.

The political balance of left and right in countries throughout Europe was overturned by the war. Many conservative parties and movements had collaborated with the Nazis and were discredited at least for a time. On the other side, socialist and communist parties benefited from their work in the Resistance. In Western Europe, the role of the Soviet Union in the victorious military campaign eclipsed Stalin's pact with Hitler that led to the outbreak of war in 1939. Few in Eastern Europe had any illusions about what Stalin would do to their countries once the war was over, but the war against fascism tilted the political balance throughout Europe to the left.

The result was evident. Conservative parties made peace with the idea of a welfare state, the foundations of which were laid by Liberal and Socialist parties in the immediate postwar years. To be sure, many of these plans to provide healthcare and unemployment benefits antedated the Second World War. But the tilt to the left during the war and in its aftermath turned plans into legislation and then into law.

In 1945 France adopted a social security insurance scheme providing healthcare to workers, employees, and retirees. Similar schemes were adopted in other European countries, incorporating pensions, family allowances, and housing subsidies into a welfare safety net that radically altered the entitlements of citizenship. In Britain, the ruling Labour party faced considerable opposition in bringing about these changes, but they were able to force these measures through. In Sweden, the Labour party pursued a policy of equalization of incomes and transfer payments in other ways.

What we now term "welfare state capitalism" was set in stone in the aftermath of the Second World War. In part this reflected American foreign aid through the Marshall Plan, and American occupation policies. What the United States engineered was a "New Deal" for Western Europe, offered to the Eastern bloc, though declined. Trade unions were drawn into partnership with management in Germany, to assure that the bitterness of major strikes and mass unemployment of the interwar years remained a thing of the past. This German development, named *Mitbestimmung* or "codetermination" gave labor an important role in the management of corporations, first in heavy industry and then elsewhere. Interestingly, these measures were first introduced by British occupation authorities in the heavy industrial region of the Ruhr in 1947, before Germany regained her sovereignty in 1949. They went well beyond what was possible to achieve in Britain. In Germany, management still retained the upper hand in framing corporate strategy, and left-wing critics hold that labor lost out by abandoning nationalization as the key to fundamental change in the way the economy was run.[4] In Britain, the coal industry, the electricity grid, and for a brief period in the 1950s and then again in the 1960s, the iron and steel industries, were nationalized, but ownership of the rest of the private sector remained untouched by the British state. Elsewhere in Western Europe, the mixed economy, tilted toward private enterprise, survived the transition from war to peace.

A second powerful support for expanding the state sector in healthcare and in industry came from the adoption of the ideas of John Maynard Keynes as the bedrock of economic thinking in the immediate postwar years. Keynes died in 1946, but his thinking continued to dominate economic planning in the first postwar decade and beyond.[5] At Bretton Woods in New Hampshire, British and American delegates set up an international lender of last resort, the International Monetary Fund, and a financial aid to development, the World Bank. Keynes was a lifelong liberal, and his life's work was to help forge a framework to stabilize capitalism, so as to avoid the repetition of the devastating depression of the interwar years. Socialists and social democrats embraced his ideas to support increased public expenditure on health, education, and housing.

In the Soviet bloc, communist authorities adopted the "Sameshko system" of state healthcare in the Soviet Union. Universal provision had its advantages, though top-heavy bureaucracies, chronic underfunding, and shortages of pharmaceutical and other products hampered the workings of the health sector.[6] This flawed system of social and health services helped reestablish the condition necessary for the revival of family life after the horrors of the Second World War. As we will see in subsequent chapters", as the the earlier sentences refer to the Soviet bloc but the rest refers to the whole world

Race and Nation: The Preference for the Native-Born

One of the most disturbing of the continuities of the 1940s is that the defeat of the Nazi regime did not undermine the depths of racial and religious stereotypes in Europe, east or west. Anti-Semitism did not disappear in 1945. On July 4, 1946, in the Polish town of Kielce, north of Krakow, 40 Jews were killed in a pogrom, following rumors that a Polish child had been abducted by Jews. The victims had recently returned home from Nazi concentration camps. Sporadic killings continued in the following days. Nine of the perpetrators were tried and executed by Polish courts, but these events triggered a flight of the few remaining Jewish survivors out of Poland.

Indeed, postwar Europe shared with the Nazi regime the idea that population planning was a critical part of national development. Pierre Pfimlin, speaking for the French Ministry of Public Health and Population in 1946, thought that there were opportunities to replenish the national stock by taking in children born during the war. He was thinking of those born not in France, but to French fathers and German mothers in Germany, where millions of French prisoners of war and workers were held. The notion of children as national resources was popular all over Europe. Here are his words:

> During the war years Germany was an immense prison, where humans belonging to all of the nations of Europe rubbed shoulders. . . . This mixing of humans without historical precedent has left human traces—children were born. A lot of children. A good number of them have French blood in their veins. . . . From a demographic point of view the child is the ideal immigrant because he constitutes a human asset whose value is all the more certain since his assimilation is guaranteed. It is impossible to say the same of any adult immigrant.[7]

Pfimlin was later prime minister, and a pillar of Franco-German reconciliation.

Here we have a key idea of the postwar years. A revival of family life meant a revival of the nation. And natural increase was infinitely preferable to immigration, since most immigrants were already formed human beings, with attributes and habits that might not be assimilable. The ideology of national rebirth through protecting and supporting families appealed to people on every point of the political spectrum.

In the two postwar decades this French preference for natural increase over immigration was deepened by the dismantling of French rule in Algeria, established in 1848 and ended in 1962 after a long and bitter insurrection. The outcome of the war was defeat for those who wanted to keep Algeria as an integral part of France. Thousands of Muslims who had fought not for Algerian independence but for France had to flee. And yet, despite rhetorical commitments to equality and fraternity, many questioned whether in the postwar period Muslims could ever become part of the French nation. Here is what a noted demographic historian, Louis Chevalier, said about Islam in 1947:

> Much more than a faith, much more than a religious practice, much more than a community pride, Islam is a manner of being, of feeling, of

> understanding, in sum, a temperament, a psychology that creates a profound refusal of all assimilation behind all the secondary appearances of Europeanization.[8]

Muslim assimilation, he and many others believed, was an impossibility. The rebuilding of postwar France was not to be accomplished by immigrants, Muslim or foreign-born Christians or Jews. It had to be done by *les français de souche*, the native-born population. And that meant an increase in the birth rate.

The preference for the native-born over immigrants was reinforced after 1945 by the survival, albeit in muted form, of a prewar scientific movement known as eugenics. There were two varieties of this movement. Positive eugenics aimed at the improvement of the biological stock of a nation. Negative eugenics rooted "social and physical deviance" in genetic defect. Distaste for anything resembling Nazi ideas reduced but did not eliminate forms of negative eugenics after 1945. In Sweden, where social democrats operated a well-developed welfare state, the sterilization of the "feeble-minded" continued until 1976. That practice was justified as a way of "removing from the gene pool the threat of offending groups."[9] Progressives advocated access to contraception and abortion as ways of protecting the poor and the handicapped from uncontrolled reproduction.[10] Once again, we see how the ideology of promoting the family fit in with very different political programs.

The underground life of eugenics in Europe after 1945 continued in other ways. Most prominent was the claim by reputable researchers that intelligence, however measured, was transmitted genetically. British psychologist Hans Eysenck, a German-born refugee from Nazi Germany, claimed in 1971 that the White race was "a superior intellectual race," and that differences between the IQ scores of White and Black British children were genetically predetermined. In some cases, Black children were sent to special schools on the basis of these now-discredited findings.[11]

The European Baby Boom

What pronatalists in all European countries dreamed about before the Second World War came true during and after it. The birth rate rose in some countries during the war and in almost all European countries after the war. To the pleasant surprise of demographers and other planners, this upsurge in births reflected a variable previously ignored in most demographic reports. That variable was the age of marriage, which trended downward in this period. In effect, the postwar baby boom was not just a reflection of deferred births but also the result of a significant change in patterns of nuptiality.

This shift in marriage patterns was detected first by statistician John Hajnal, the son of Hungarian refugees who had fled Nazi Germany for Britain in the 1930s. In 1953, Hajnal reported a sustained rise in marriage rates in Central, Northern and Western Europe, and in the English-speaking world outside of Europe. What made the shift striking was that it occurred in many countries terrified by the specter of "depopulation" through declining birth rates before the war.[12]

Hajnal's analysis went two steps further. First, he showed that the critical difference between the prewar and the postwar periods was a striking decline in the proportion of women remaining single both by the time they were 30 years old and when they left the child-bearing period of life at or about age 50. Thus, there were far fewer never-married women in Western and Central Europe after 1945 than before the war. Second, he showed that changes in attitudes to marriage itself were important elements in the unfolding of the baby boom after the war.

The implications of Hajnal's pathbreaking work are fundamental for our understanding of the population history of Europe as a whole. He claimed that in the 1940s there occurred a form of European unification well before the European Union got off the ground. What he had in mind was that before 1940, there was a line running roughly from Stettin on the Baltic Sea to Trieste on the Adriatic. By sheer coincidence, Winston Churchill pointed to the same line in a celebrated speech in Independence, Missouri, in 1948, as the division of Europe by the Cold War. He was not aware that the same line described a demographic divide. To the east of that line, and for two centuries, marriage tended to be early and the proportion of women who never married was very low. Hajnal called this the domain of the Eastern European marriage pattern. To the west of that line, until 1940 or so, marriage tended to be late and the proportion of unmarried women tended to be high, perhaps one in five or so. But after 1940, the European divide in terms of marriage patterns faded away.[13]

Hajnal's narrative of the end of what he termed "the Western European marriage pattern" offered many fresh insights into an understanding of the post-1945 baby boom. On top of registering marriages and births deferred by the dislocations of war, postwar Europe went through a period in which women's attitudes changed on both when to marry and whether to enter the marital state at all. The decline in the age of first marriage and the decline in the proportion remaining unmarried after the age of 50 by and large accounts for the phenomenon we call the European baby boom.

In seeking the causes of this change in attitudes to marriage, it is best to adopt a broad approach, for what happened in Europe happened even more strikingly in the United States, Canada, Australia, and New Zealand. Finding a single cause of this ecumenical movement toward early marriage and larger families is likely to be impossible. The postwar economic boom must be part of the explanation. Similarly essential is to acknowledge the importance of the extension of social and educational provision, and in particular the expansion of healthcare and affordable housing. In the European case, a third element is that of the revaluation of family life in the aftermath of the upheaval of war. However deep the impact of war was on the United States, Canada, Australia, and New Zealand, their happy escape from virtually all of the direct effects of combat places them in a different world of injury, destruction, suffering, and mass death. The evisceration of European society between 1939 and 1945 was a case apart.

The End of Empire and Non-White Immigration to Europe

By the end of the 1960s, Europe's imperial history had entered its final phase. From being a net exporter of populations in the 19th century, Europe became an importer of people, mostly from Asia and Africa after the Second World War. One scholar terms this movement an imperial "reflux" of roughly 16 million people: Dutch from Indonesia starting in 1949, French from Vietnam in 1954 and North Africa in 1962, British from their worldwide colonies from 1947 to 1999, Belgian from 1960, and Portuguese from 1974, after which 1 million Portuguese left her African colonies for Portugal. A second phase was characterized by an "influx" of approximately 13 million workers to expanding economies: Turks to Germany as 'guest workers', West Indians and people from the Indian subcontinent to Britain, and North Africans and Africans to France. A third phase represented "overflow" and a search for refuge. Estimates vary, but between 1980 and 1991, perhaps 2 million refugees came to Europe; most were from the Global South. In the 1990s, those displaced by the civil war in the former Yugoslavia tipped the balance toward "European" refugees seeking asylum. These distinctions must be treated with caution, since people moved for multiple reasons. For example, the "reflux" from British colonies in East Africa included Asian workers earlier imported by British administrators and later expelled by post-colonial governments in Kenya and Uganda.[14]

Public responses to these three forms of population movement varied substantially too, but one way to characterize them is to say that those who came home were greeted with sympathy, those who came to work found grudging acceptance, and those who sought refuge found a range of responses, from an initial welcome to later panic.[15]

We will treat the problem of refugees and asylum seekers after the turn of the 21st century in chapter 2. Suffice it to say for now that in the second half of the 20th century Europe's imperial history left a residue of racism in Europe that lasted for decades after the formal end of empire. Even after the British Empire mutated into the "family" of the British Commonwealth of Nations, the habits, sometimes unconscious, at other times egregious, of White superiority remain visible and palpable.

One indication of this problem is in the great difficulty former colonial countries still have in accepting the historical record of violence and cruelty embedded in colonial rule. It took 50 years and a lot of luck for historians to find and publish the archive of torture and other cruelties in the last years of colonial rule in Kenya.[16] The subject of torture in the Algerian war is still politically explosive in France, even 60 years after the end of French rule. The same is true in Belgium, where the history of colonial cruelties in Africa is still hidden.

What makes this point relevant to our story is that immigrants of color brought these stories with them to Europe. They passed them on to their children over the dinner table, and provided young people with a context, at times exaggerated, in which they could comprehend perceived racial and religious discrimination in their new homes in Europe.

One example can stand for many others. On October 17, 1961, in the last years of the Algerian war of independence, when the French government was still holding on to Algeria, there occurred a massacre of Algerian-born French citizens in Paris. Thousands of supporters of the Algerian side in the war decided to hold a peaceful demonstration, despite the imposition of a curfew in Paris. The demonstrators were attacked by police in many parts of the city, and perhaps 200 were killed, most by drowning in the Seine. The truth was hidden by the government, one of whose high officials, Maurice Papon, prefect of Police, had orchestrated the police repression of the march.[17]

The cover-up lasted for 35 years. The truth came out in a defamation trial launched by Papon after the publication of a book and later an article in the newspaper *Le Monde* accusing him of responsibility for these deaths. The court found that the author of the book, Jean-Luc Einaudi, had exposed the absurdity of the official version of events. He had told the truth. He had done his research and had acted in good faith. To call the events a massacre may have been harsh, but it was not libelous to do so.[18]

Papon brought this judgment on his own head. The prior year he had been convicted of crimes against humanity for his actions in the 1940s in Bordeaux as a bureaucrat who oversaw the paperwork surrounding the deportation of Jewish children to their deaths. Historian Einaudi had served as a prosecution witness in that trial, an act which may have pushed Papon to sue him unsuccessfully for libel in 1999. What Papon had done in Paris in 1961 was to repeat the moral bankruptcy he had shown during the war.[19]

The same 35-year delay in judging Papon's crimes during the Vichy regime had hidden his guilt for directing the murder by the French police of Algerians in Paris in 1961. Justice delayed is indeed justice denied. Even when the truth had come out, the sour taste of the cover-up remained in the mouths of the descendants. Today a further 30 years have passed, and yet every time a person of North African origin is killed by the French police, these older stories return to give them a bitter meaning.

It is apparent that even when population growth rates were positive, and economic growth robust in the 1950s and 1960s, immigration injected multiple ideological currents into the language of politics throughout Europe. Even in liberal Britain in 1968, immigration and bloodshed were braided together in public discourse. A Conservative member of Parliament and former classics scholar, Enoch Powell, drew on Virgil's *Aeniad* when he contemplated Black immigration to Britain. "As I look ahead, I am filled with foreboding; like the Roman, I seem to see 'the River Tiber foaming with much blood.'"[20] Powell delivered this speech in the Midlands city of Birmingham, home to a large non-White immigrant population. He spoke precisely two weeks after the assassination of Martin Luther King Jr. in the United States. He was also referring indirectly to his opposition to the Labour government's proposed Race Relations Bill, then winding its way through Parliament. That bill forbade the denial of housing, employment, or public services to a person on the grounds of race, religion, ethnicity, or national origin. It passed, but did nothing to erase Powell's message. Though the day following his speech he was dismissed from the front ranks of the

Conservative party by the party leader, Edward Heath, his views resonated with a certain kind of English patriotism, cultivated in India, where Powell had spent the war as a soldier. Powell's racially charged rhetoric is a prime example of the lingering afterlife of empire in postwar Britain.

Eastern Europe 1945–1970

In Soviet-dominated Central and Eastern Europe, a baby boom was restricted to the immediate postwar years. From the early 1950s in most of these countries, the drop in the birth rate came well before that in Western Europe. One of the causes of this decline in fertility in the 1950s was the radical effects of the war on the age composition of the population.[21] In the German Democratic Republic and in the Soviet Union, the ratio of women to men aged 15–39, at prime child-bearing ages, fell from 130–135 in 1950 to 101–2 in 1960.[22] The sharp decline in the number of women born during the Second World War helps explain the early onset of postwar fertility decline in Eastern Europe.

By the early 1960s, fertility was declining throughout Eastern Europe, though from higher rates in Poland and the Soviet Union than in Romania and Bulgaria. In one case, that of Romania, a very liberal policy on abortion had been promulgated in 1957, consistent with Soviet practice and longstanding Marxist-Leninist ideology. Subsequently, Romanian period total fertility rates declined sharply to 1.80 by 1966, about 15 percent below replacement level. Most of this fertility decline could be attributed to the use of abortion, which had come to be routine under the 1957 policy and in the absence of widespread availability of effective contraception.

In 1965 Nicolae Ceaușescu became the Romanian leader, and expressed alarm about the implications of these fertility declines for the future of the Romanian nation. In 1966 he abruptly issued a decree that banned most abortions and contraceptives and instituted a series of pronatalist measures. As one of the authors of this book has shown, this decree had dramatic effects on fertility rates over the short term.[23] Over a single year from 1966 to 1967, Romania registered one of the largest national fertility increases in human history – more than a 100 percent increase in the total fertility rate, from 1.80 to 3.66. Maternal and infant mortality rates also increased sharply, as the surge of births overwhelmed the Romanian medical system and in subsequent years its daycare facilities, primary schools, secondary schools, and entry-level job markets.

Despite such problems, the provisions of the 1966 decree were sustained, but fertility rates began to decline from their 1967 peak. Given lack of access to most contraceptive methods, it appears that abortion continued to be the preferred method for regulation of fertility, through a kind of medical black market. By the early 1980s Romanian fertility had returned to its 1966 level, provoking even harsher pronatalist measures from the government. These measures were among the first government policies to be dismantled after Ceaușescu's fall and execution in 1989. Further declines in the birth rate in Romania after abortion was relegalized in 1990 showed that, like their sisters elsewhere in Eastern Europe, Romanian women were having fewer children in the 1990s than before the war.[24]

Berent showed that urbanization was a significant factor in accounting for fertility decline in Eastern Europe. In Hungary and Poland fertility rates fell much more rapidly in towns than in the countryside.[25] Nonmanual workers' fertility was lower than that of manual workers; and agricultural workers' fertility was higher than both. Both social mobility and education were positively correlated with fertility decline in postwar Eastern Europe, as elsewhere.[26]

Access to abortion under the law was generally freer in Eastern Europe than in the West. There were exceptions, and available statistics are unreliable in many cases. On the whole, though, it is safe to say that abortion probably played a more significant role in fertility control in Eastern Europe than in the West. For instance, in the late 1960s, there were reported in the Soviet Union 7,500,000 abortions each year, a figure 80 percent higher than the number of live births.[27]

Social policy throughout the Eastern bloc favored large families, but was ineffective in increasing fertility. Rigidities in housing provision and employment opportunities for women were partly to blame. Perhaps most strikingly, the earlier onset of fertility decline in Eastern Europe compared to Western Europe reflected material constraints and shortages in everyday family life. And yet after the mid-1960s, declining fertility once again became the rule in both Western and Eastern Europe.

The arrival of socialist regimes throughout the east of Europe after 1945 certainly did not produce an environment in which rising levels of fertility became the norm. In Eastern Europe there was a postwar recovery of postponed marriages and births, but underlying social conditions and not ideology determined demographic outcomes.

Rigidities in every facet of the Soviet way of doing things were apparent from the onset of the new socialist order in Eastern Europe. Opposition turned violent in East Germany in 1953, in Hungary in 1956, and in Czechoslovakia in 1968. And yet the nuclear stalemate between the two superpowers gave to the division of Europe an air of permanence that was misleading. The Berlin Wall, symbolizing the political divide of Europe, was erected in 1961, but in demographic terms, Europe east and west were moving in the same direction.

Part 2: Europe 1970–1990: The Turbulent Years

The Political Economy of Europe, 1970–1990

There were two parallel developments in Europe in the post-1970 period, one destabilizing, the other restabilizing. First, *Les trentes glorieuses*, the robust economic recovery of Europe after the war, abruptly came to an end. In the 1970s, economic instability and turbulence led to bitter political conflict tending toward conservative rather than social democratic rule in many countries. Inflation, unemployment, strikes—the signature of the 1930s—had returned.

What made the 1970s different, and less destructive of democratic institutions, was the existence of the European Economic Community (EEC), founded in 1957 through the Treaty of Rome. In the 1970s and 1980s, the EEC consolidated its place in Europe and expanded its reach. Britain, Ireland, and Denmark joined in 1973. Then a decade later came a second wave of countries whose leaders saw in the EEC a pathway to stable democratic rule. Spain, Portugal, and Greece shed dictatorship and joined the European community of nations in the 1980s. These transitions from dictatorship to democracy set the precedent for the later expansion of Europe to include the former members of the Warsaw Pact. That process will be dealt with in the following chapter.

In the 1970s and 1980s European integration was a goal, not an achievement. The task for Europe's leaders was to make the EEC a kind of life insurance for democracy, and not a replacement of it by a vast, unelected bureaucracy. Resistance to it remained stubborn, based in part on national pride and assumptions of superiority over the neighbors. Britain needed no protection for its democracy or for its currency, which it never gave up. In many respects, the marriage of Britain and the EEC remained unconsummated until divorce through Brexit in 2016. In contrast, the existence of the

EEC tended to reduce the harsh effects of the economic downturn of the 1970s and 1980s.

And downturn it was. In the two decades of the 1970s and 1980s, the robust growth trajectories of the immediate postwar years came to an end. Replacing them were a host of problems that were partly political in origins. These difficulties brought the postwar period of rapid and robust economic and demographic growth to an end. In all domains, demographic as well as economic and political, the years 1945 to 1990 are divided sharply between an upswing and a downswing, each lasting roughly for two decades.

The exogenous shock of the 1973 Arab-Israeli war led the organization of the oil producers' cartel OPEC to impose an oil embargo on nations supporting Israel—the United States, the United Kingdom, the Netherlands, Canada, and Japan—and to raise the price of oil. The embargo ended in 1974, but the price of oil stayed high. The average price of crude oil was $3.22 per barrel in 1972; in 1980 it stood at $33.86. Inflation rates rose in many countries and rocketed upward in others. In Italy, inflation reached 20 percent in 1974; in Britain inflation rose to 25 percent the following year. This dizzying rate of inflation destroyed the future for many people. It wiped out the real value of the savings of those living on fixed incomes, like the elderly, and made life particularly difficult for first-time house buyers, those starting a family.

The volume of exports and imports from and to Europe dropped rapidly in the 1970s. GDP growth in the 1960s was reduced by between a quarter and a half in the 1970s not only in Europe but also in important trading partners like Japan. These trends were ominous in another way. They signaled a crisis in European manufacturing. Compared to the good years of 1964–1973, the growth rate of manufacturing capital stock in Britain, France, and Germany was halved in 1973–1979, and then halved again in 1979–1989.[28] Investment in extractive industries shifted to locations where deposits are rich and environmental regulation weak. We need to look not at Europe but at China or Mexico to see a robust manufacturing sector, exploiting lower wages and benefits, on the one hand, and state policies favoring exports. Manufacturing has not disappeared completely, but its share of both overall investment and the labor force declined radically in the late 20th century. Britain led the way downhill. Its labor force in the manufacturing sector declined by half between 1973 and 2000.[29]

The domestic political turbulence of the years 1970–1990 in part emerged directly from this economic turbulence. "Stagflation" was the term of the day used to describe the worst of both worlds—a slowdown in rates of economic growth and an acceleration in prices. Under these conditions, unemployment rates rose rapidly too. They kept going up in the 1980s, reaching levels not known since the interwar depression.[30]

As early as 1856, Alexis de Tocqueville had pointed out the destabilizing effects of a tabling off or decline in economic growth. In 18th-century France, he observed, as conditions improved, discontent rose. The parallel with post-1945 Europe is evident. After the boom years of the 1945–1970 period, contemporaries were bound to anticipate further growth. Their frustration arose not out of absolute deprivation, since they were better off in 1980 than in 1950. It arose out of *relative* deprivation, a loss in terms of their hopes, their expectations. Economic growth fueled the politics of entitlements; the tabling off or reversal of patterns of material gains fueled the politics of resentment, characteristic of the 1970s and 1980s.

It is one of the ironies of political history that left-wing parties need a strong capitalist world order and economic growth in order to pay for a welfare state. When bad times come, right-wing parties prosper. Deep instability in economic affairs undermined center-left political parties and gave the center-right a new lease of life. This was not true everywhere. In Germany and Britain, as in the United States in the late 1970s and 1980s, strong conservative leaders took on and defeated working-class organizations and social democratic parties.

This was the moment of the emergence of neoliberalism—meaning in the European context, two core beliefs. The first was that free markets were preferable to restricted or controlled ones. The second was that governments had to reduce the size of the state sector of the economy. That meant reducing real levels of funding of state-run social services, and whenever possible, ending state control or ownership of industry. It was time, neoliberals believed, to jettison Keynesian ideas about priming the pump or demand management; to neoliberals, dreaming of the halcyon years of free trade liberalism in the late 19th century, markets were better than states in guiding the economic destinies of nations.[31]

With some exceptions, neoliberalism was a popular political platform in Western Europe in the 1970s and 1980s. France was an exception, possibly due to the high proportion of the French labor force in the public sector. Unsurprisingly, it became impossible to privatize the massive French civil service. Thus, we need to set on one side François

Mitterrand's 14 years as a socialist president of France between 1981 and 1995, and on the other, the 11 years that Margaret Thatcher served as British prime minister between 1979 and 1990, and the 16-year period in which Helmut Kohl served as German chancellor between 1982 and 1998.

Neoliberals like Thatcher shifted the center of the political spectrum to the right. She believed that there was no such thing as "society," only individuals whose achievements arose from their innate talents. Time and again trade unions lost bitter industrial disputes in both the private and public sectors. She broke the back of the miners' union, and then dismantled the coal industry itself. Free market competition determined which sectors of the economy lived and which were left to die.

It is at this point that we can see the balancing function of the European project. The European Parliament provided a home for socialists and social democrats voted out of office at home. In Brussels, they could build on the European Social Charter, which came into effect in 1965. That document extended the European Convention on Human Rights to the domain of social and economic rights. The positive rights assured to all those in the European Economic Community included social security, education, healthcare, full employment, and equal pay for equal work. Migrant workers' rights and trade union rights were also assured in this document. It is hardly surprising that neoliberals like Thatcher treated the European project as a misfortune.

Political Violence in Europe

Economic difficulties dominated political conflict in Europe in these years. But what made matters worse was the recrudescence of political violence in Europe. Small groups of extremists, usually termed "terrorists," appeared in many countries. These activists were against the West, but most were hostile to the Soviet Union too. Their commitment to at times spectacular and bloody acts of violence destabilized European political life in these years.

After the wave of student-led demonstrations in May 1968, and the recognition thereafter that not much had changed in the world of education or politics, small groups of radicals, mostly on the left but some on the right, broke away from mass movements and took the path of violence for its own sake. Their descent into nihilism fueled waves of urban bombings, kidnappings, and murders particularly in Italy, France, and Germany. Right-wing atrocities shook public confidence in the police, the courts, and the government as a whole. That was in part their purpose. On August 2, 1980, right-wing terrorists detonated a bomb at the Bologna Central Rail Station, killing 85 people and wounding over 200.

At the end of the economic and demographic growth spurt of the postwar decades, democracies broke down in Europe and in other parts of the world. Greece was ruled by a military junta between 1967 and 1974. Opponents were routinely arrested and tortured. The same was true in Turkey, where military coups took place in 1960, 1971, and 1980. Democratic regimes were overthrown in Chile and Uruguay in 1973, and in Argentina in 1976. Coordinating their repressive measures, all three launched their own "dirty wars" against the enemy within. Thousands were arrested, tortured, and "disappeared."

To European conservatives, and to their American friends, these campaigns of violence prevented communist subversion of the West. Secretary of State Henry Kissinger later admitted participating in the "destabilization" of the Chilean regime under socialist president Salvador Allende, murdered in a coup on September 11, 1973. Even after the American defeat in Vietnam in 1975, diehard Cold Warriors clung to the illusion that falling dominoes topple other dominoes. But the truth was more complicated. Much of the violence in Europe was not communist but separatist in character. In 1968, there was an upsurge in violence in Northern Ireland, where a Republican insurgency was repressed by the British army. Thirty years of sectarian violence followed. Similarly, in the 1970s and 1980s the Basque separatist movement ETA pushed the new democratic Spanish regime to wage a kind of "dirty war" against it.

Troops were on the move in Eastern Europe too. In August 1968, the democratic socialist government in Prague was overthrown by Soviet tanks. Roman Catholic and trade union opposition to Communism in Poland was repressed by the army and the state in the 1980s, but cracks in the edifice of communist authority appeared everywhere in Eastern Europe. Still, the control and manipulation of Eastern European economies by the Soviet Union in its own interests and the maintenance of substantial numbers of Soviet troops in its satellite nations during the period of détente hampered innovation and economic growth in the Warsaw Pact region as a whole.

The communist bloc fell behind the West in terms of per capita GDP between 1950 and 1989, first of all in the Soviet Union and then in Czechoslovakia and Poland. In contrast, Hungary, Bulgaria, Yugoslavia, and Romania, while still well below half the level of GDP per capita in the West, closed the gap between East and West in the postwar decades 1950-90. In sum, the economy of Western Europe outperformed that of Eastern Europe in almost every respect, but within that contrast, some communist states did better than others.

At the same time older currents of anti-Semitism resurfaced in the Soviet Union and the Warsaw Pact countries. One cause of this recrudescence of hatred of Jews was the belief that they were all closet Zionists or agents of Israel, by then transformed into a regional superpower by military victories in 1967 and 1973. Where feasible outmigration followed persecution in these years of state-sponsored oppression.

Migration in the 1970s and 1980s

Western European economic dynamism led to a search for low-skilled migrant labor from the mid-1950s on. Economic growth outstripped population increase at working ages. In addition, the expansion of educational provision within Europe took young workers out of the labor force, and rising wages attracted people to better-paying jobs, leaving other less skilled posts unfilled. Consequently, employers looked outside their own domestic population for additional workers. In Germany and elsewhere the initial policy was to promote immigration on short-term contracts for a year or two, and then rotate these workers with others who would take their place for a similarly limited period. But once initiated, these rotational "guest worker" programs did not work as planned. A short-term solution to expanding the labor force had long-term consequences, since once-established, employers of lower-paid guest workers preferred to retain them and the workers themselves were reluctant to return to their lower-wage countries. In West Germany, these workers came from many countries.

Initially, the largest group of migrant workers in Germany were Italians. By 1972, Turkish workers were the most numerous, and their number continued to grow substantially in the following decades. The bilateral agreement signed in 1961 between Turkey and West Germany on the recruitment of these workers lapsed in 1973, when spiking energy prices increased German unemployment. About half of the Turkish work force in Germany returned home, but the rest stayed and brought their families in Turkey to live with them in Germany. The result was that these people became a permanent part of German society. There were 2 million guest workers in Germany in 1980, but together with their families, they numbered over 4.5 million people.[32]

Growth in the service sector stimulated further the recruitment of both high-skilled and low-skilled immigrant workers, even during times of industrial downturn. In the 1980s Chancellor Helmut Kohl wanted to reduce by half the size of the Turkish community in Germany, but he failed to realize his plan.[33] What the chancellor disclosed was the common view among conservatives that guest workers were a liability that had outlived their usefulness to Germany. Germany was stuck with a trade-off between "immediate selective economic benefits but deferred general socioeconomic costs" of integration. By the 1980s there were more non-working dependents in immigrant families than workers, and higher fertility among these families set up the clash that was to come in the 1990s and after.[34]

There were similar patterns of recruitment and resentment of seasonal or short-term immigrants from the Mediterranean region, as well as from Ireland to the United Kingdom and Finland to Sweden. In 1980 there were the same number of immigrants in French society—roughly 4.5 million—as in Germany.[35] What made the Turkish 'guest workers' and a part of the French immigrant community more difficult to assimilate than other groups was that they were Muslim. We shall return to this difficulty below.

One facet of the problem of immigration in the 1970s and 1980s is that high unemployment rates fueled the view that foreigners were taking the jobs of the native born. This point of friction became explosive when it was combined with frequent clashes between White police and Black city dwellers.

In 1981 and in 1985 there were race riots in working-class districts of London, Liverpool, Birmingham, and Leeds. Many of these districts had large populations of immigrants who had been recruited to help rebuild Britain after 1948. They were termed the "Windrush generation" after a transport ship that brought men and women from the Caribbean to London. They were Britain's guest workers, though more assimilable, everyone thought, because they were Christian. Their later treatment in Britain has been scandalous, in that many lost the right to domicile in Britain through bureaucratic incompetence and casual racism.[36]

Fertility

Massive refugee flows took place in the 1960s and after against the backdrop of substantial population growth in the developing world. International violence added menace to the threat of "the population bomb," the title of a best-selling book published by Stanford University biologists Paul and Anne Ehrlich in 1968. It opened on an apocalyptic note. "The battle to feed all humanity is over . . . nothing can prevent a substantial increase in the world's death rate." Its recommendations were draconian. After considering and rejecting "temporary sterilants" in the water supply, as too dangerous under present knowledge, they advocated tax breaks for those who accepted sterilization, and tax charges for large families. Foreign aid should go to countries working toward self-sufficiency in food, and denied to those like India unwilling or unable to reach this goal.[37] The book sold 2 million copies, and captured an important current of opinion about fertility trends in the 1960s and after.

Neo-Malthusians like Ehrlich were strong advocates of both contraception and abortion, the political and legal conflicts over which have lasted. In one respect, though, the alarmist school that Ehrlich's book well represented had two major flaws. The first was that its prediction of a major increase in death rates due to food shortages for growing populations did not occur. The second was that at the very time they were writing their book, a contraceptive revolution was taking place which, together with expanding education and other changes, would yield declining fertility rates all over the world.

Fundamental research in the United States and in Mexico led to the development of drugs in the late 1950s that received cautious approval in 1960. Carl Djerrasi's synthesis of progesterone in 1951 was an important step in this process. In this ongoing effort Gregory Pincus at the Worcester Foundation for Experimental Biology played a leading role. Backed by the pioneer family planner Margaret Sanger and financed by Katherine McCormick, Pincus developed a contraceptive tested in Haiti and Puerto Rico in 1956. The discussion of the safety of the drug (US name Enovid, UK name Enavid) became entangled with the disclosure in 1961 of birth defects in the children born to women who took the unrelated drug thalidomide. Researchers showed that the contraceptive pill, taken in moderate doses, was no danger to the health of women or to the children they would have once off the pill. Congressional hearings in 1969 helped clear the air and allay women's fears both that they had been used as guinea pigs in the development of the drug and that they were not being told the truth about its risks.[38] From the mid-1960s, the pill became the first easily accessed and effective oral contraceptive in history.

From the mid-1960s, fertility rates in Europe and elsewhere in the developed world began to decline. The end of the postwar "baby boom" was both a return to the pattern of fertility decline evident in the interwar years and a major departure in contraceptive practice. It would be absurd to adopt a single-cause explanation for these trends; demography is messier than that. A balanced claim is that safe and inexpensive contraception was an essential, though not the only, element in the decline of fertility from the 1960s on. In Britain, the decline in fertility since the 1960s was not due to changes in the age at marriage, a variable of great importance in the 1940s.[39] Patterns of women's work and education must be considered in any full account of the decline in 20th-century European fertility.

Before the introduction of the pill, though, abortion served as a common practice of family limitation in most of the world. In Eastern Europe and East Asia abortion was legal and open, though there were variations in official policies in some countries like China.[40] Even after the pill became available, in some countries and despite its risks, abortion continued to be an alternative to contraception. Abortion was legalized in Britain in 1967. Thereafter the National Health Service provided abortions for free. Germany and Sweden legalized abortions in 1974. The following year the Veil Act legalized abortion in France up until the 10th week of pregnancy, a subject we will discuss below. Three years later the Italian Senate legalized abortion. In the Eastern bloc, abortion was legalized earlier, in 1920 in what would become the USSR, and in its satellites, in the 1950s. There were still countries that refused to follow these trends; Ireland legalized abortion only in 2019. But the move toward liberalization in Western Europe was roughly simultaneous with the US Supreme Court decision on *Roe v. Wade* in 1973.[41]

Women's strategies of achieving desired family size were multifaceted. Contraception complemented, but did not entirely replace, abortion. Women's choices arose from multiple sources. As demographer Judith Blake observed at the time, "individuals will employ such methods only when they have, in their judgment, good reasons for doing so."[42] In accounting for the decline in fertility from the mid-1960s on, we must recognize that minds and attitudes matter as well as the availability of effective contraception or the legal status of abortion.

There are many interpretations that emphasize women's attitudes as the primary, though not the sole, source of fertility decline. Some emphasize a flight from risks faced primarily by better-educated women forced to choose between family responsibilities and career aspirations. Smaller family size keeps options open for women who are the primary carers of children.[43] Others find the source of these changes in rampant individualism and a decline in a belief that sex, marriage, and childbearing are necessarily linked.[44] Still others see fertility decline as the assertion of gender equity and of women's rights as human rights.[45] Urbanization and changes in the skill composition of the labor force appear important to scholars of fertility decline in Eastern Europe in the period 1960 and after.[46] It is evident that fertility decline in Europe is part of a broader set of changes that now, with exceptions, have gone global.

Mortality

In the 1940s and 1950s, Europe east and west benefited from major advances in the chemical treatment of bacterial and viral infection, primarily through antibiotics and vaccines. Free or inexpensive healthcare, better nutrition, and improved housing conditions in both Eastern and Western Europe accounts for a striking convergence between mortality rates on both sides of the Iron Curtain between 1945 and roughly 1965. Thereafter, the Eastern bloc countries fell behind the West. In both Poland and Russia, life expectancy at birth for males and females approached that of Italy around 1965. Subsequently, Italy reached the higher levels of Sweden, while there was a rough plateau in life expectancy in Russia and Poland. Meslé, Valin, and Andeyev ascribe this divergence between Europe east and west, primarily to advances introduced in the west in the prevention and treatment of cardiovascular disease.[47]

The same scholars' research helps us see the age structure of the disparity between survival chances in Western and in Eastern Europe in 1965 and 1995. At ages 15–70, males in the former Soviet Union in 1995 had up to twice the probability of dying than that same age group had in 1965. Women ages 15–70 in the former Soviet Union in 1995 had up to 1.5 times the chances of dying than did the same age group 30 years before. In the former Warsaw Pact countries, men at ages 20–60 in 1995 had higher probabilities of dying than the same cohort in 1965. In contrast, women at all ages made gains in survival chances between 1965 and 1995.[48] It is evident that a deterioration in the survival chances of male adults at working ages accounted for the overall worsening of survival chances in the Soviet Union, and to a certain extent in her satellites as well.

One problem in interpreting these data is that they straddle the years when the Soviet Union and its empire collapsed. There seems to have been a short period of improvement in life expectancy before 1990, before a downturn in the chaotic years of the 1990s. Levels of consumption of vodka were high in many parts of Eastern Europe, and very high in the USSR. Mikhail Gorbachev's antialcohol campaign of the late 1980s may have been one of the causes of a decline in infectious and respiratory diseases.[49] On the other hand, the nonexistence in the Soviet Union of anything like the public campaigns against smoking in the West may account for the persistence of high rates of death due to lung cancer in Russia, both before and after the collapse of communism.

This divergence between improving health indicators in the west and deteriorating health indicators in the east constituted nothing less than a public health disaster in the communist world, one especially marked in the Soviet Union. By the end of the Cold War, Polish and Russian cardiovascular mortality rates were between four and five times higher than those rates in Britain or France. The communist regime collapsed for many reasons. We leave open the question as to whether these catastrophic developments in the survival chances—in particular those of men—were the cause of regime change or a reflection of a more general breakdown of the communist system.

Population Polemics

Demographic distortion is the art of hijacking informed discussions of population questions with the intention of proving a political or an ideological point. We explore two instances in which public figures created and disseminated caricatures of debates over demographic phenomena in Europe in the 1970s. The first is the story of a French satiric novel published in 1973. Its theme is a nightmare in the form of an invasion of France by an armada of starving Indians. The second concerns the polemics surrounding a highly contested government campaign in France to decriminalize abortion in 1974.

Jean Raspail and the Great Replacement Theory

What we now call "the Great Replacement" theory emerged in Europe in the 1970s. It was a moment when the "population bomb" was on people's minds, after the publication of a book of that title in the United States and elsewhere, in 1968. Major declines in mortality rates after 1945 had indeed led to massive increases in numbers in the developing world. As we have seen, European populations recovered rapidly from the devastation of the Second World War, but their growth rates were lower in Europe than in the Global South. This disparity between the fertility of the developed and the developing worlds provided the soil in which the Great Replacement theory germinated and flourished in the 1970s and after.

One pioneering literary work helped turn replacement theory into a subject of transnational conversation, especially on the extreme right of the political spectrum. French writer Jean Raspail's *Camp of the Saints*, published in 1973, and republished three times since, is a demographic dystopia. It is also one of the most instructive examples of how fertility rates in different parts of the world, or rising numbers of documented and undocumented migrants from the Global South to the Global North, become the foundation on which an edifice of alarm, pessimism, disgust, hatred, and apocalyptic violence rests.

There are very specifically French features of this work of fiction. The author, a Catholic royalist, led a respectable life as a novelist and travelogue writer. His forays into racist fantasy did not put off most reviewers or admirers. Indeed, he came very close to election to the *Académie Française*, just missing becoming one of France's "immortals." Raspail was no wild man; he was at the center of French culture, though he held views he termed on the right wing of the right wing. In a sense, he seemed to be a more civilized version of Louis-Ferdinand Detouche, who took the *nom de plume* Céline, a celebrated author of racist prose blaming Jews for whatever was wrong with the world. Céline's pamphlet raging about the Jews, published in 1937, is titled *A Trifle for a Massacre*. What is intriguing is that Raspail railed not against the Jews but against what Frantz Fanon termed "the wretched of the earth." Fanon's study of the damage colonization caused both colonized and colonizers was published in 1961, during the Algerian war of independence from France. That war was lost by France, and created not just a massive exodus of European settlers and Algerian supporters of France, but also a wave of bitterness among those nostalgic for the racial ordering of empire and wedded to a belief in the superiority of Europe over Africa and Asia in general and France over Algeria in particular.

There were other elements in the cultural construction of Raspail's dystopia we need to recognize as particularly French. The author pours into his novel his own fears through an old professor Calguès, who sees firsthand the arrival of an "anti-world bent on coming in the flesh to knock, at long last, on the gates of abundance."[50] Calguès is a reactionary French Catholic, sick of the moral cowardice of his country. He dreams of the Crusades. He imagines that in the Middle Ages, he "would have shown a certain zeal in poking my blade through Arab flesh." And centuries later, he would have been a Confederate during "the War Between the States, when my side is defeated and I join the Ku Klux Klan to murder myself some blacks." He dies in a last stand for Christian Europe.[51] Like Céline, Raspail is an *agent provocateur*, a racist proud of his capacity to slay what he took to be the sacred cows of the French Republican tradition.

What did Raspail detest? His revulsion is directed primarily at two targets. The first is the French Revolution and its legacy of liberty, equality, and fraternity. The second is the Roman Catholic Church and its major transformation at the time of the Second Vatican Council. The Council's opening of the windows of the Church to the world of the 20th century was, in Raspail's view, a betrayal of Christianity itself. He blames the invasion of France on "those worker types, from the wrong side of town," who reduced Christianity to the worship of the poor.[52] His reference is to the left-wing worker priest movement of the 1960s and 1970s.

The novel is a savage and uncompromising satire about race and immigration. The setting is the year 2000. Catholic priests in India urge Catholics in Belgium to adopt Indian children and to bring them to Europe. This gesture triggers a mass movement to Europe of boat people, engaged in one vast orgy on their journey. One Catholic aid worker agrees to go to Europe with a waste remover in Calcutta, the lowest of the low. He is called "the turd eater" by Raspail, and together with a horribly deformed child, they join hundreds of thousands of Indians who head for Europe by ship. Their aim is conquest and destruction.

The central question of the novel is whether Europeans will resist this human wave of misery, this stinking "river of sperm," desperate to come ashore in southern France? The French president addresses the nation about this crisis. He refuses to defend his country, urging citizens to follow their conscience in deciding how to treat the army of the poor begging for entry to their country. The French army disintegrates, and the south of France is flooded by violent and voracious migrants. One small band of true Frenchmen fight to defend their country, but they are wiped out by the French air force. Asians and Africans already living in France and left-wing and anarchist groups rally to the side of the newcomers. The new French government, given by Raspail the name of the "Paris multiracial commune," oversees the full takeover of France by non-White people, whose fertility is much higher than that of the locals. Thus White "civilization" is overwhelmed and destroyed by a non-White invasion of pullulating poverty.

The same fate awaits London, led by a "Non-European Commonwealth committee," who force the Queen to instruct the Prince of Wales to marry a Pakistani woman. Miscegenation will wipe out the remains of White Europe. Elsewhere, Chinese peasants overrun Siberia, defended by a single drunken Soviet soldier. The last state to hold out for Europe is Switzerland, whose government refuses to open its borders to the Asian hordes. Deemed a "rogue state" by the rest of Europe, Swiss resistance collapses. Hell on earth triumphs.

In short, Raspail's novel is an explicitly racist tract pointing out that in Europe non-White immigration is an act of suicide. Immigrants are agents of genocide, and so are their European allies and friends. Their aim is not assimilation but conquest and the subjugation or elimination of White Europe. Later we will describe similar outbursts of anti-immigrant prejudice in other parts of Europe, but first we need to specify the particularly French features of the "replacement theory" that spread on the extreme right of the French political spectrum in the last decades of the 20th century.

Raspail noted that the idea for the book came to him while gazing out to sea from a village on the French riviera. On the other side of that span of water is Algeria, the site of a vicious anticolonial conflict. After Algeria was freed from French rule in 1962, approximately 800,000 "Pieds noirs" fled to France. The term "Pieds noirs" meant many things; one usage was shorthand for Europeans who wore shoes instead of sandals. Raspail saw that army of refugees as White Europeans, and therefore acceptable immigrants; it is the African and Asian migrants, people of color, who are anything but Christian, who will overwhelm *les français de souche*, real French men and women, who in their childhood soaked up the soil and culture of France. We should note that to him, Jews in Algeria were *pieds noirs* too; Raspail was innocent of anti-Semitism.

The fact that the novel starts in Belgium points to another part of its ideological message. The city of Louvain was the location of a school of liberation theology in the 1960s and 1970s. There were similar groups in Paris that formulated a new direction for the Catholic Church. The Church, these left-wing Catholics stated, had to have a preference for the poor. Christ the child had to flee persecution, and it was in service to impoverished immigrants that the Church would leave behind its attachment to wealth and privilege. These developments made Raspail nauseous. To him, liberation theology was a pathway to the extinction of White European "civilization," understood as being held together by a hierarchical Christianity systematically destroyed by fools hypnotized by the illusion of racial brotherhood and equality.

Raspail wrote about many themes in his long literary career. His travel writing is full of insight, though with asides telling us what really was on his mind. He admired Costa Rica, he said, a country with very few "mulattoes, Indians or blacks. The Costa Rican nation is 75 percent pure white and the nation tries to preserve the homogeneity of the race by all means."[53] Race is at the heart of many of Raspail's satires. One story is set in Paris in a typical August, when French workers (that is, White workers) are on holiday and flee the city. Immediately, line 7 of the Paris metro, traversing northeastern Paris, reverts to Black Africa, "replete with improvised African drums. A hundred years of Westernization is wiped out in 10 seconds." In "A Strange exploration in the African forest in 2081," a "mongrelized" European population visits Africa. What they find is military despotism and murder on a grand scale. Raspail turns Joseph Conrad's idea that Europe degraded Africa through colonialism into its opposite. Africa is where evil has reached a pinnacle; its savagery is racially determined and lethal to the survival of Christian Europe. In this apocalyptic ideology, older tropes of Black and Brown people literally devouring their imperial overlords are turned into the stuff of nightmare about racial violence descending on an innocent and naive Europe with no imperial past. Ideologies simplify the world and whitewash history so completely that they make racial prejudice into an act of civilizational survival.

Is Raspail's satire an act of pure imagination, and therefore no more reprehensible than Jonathan Swift's 17th-century recipe book on how to cook Irish children and thereby to reduce the problem of poverty in Ireland? The answer is yes and no. His writing challenged conventional assumptions of racial equality. But he also made it clear that his was a zero-sum universe. Either Whites would survive or they would be exterminated. This is the "looming tragedy" to which he draws attention, the tragedy of the replacement of Whites by non-White immigrants.

Raspail, who died in 2020, lived into his 90s, and was surprised by the attention his book received as late as 2017. One reason for the resurrection of his fantasy was its adoption by Steve Bannon, then an advisor to President Donald Trump in the first year of his administration.[54] Bannon had discovered *The Camp of the Saints* a few years earlier, and was drawn to its portrayal of immigration as invasion. As Bannon understood Raspail's message, the West is White, and will collapse if White supremacy is lost due to non-White immigration.

Raspail's message has been echoed by others in contemporary France. Writer Renaud Camus started out on the political left, and became active in homosexual politics. He adopted many other causes, some of which had anarchist or antistate elements. In the 1990s, he became convinced that French society was undergoing a revolution, in that its native stock was being replaced by immigrants. A decline in the birth rate of the native-born French population, matched by higher fertility rates among rising numbers of immigrants would bring about what he termed "genocide by substitution." This was the aim of an elite, dreaming of installing what Camus and like-minded militants called "replacist totalitarianism."[55]

The Great Replacement theory of Raspail and Camus has been adopted both by some Jews and by some anti-Semites in France.[56] Eric Zemmour, an extreme right-wing candidate for the French presidency in 2022, and a French Jew of Algerian origins, has recently decried the "Islamicization" of France. Not to be outdone, a Catholic militant Pierre Hillard pointed out in August 2023 that the granting of citizenship to Jews in 1791 had opened the door to the immigrant flood. Perhaps, Hillard wondered, it is time to reverse the measure of 1791 on the Jews in order to restore French Catholicism to its rightful place in the state and at the same time to halt the immigrant invasion.[57]

And as we note in other parts of this book, the Great Replacement theory has echoes all over the world. Locating the origins of this splenetic mix of demography and demagogy in France in the 1970s is instructive. It shows that the conditions of political and economic instability matter in the reception of ideas about the decline of the West or Christian Europe or the replacement of the White race by others. In the following chapter we shall listen to echoes of this message in the politics of the Hungarian prime minister Victor Orban in 2023. He is not alone.

343 French Women

The specter of the decline of the White race is one instance of polemical fantasies and exaggerations of demographic issues in late 20th-century Europe. Another is abortion. In the 1970s in France abortion reform became an emotive symbolic issue that was distorted time and again by invective, misinterpretation, and calumny. We can see the nearly hysterical atmosphere in which the issue of abortion reform was discussed in three highly publicized moments. To be sure, there was a long preparatory phase in which opponents of the strict 1920 French law forbidding abortion under any circumstances prepared the ground for public contestation. In particular the French Movement for Family Planning (MFPF), through its local centers, educated young people and married couples about contraception, legalized in 1967.

For many Catholics and other traditionalists, that was as far as they would go in liberalizing laws dealing with sexuality and childbearing. When Simone de Beauvoir gathered together a group of 343 prominent French women prepared to sign an open letter that they had all had abortions, and published the letter in the left of center *Nouvel Observateur*, the fight was on.[58] It opened with this declaration:

> One million women in France have abortions every year. Condemned to secrecy, they do so in dangerous conditions, while under medical supervision, this is one of the simplest procedures.
>
> Society is silencing these millions of women. I declare that I am one of them. I declare that I have had an abortion.
>
> Just as we demand free access to contraception, we demand the freedom to have an abortion.

The point was that everyone knew that millions of French women—including the signatories of the declaration—had broken the law; most were married and did so secretly and out of necessity. Calling them criminals was not only absurd; it was itself a scandal and a crime.

The satirical journal *Charlie Hebdo* added fuel to the fire. One of its targets was the conservative Minister of Defense, Michel Debré, a former Prime Minister and an opponent of liberalizing the laws on abortion. A cartoon by celebrated caricaturist Cabu shows Debré responding to a question posed by other conservative politicians: "Who got the 343 sluts signing the abortion manifesto pregnant?" Debré's answer was that he had "done it for France."[59]

Here Cabu was mocking Debré and a long line of pronatalist politicians who did everything they could to increase the French birth rate, as a matter of importance in defense of their country. The language of the caricature stuck. The signatories were from that moment on known as the "343 *salopes* (sluts)."

One of the signatories was a firebrand lawyer, Gisèle Halimi, who was, like Debré, of Jewish origins, and who had defended women raped in detention during the Algerian war. In 1972, Halimi created an organization to defend women accused of abortion. In the same year she took up the defense of a poor 16-year-old girl, Marie-Claire Chevalier, who had been raped, and who had secured an abortion with the help of her mother and some friends. Her rapist, picked up by the police for another crime, wanted to trade information. He informed them that Marie-Claire had had an abortion. The police reported the matter, and charges were brought against Marie-Claire, her mother, and the friends who had helped her. Marie-Claire was judged as a minor, but the others faced charges as adults. They secured the services of Gisèle Halimi as their lawyer.

In juvenile court, closed to the public, Marie-Claire was acquitted, on the grounds that she had not sought out an abortion. Halimi made sure Marie-Claire's photograph appeared in the Parisian press, and that Simone de Beauvoir's denunciation of all aspects of the first trial was published too. Then came the second trial, open to the public, of the mother and her friends. Halimi turned it into a public denunciation of the law. The doctor who had performed the abortion, who was a practicing Catholic, did so, he said, out of compassion for the girl. Halimi called as witnesses an impressive list of the good and the great, including Nobel prize-winners and actors who had signed the *Nouvel-Obs* letter the year before. The verdict was mixed but light. Marie-Claire's mother was found guilty, but her fine was suspended; the woman doctor who had performed the abortion was found guilty and given a suspended sentence of one year. No one went to jail. Instead, the law was exposed as absurd and unenforceable.

This case added to the momentum behind a government decision to end the criminalization of abortion. Here is where we see the most spectacular examples of the ideological hijacking of a practice that French society in general and poor people in particular had already adopted, whatever said the law. The scene of this debate was the French National Assembly. On November 26, 1974, the minister of health, Simone Veil, a centrist conservative, and a Jewish survivor of Auschwitz, introduced a bill to decriminalize abortion. She faced an assembly of 481 men and 9 women. Her first words were personal:

> First of all, I would like to share with you a woman's conviction—I apologize for doing so in front of this Assembly almost exclusively composed of men: no woman resorts to abortion with light heartedness. Just listen to women. It is always a tragedy and it will always remain a tragedy. This is why, if the project presented to you takes account of the existing factual situation, if it admits the possibility of an interruption of pregnancy, it is to control it and, as much as possible, to dissuade the woman from doing so.[60]

These words opened a ferocious debate that lasted for three days. What is striking about the debate is the way so many deputies presented veiled attacks on Veil, not just as the author of a measure they opposed, but as a woman and a Jew. Later a number of them said that they had not known that Simone Veil was a survivor of Auschwitz, who lost her father, mother, and a brother in the camps. Consider these extracts from the debate, and see if such protestations of innocence make sense.

Two right-wing deputies, one a doctor, played in the chamber of deputies a recording of the sound of the heartbeat of a fetus. Start with abortion, they said, and euthanasia is not far behind. Those who suffer will be the same groups murdered under the Nazis. A centrist deputy, Jean-Marie Daillet, went further still. These are his words:

> Suppose we find one of the Nazi doctors who still escaped punishment, one of those men who practiced human torture and vivisection. Is there a difference in nature between what he did and what will be practiced officially in hospitals and clinics in France [under the new law]? [. . .] We have gone so far as to declare that a human embryo was an aggressor [against the mother]. Well, as for these "aggressors," will you accept, Madame, as happens elsewhere, that they will be thrown into the crematorium or fill garbage cans?

Then, the right-wing deputy from Nice, Jacques Médecin, dipped into the muddy waters of the Second World War again. The law does not deserve the title of a law; it is a recipe for chaos. "That is no longer called disorder, Madam Minister. It's not even called injustice anymore. It is barbarism organized and covered by the law, as it was, alas! thirty years ago, by Nazism in Germany." In case anyone had missed the point, de Gaulle's former minister of justice, Jean Foyer, made this prediction: "The time is not far when we will know in France these 'abortion houses' [*avortoirs*], these slaughterhouses where the corpses of little men are piled up and that some of my colleagues have had the opportunity to visit abroad."[61] Hector Rolland, a deputy who had been abandoned by his mother as a child, condemned Veil and her law for making "the choice of genocide."

When questions about her patriotism or subtle jabs at Veil's Jewishness would not do, then accusations of her inhumanity came to the fore. The same Michel Debré who had been caricatured by Cabu, joined the ranks of opponents of the bill. Debré came from a distinguished Jewish family. His father was a celebrated pediatrician. In the debate on the abortion bill, Michel Debré framed his position as that of a humanist:

> Respect for human life is the first stage of respect for freedom. A memory came back to me when I was preparing this speech. It was during military operations in Algeria, in Constantine, when attacks and ambushes killed people every week. Visiting a hospital, I saw, under an incubator of the latest model, two twin girls from a Muslim family, born prematurely—before six months—and whom a helicopter, at the request of the gendarmerie, had gone to pick up in a mountain village. In the midst of hatred and fighting, France strove to maintain the demands of modern consciousness regarding respect for life.[62]

The law passed on November 29, 1974.[63] What did not pass were the personal attacks and prejudices aimed at the woman who presented the bill. There is a simple lesson here, as true in 2024 as in 1974: anyone who enters the always heated public discussion of this highly charged subject will be a magnet for malice and calumny.

2

The New Europe, 1990–2024

Introduction

In periods of political upheaval, discussions of population questions are hijacked time and again by partisans worried about challenges to national identity or the changing ethnic, racial, or religious composition of a nation. Demographic distortion of this kind was particularly evident in the 1990s, when the Cold War came to an end and a new European Union was born.

Endgame

Europe left communism behind in 1989. To many observers, the collapse of the Soviet regime was a surprise, although everyone could see the fault lines. Rigidity, corruption, and inefficiency were evident, but the binary division of the Cold War and the maintenance of nuclear arsenals on both sides gave to the Soviet Union joint responsibility with the United States for ensuring that the nuclear standoff endured. Still, as historian Charles Maier has argued, the West was able, at considerable political cost in the 1970s and 1980s, to restructure the model of industrial growth that West and East had shared between 1940 and 1970. In contrast, the Soviet system put off confronting the need for economic and political reform until it was too late to do so within the communist system.[1] Slowly but surely the Soviet Union lost the support of its own people, as well as that of its satellite states in Eastern Europe. A disastrous military intervention in Afghanistan starting in 1979 and continuing in the following decade exposed not only its military weaknesses but also the structural rigidities of the regime. By the late 1980s, the Soviet system carried on largely through inertia.

When the end came, it deepened an already major social crisis with significant demographic consequences. In this chapter we explore these post-1989 developments and link them to the emergence of an enlarged European Union, forced to cope with refugee flows and the emergence of radical Islam

Toxic Demography. Jennifer D. Sciubba, Michael S. Teitelbaum, and Jay Winter, Oxford University Press.

DOI: 10.1093/oso/9780197745038.003.0003

within Europe itself. In a major departure from its earlier history, Europe in the later 20th century was a net receiver of migrants, and had to cope with the consequences of this change, in particular as it affected the ethnic, racial, and religious composition of the population.

The Fall of the Soviet Union

On December 25, 1991, Mikhail Gorbachev resigned as president of the Soviet Union. It was a gesture without consequences, since the Soviet Union he had led had ceased to exist before he resigned. He fell, as it were, because his seat of power simply had disintegrated.

This revolutionary moment was bloodless, and so was the fall of all but one of the satellite communist regimes in Eastern Europe. The exception was Romania, whose dictator Nicolai Ceaușescu and his wife were tried and executed publicly on Christmas Day 1989; roughly 1,000 people lost their lives during the collapse of the communist regime.

There are many competing interpretations of why the constituent elements of the Soviet Union fell apart. One school of thought is that the last leader of the USSR, Gorbachev, had launched a program of political reform without first addressing the difficult task of economic reform. Deng Xiaoping, leader of the Chinese Communist Party, thought Gorbachev's order of priorities was "idiotic";[2] China followed a different strategy and survived the challenge of 1989. A second school holds that the problem was that Gorbachev wanted to retain and reform the communist system while maintaining his commitment to humane democratic principles. He could not square this circle, and maybe no one could do so. Consequently, his authority in the communist system vanished to the point that some of the old guard attempted a half-hearted coup in August 1991. Their failure opened the door to the anticommunist approach of Boris Yeltsin, who took on the presidency of the Russian Republic. In 1991 Yeltsin declared that there was now a Commonwealth of Independent States in place of the old Soviet Union.

There is a third school of thought that emphasizes the multinational character of the Soviet Union as the key problem. Many observers, especially in the West, have seen the years 1989–1991 as the moment when the last great empire of the 20th century collapsed. One of the problems with this interpretation is that the collapse came from within the "mother country" and was followed in the supposed former "colonies" or satellites of the old USSR.

There were exceptions. The Baltic states were nations forcibly absorbed into the Soviet Union in 1940. Georgia was absorbed into the USSR at its inception. Most of the new Republics were multiethnic states rather than ethnically homogeneous nations, but their new leaders quickly learned the vocabulary of the new language of nationalism of the day.[3]

The collapse of the Warsaw Pact preceded the collapse of the USSR. In 1989, when Gorbachev made it clear that he would not intervene to keep these dictatorships intact, the Communists who had dominated this region since 1945 lost their hold on power. New nationalist leaders, or old leaders who rediscovered nationalism, emerged to replace them. Most of them promised a return to independence and a democratic order that had been destroyed by Hitler and Stalin in the period of the Second World War. Russia had no such democratic path to resurrect. Instead, after a decade of profound economic and social upheaval, a new dictatorship emerged. Boris Yeltsin appointed Vladimir Putin as his prime minister in 1999. A year later Putin was elected as Yeltsin's successor. He was still in power in 2025, having inherited the authoritarian politics of the Soviet Union and a brand of Russian nationalism based on nostalgia for the hegemonic status lost in 1989–1991.

In this chapter we first look at the demographic, social, and political consequences of this upheaval, first in Russia and then in Eastern Europe. We then turn to Western Europe in the same years to chart the rocky but successful incorporation of many of the new nations of the east into the European Union. Finally, we address the implications of the arrival in this period of radical Islam both on the periphery and at the center of Europe life.

Russia's Mortality Crisis

In chapter 1 we discussed the emergence after 1965 of a growing gap in life expectancy at birth between Western and Eastern European countries. The gap between Eastern and Western Europe was striking: Swedes and Italians had a life expectancy about 20 years greater than Russians, and 10 years greater than Poles. In Russia there was a steep fall in life expectancy at birth during the crisis decade of 1985–1995.

High mortality due to cardiovascular disease among males was the main source of the mortality crisis, followed by related causes of death like accidents, violence, and suicide. What was going wrong? Since the 1960s the healthcare system had been breaking down, due to supply shortages and inefficiency.[4] At the same time, observers pointed to high levels of alcohol consumption, stress, and uncertainty about living in a social order that was in the process of unraveling.

It appears that women adapted better to the social crisis of the post-1960 period in Russia than did men. Life expectancy for women in Russia went down by roughly two years during the social crisis of the early 1990s, whereas men lost roughly six years over the same period. Neighboring Belarus also reported the same steeper decline in life expectancy at birth for men than for women in these years. Eastern Europeans were denied the steady improvements that were registered in the West, in particular in France and West Germany.

In 2005, Rifat Atun, a prominent British physician and healthcare specialist at Imperial College London (now at Harvard) wrote an editorial in the *British Medical Journal* titled "The Health Crisis in Russia."[5] His analysis was alarming. Russia's population, he noted, was becoming "smaller and sicker"; this was a departure from the widely accepted notion of a demographic transition from high to low fertility and mortality. In the decade from 1992 to 2003, Russia's population dropped by 6 million, or 4 percent.

Even if we forego comparisons between Eastern and Western Europe, the Russian case remains disturbing. In the early 21st century, the probability that a 15-year-old boy in Russia would die before he reached the age of 60 was twice that in Turkey. Morbidity and mortality rates from noncommunicable diseases for Russian men were three to five times higher than similar rates in the European Union. Smoking, alcohol abuse, and stress due to the transition from one economic system to another again were identified as among the causes of the Russian mortality crisis. And on many occasions, Russia's healthcare system was blamed for largely ignoring prevention to focus on cure.[6]

For once, fears of population decline appeared to be substantive rather than the stuff of fantasy. Not only had Russians lost the prestige of being one of the two hegemonic superpowers, but after the collapse of the Soviet Union they also seemed to be in a crisis of health and welfare of major proportions. President Putin himself admitted that the future of Russia depended on finding a better solution to this demographic crisis.[7] Here is another instance of a political leader insisting that demography is destiny for his nation.

After the turn of the century, there was some evidence that the worst of the health crisis was over. Male cardiovascular mortality rates began to decline in Russia after 2003.[8] The drop in this cause of death was significant, at

3 percent per year, yielding a 50 percent decline between 2003 and today.[9] And yet the gap between Russia and the EU, as well as the gap between Russia and Eastern European countries, remains striking. Cardiovascular death rates for males are still five times higher in Russia than in France or Germany and twice as high as these rates in Poland and Croatia.[10] However we rate the importance of nutrition, medical care, and health administration in generating these vast differences, it is clear that the Russian people suffered both under the old Soviet system and in some respects even more under the capitalist order that replaced it. How President Putin has tried to rally the nation and restore its prestige to the dignified and feared position it once occupied will be discussed below.

The European Union East and West, 1990–2008

The collapse of the Soviet empire had catastrophic consequences for Russian society. Russia's former satellites were similarly disrupted by the arrival of market economies. This is reflected in trends in both fertility and mortality. Demographer Tomas Frejka has shown that after 1990 while mortality rates in Eastern Europe were higher than in the West, fertility rates were significantly lower in the East of Europe. Fig. 2.1. shows that by 2000, the two groups of lowest below-replacement fertility countries in Europe were the old Warsaw pact region and a cluster of nations in southern Europe, including Spain, Italy, Greece and Portugal. German-speaking nations were not fare behind. They include now-united Germany and Austria. In sum, around the turn of the 21st century, the further east and south you go in Europe, the lower the total fertility rate.

Another way of putting the same point is to say that strikingly different regional clusters of total fertility rates appeared in Europe after 1990. There was a near-replacement cluster in Northern and Western Europe, and three lowest, low-fertility clusters, one in Eastern Europe–Belarus, Moldova, Russia, and Ukraine, a second in Central-Eastern Europe–Croatia, Czech Republic, Estonia, Hungary, Latvia, Lithuania, Poland, Slovakia, Slovenia, Bosnia-Herzegovina, Bulgaria, Macedonia, Montenegro, Romania, and Serbia and Kosovo, and a third in the Mediterranean, from Portugal and Spain to Italy and Greece.[11]

What accounts for this regional pattern of total fertility rates? There is no one answer to this question. In some places, relatively liberal abortion policies in the former Soviet bloc were maintained after 1989, and material conditions help explain why women in Eastern Europe deferred first births

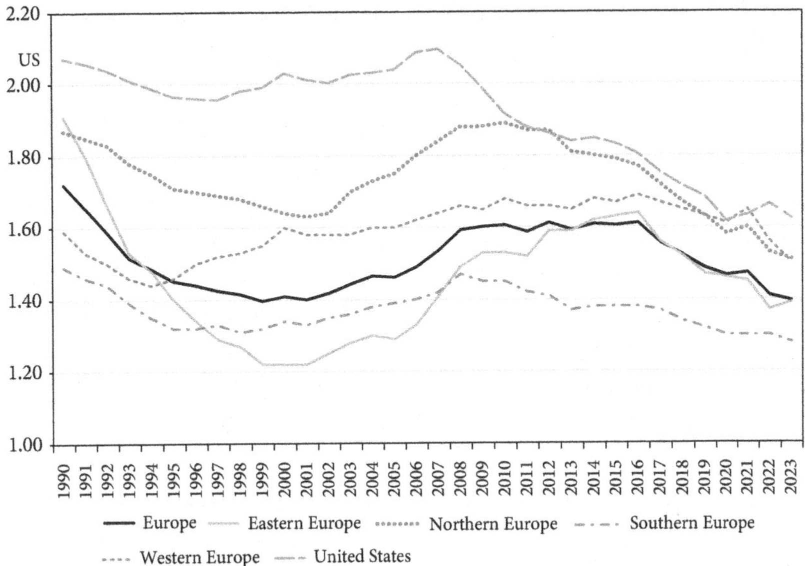

Fig. 2.1 Total Fertility rates Europe and the United States, 1990–2023.
Source: UN *World Population Prospects, 2024 Revision.*

significantly longer than did women in Western Europe. Motivations for doing so varied, but the harsh economic climate in transitional economies played a significant role. In this context it was understandable that women would avoid or defer childbearing, given the risks of raising children as a single mother in countries with relatively low ages at first marriage and high divorce rates. Russia and Ukraine registered the lowest age at first marriage and the highest divorce rates in Europe in 2000. Even in countries with lower divorce rates—Poland, Romania, and Hungary, for instance—the total fertility rate reached historically low levels at the end of the 20th century and beyond.

In the 1990s, population decline became a reality in the states that turned away from communism. The combination of fertility well below the replacement level and relatively high mortality rates ensured negative rates of natural increase. In addition, out-migration, in particular to Western Europe, reduced further the prospects for population growth in the East of Europe.

Part of the story of differential population growth in Europe was political in character. The expansion of the European Union to incorporate the former communist domain in Eastern Europe provided pathways of migration from east to west that have continued until the end of this period (2025).

Migration, Refugee Flows, and the European Union, 1990–2008

In 1985, the European Union promulgated the Schengen agreement. This accord abolished internal border controls in Belgium, France, Germany, Luxemburg, and the Netherlands. In the 20 years that followed, the Schengen area expanded to include Italy in 1990, Spain and Portugal in 1991, Austria in 1995, Greece in 1992, and Denmark, Finland, Sweden, Iceland, and Norway in 1996. A decade later more countries joined: the Czech Republic, Estonia, Latvia, Lithuania, Hungary, Malta, Poland, Slovenia, and Slovakia. The economic advantages in terms of the free movement of people, goods, and services have been significant. The creation of areas of trust in places marked indelibly by bloody wars and frontier and border disputes is one of the greatest achievements of the European Union.

But the political costs have been high. The free movement of labor disrupted traditional labor markets and undermined the ability of trade unions to negotiate agreements on wages and conditions of labor. In some parts of Western Europe, newcomers from the East depressed wage rates, and their presence stirred up nativist resentments among working people. From the mid-1990s until today, political campaigns spread throughout Europe with slogans like "Keep France for the French" or "Keep Ireland for the Irish." Right-wing political parties took up this cause, and when they did not move with sufficient speed or ardor, factions split off from them to speak for "the people" threatened by the inflow of immigrants.

Of equal or even greater importance is the way Schengen affects popular notions of security in many parts of Europe. A common external border means that breaches of one state's secure borders become breaches of all states' borders. Not only does the Schengen agreement lay at the heart of disputes over those seeking refugee and asylum status, but it also makes it very difficult for one nation's police system to keep track of those who have either committed crimes or have been denied the right to settle in Europe.

In the years from 1990 to 2008, there were two periods of political and social tension over the common internal border in Europe. The first was the period of the breakup of Yugoslavia. The second was the debate over the possible entry of Turkey into the European Union.

Civil War in the Former Yugoslavia

After communism, what kind of political forces took the reins of power? By and large the answer was that nationalists came to the fore. Some of them were the very same people who had operated as communists within communist states. This was strikingly the case in Yugoslavia, where by the late 1980s, the patina of communist rule had given way to various forms of ethnic nationalism adopted by former communist politicians in new ideological clothes. Catholic Croats in Croatia confronted Muslims in Bosnia, and both were menaced by Orthodox Serbs, who constituted 70 percent of the former Yugoslav army.

Between 1989 and 1995, these three groups waged a savage civil war, not just for independence or dominance, but for survival. Ethnic cleansing was a weapon of civil war, reaching its nadir in the genocidal treatment of Muslim prisoners of war in Srebrenica. In July 1995, approximately 8,000 Muslim men and boys were murdered; a decade later Serb officials admitted planning and carrying out this crime.[12]

Given the breakdown of the legal order and the savagery of ethnic warfare, it was inevitable that a mass exodus of refugees would take place. That refugee flow challenged the reinforced European Union at the very moment it opened its internal borders to free movement. The reason was that refugees entering one country perforce could enter every other country of the Union.

The number of asylum applicants to industrialized countries soared in the early 1990s. Of close to 1 million applicants, three-quarters applied to members of the European Union.

What was different in the 1990s was that a reunited Germany had to adjust to an unprecedented wave of asylum claimants. As we can see in Table 2.1, applicants in Germany constituted between two-thirds and three-quarters of all such applicants to Europe in the mid-1990s. When the wars in the former Yugoslavia came to an end in 1995, Germany still fielded a majority of all asylum applications to Northern and Western Europe. While only about 15 percent of all asylum applications were approved in Germany,[13] many of those rejected found ways to avoid deportation and remained in the country.

Table 2.1 shows too that among these applicants, a clear majority applied from within Europe. This asylum crisis was clearly triggered by the war in the former Yugoslavia and the social and economic upheaval of postcommunist states in Eastern Europe. Economist Tim Hatton has shown that of these

Table 2.1 Asylum applications in the EU, 1970–1999.

Year	1970–74	1975–79	1980–84	1985–89	1990–94	1995–99
Total EU applications (000s)	64.5	213.7	540.2	1012.3	2419.8	1613.5
Country of application						
Austria	8.7	14.7	63.2	64.4	76.1	53.5
Belgium	1.7	6.6	14.5	32.1	87.0	93.4
Denmark	3.7	1.3	5.6	42.1	76.4	36.0
Finland	–	–	0.1	0.3	11.4	6.9
France	5.1	40.5	106.3	178.7	184.5	112.2
Germany	34.3	121.8	249.6	455.3	1374.7	749.6
Greece		9.2	6.4	24.0	12.8	11.8
Ireland	–	–	–	–	0.5	21.2
Italy	11.0	9.2	16.5	26.3	40.8	48.8
Luxembourg	–	–	–	–	0.1	5.7
Netherlands	–	5.3	8.8	46.4	151.1	170.4
Portugal	0	1.7	4.3	1.3	3.9	1.7
Spain	–	–	5.4	15.7	53.1	30.4
Sweden	–	–	41.9	97.1	197.0	48.5
UK	–	3.4	17.5	28.5	150.8	223.3
Region of origin						
Africa	–	–	57.8	169.0	452.2	292.4
Asia	–	–	278.3	464.1	677.3	672.0
Europe	–	–	141.1	291.3	1164.1	483.2
Latin America and Caribbean	–	–	12.1	28.9	31.7	19.2
Other/Unknown	–	–	50.9	58.9	94.5	146.7

Source: *UNHCR* (2001a), Tables I.2, II.2, III.2, IV.4, and VI.5

applicants, only 15 percent were successful.[14] The adoption in Germany of restrictive policies on the admission of asylum seekers helped stem the flow of asylum applications to Germany; the numbers for 1995–1999 are roughly half those of 1990–1994. This decline in applicants helped Germany survive hostility and violent incidents against immigrants in general and asylum seekers in particular.[15] Other European leaders watched Germany closely, and saw the way the explosive political and social implications of a surge in the number of asylum seekers could be defused by adopting restrictive policies.

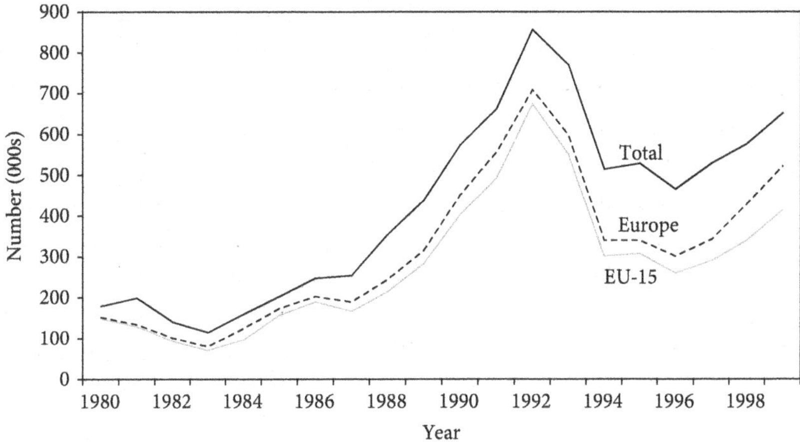

Fig. 2.2 Asylum applications in Europe and in all industrialized countries, 1980–1999.

Source: Timothy J. Hatton, "Seeking Asylum in Europe," *Economic Policy* 19, no. 38 (2004): 9.

Europe and Islam

The second instance of political conflict in Europe with direct demographic consequences in the period after 1989 is the debate over the entry of Turkey into the European Union. The first time a Turkish government entered into negotiations on membership was 1987. From December 2004, another set of negotiations opened on that issue. The obstacles were formidable. One commentator listed them seriatim: Turkey was too big, too poor, too agricultural, too authoritarian, and above all, too Muslim.[16] Its legal system did not conform to the norms of European law. All true, but there were other reasons why negotiations stalled time and again. Inclusion of Turkey would insert the EU directly into the cauldron of Middle Eastern politics. After all, the American and British invasion of Iraq had begun only one year before.

Turkey had been a member of the Council of Europe since the latter's founding in 1950. It was also a member of NATO, and had been a keystone of the anti-Soviet military bloc. Turkey also occupied a strategic position in the Middle East, one that successive Turkish leaders exploited in discussions about ties to Europe. In November 2002, the Turkish government under Recep Tayyip Erdoğan decided to pursue actively an application of membership in the EU.[17] A decade later, negotiations were still incomplete, and yet Erdoğan was optimistic. He promised to complete all necessary steps by 2023, the centenary of the founding of the Turkish Republic. That goal has proved unreachable for both sides, though there are numerous bilateral agreements that govern the relationship between Turkey and the EU on visas, refugees, migrants, police and security cooperation, and other topics.

Why was it so difficult to find a way to incorporate Turkey into the European Union? Differences over human rights or the Cyprus problem or other sensitive matters were apparent, but the critical problem was Islam. Adding 60 million Muslims in 2000 or 80 million Muslims in 2020 to the population of a European Union with open internal borders was and is politically impossible.

Radical Islam in Europe, 1990–2008

In the early 21st century, it became even more difficult to advocate a major increase in the Muslim population of Europe. The reason: the threat of radical Islam, both on the European periphery and within Europe itself.

The first region to be hit by systematic and sustained Islamic terrorism in Europe was the territory of the former Soviet Union. The break-up of the Soviet Union had been the occasion for the emergence of Islamic nationalist parties and armed groups in the Caucasus region between the Black Sea and the Caspian Sea. These groups used the tactics of terror to fight against Russian or Russian-backed forces, whose savagery in counterterrorist operations matched that of their adversaries.

On September 4 and 8, 1999, two apartment buildings, one in Dagestan and the other in Moscow, were targeted by Islamic militants from Chechnya.[18] Two separate wars between Chechen nationalists and Russian and pro-Russian forces in the mid-1990s had devastated Chechnya. Hostage-taking, assassinations, and the rape and torture of civilians became regular facets of the conflict. A second war in Chechnya lasted from 1999 to 2009. Once again, combat was indistinguishable from terrorism. On October 23, 2002, 50 Chechen militants seized a Moscow theater; the terrorists were all killed, but so were 124 hostages, victims of gas used by security forces to overwhelm the militants. Two months later, suicide bombers killed 72 people in Chechnya's pro-Moscow-government building. On February 6, 2004, an explosion in the Moscow subway took 40 lives. Chechen separatists claimed responsibility for the crash of two Russian passenger jets in late August 2004. A few days later, in the most lethal of such attacks, 50 Chechen terrorists attacked a school in Beslan in neighboring North Ossetia. They took 1,000 hostages, and after a siege, 330 people, mostly children, died in the police rescue operation. While these separatist movements failed to achieve their political objectives, they introduced an element of permanent insecurity into the Russian Federation that continues to this day.

There was a second theater of violence that had significant repercussions in the 1990s. Commercial and political ties between North Africa and Southern Europe have been strong for centuries. Migrants have moved from south to north for centuries. In the mid-1960s over 1 million mostly Christian and Jewish residents of North Africa fled Algeria after it won independence. Thereafter labor flows of both North Africans and sub-Saharan Africans continued from Morocco, Tunisia, and Algeria to Southern Europe, linking families in the two continents in a permanent embrace.

The threat posed to Europe by radical Islam became more ominous during the 1990s, when radical Islamic groups engaged in a vicious civil war with the state in Algeria. In 1990, after the Islamic Salvation Front (FIS) took a commanding lead in local elections, the Algerian army suspended elections, and declared the FIS an illegal organization, thereby triggering a decade-long civil war that took a toll of roughly 250,000 lives. The same pattern of massacres of civilians and torture practiced in Chechnya marked the Algerian civil war.[19] Muslim militants committed atrocities against Christians, and in particular against French missionaries who had been there for decades. One French film following the story of a group of monks decapitated in Algeria, *Of Gods and Men*, won the grand prix of the Cannes film festival in 2010.[20]

The war led to an outflow of Algerians escaping the civil war to France and to the spread of some militant Islamic groups with them. One demographer put the number of French residents of Algerian origin in 1999 as 1.5 million; thereafter much higher estimates have been published. The ambassador of France in Algeria put the number at 7 million in 2017.[21] Recent estimates of residents of Algerian extraction living in France also go as high as 7 million, or above 10 percent of the population of France.[22] The tide of violent conflict within Islam reached the shores of Europe at the end of the 20th century and continued to take lives thereafter.

Islamophobia

Islam has been part of European culture for over a millennium. What distinguishes the period since the 1990s from the past is the level of violence imported into Europe by Islamic radicals engaged in a global civil war within Islam. Fear and loathing were unavoidable when commuters were murdered in Madrid and in London by Muslims who lived alongside non-Muslims in these European capital cities.

The phenomenon of Islamophobia arises when rational fears of violence are transformed into essentialist fantasies about the intrinsically murderous character of Islam itself. Jihadi violence provoked understandable public outrage, but some went further and saw Islam itself as a time bomb threatening Western society. Such dangerous caricatures were reinforced by the periodic explosion of violence in Israel, the West Bank, and the Gaza strip. Ongoing war in the Middle East has spilled over into European politics and has added bitterness and invective to the discussion of the threat posed by Islamic radicalism in Europe. Ideologists of national identity respond to these perceived dangers all over the world. But in Europe, the memory of the Holocaust is a political reality, especially, though not only, in Germany. Anti-Israel protests slide into anti-Semitism there as elsewhere, and because of Germany's commitment to the security of the state of Israel as a foundational belief, German politicians and civil servants react swiftly to any recrudescence of anti-Jewish sentiment.

Populist Pessimism

On December 13, 2007, all members of the European Union (EU) signed the Treaty of Lisbon, strengthening the central institutions of the EU. This event marked two decades in which Europe went through the most radical political reorganization since the First World War. The collapse of communism and the Warsaw Pact coincided with the consolidation of moves toward European integration begun with the Treaty of Rome in 1957.

These massive structural changes in sovereignty and political power effectively created a new Europe. Nationalists east and west were troubled by these events, and found in demographic trends reasons to mobilize in opposition to them. The problems associated with migration, refugee flows, and asylum seekers reflected the anguish of nationalists in the west of

Europe who felt threatened by the European project, understood as a loss of sovereignty and identity. In the east, Europe stopped at the borders of Russia, Ukraine, and Belarus. In the Russian sphere of influence, the collapse of the old order created conditions in which resentment grew at the humiliation of Russia as a former great power.

We shall have more to say below about populism, but a few introductory remarks here may be useful. "Populism" is a flexible term, with a long history, but its most recent incarnation occurred in the 1990s and after. What populists shared was a resentment at the failure of traditional political parties to defend the old order. Populists mourned a decline in national, regional, or local power and prestige. The "people" for whom they claimed to speak, they hold, have been betrayed by elites, responsible for standing by or even engineering the eclipse of the nation.

Populism took many different forms, and yet what links the outlook of many populists is their tendency to see national decline in demographic terms. Time and again they seized on high migration in the context of low fertility to frame their accusations. While international migration did moderate population decline in Europe,[23] populists were right in claiming that it changed the ethnic and religious composition of national populations. And that is what they could not abide. Later in the chapter, we shall discuss more fully the growth of populism in the last 20 years, but it is important to note that the phenomenon appeared earlier.

From the 1990s on, Islamophobia became part of the populist's arsenal. The best way to understand Islamophobia is to see it as a cultural code in which non-Muslim Europeans express their general fears for the future at a time of political and economic instability. In this respect, Islamophobia was similar to anti-Semitism in the pre-1945 period. The fear of the Other, whose religion and loyalties were suspect, was hardly a new phenomenon,[24] but it took on new forms in the context of the massive shifts in the political structure of Europe at the turn of the 21st century.

Cultural pessimism works best when it posits a prelapsarian myth, a story of innocence before the fall. There was a time, such pessimists muse, when there was order and justice in the world. Then came the arrival of alien elements. Their presence offers uneasy or desperate groups a streamlined explanation for their perceived vulnerability.

Cultural codes work as metaphors for decline. They reduce multiple challenges to one big problem, and make that the source of all that ails their world. And yet codes of cultural pessimism work best when they give to aliens a special power to undermine the society to which they have come. That attribution enables the fearful to focus on the outsider as the chief menace to the nation or to their community. As we shall see below, echoes of these sentiments reverberate in Europe today.

Populism and Population Anxieties in Europe, 2008–2024

Political instability marked the European continent in striking ways in the first quarter of the 21st century. In many cases, the mainstream mass parties of left and right have lost their hold over many of their supporters. New groups of angry militants, representing "the people," supposedly neglected by the old parties and their leaders, came to the fore. We call them "populists." In the west, populists led the charge in the effort to end Britain's membership in the European Union. In 2016 they won a referendum, the populist's preferred form of direct democracy, on "Brexit", or British exit from Europe, which duly took place in 2016. In the east, a people's revolt of another kind overthrew the dictator of Ukraine, triggering armed conflict with Russia first in 2014 and then more violently, since 2022. The war in Ukraine sent shock waves throughout Europe, posing disturbing questions about the future of the continent. And to make matters worse, the COVID pandemic took 2 million lives in Europe alone, paralyzing social and economic life for several years.[25] What is striking about many of these upheavals is the manner in which demographic issues—matters of births, marriages, migration, and deaths—became weapons of political warfare.

Inequality in the Twenty-First Century

In 2013 French economist Thomas Piketty produced a learned tome that unexpectedly became a global bestseller.[26] *Capital in the 21st Century* showed how capitalism worked 150 years after Marx's classic analysis. And like Marx, Piketty argued it worked effectively only for a small minority and consigned the rest of us to living in an increasingly inegalitarian world. Piketty used the voluminous archives of the French Ministry of Finance to show that inequality of wealth and income had increased significantly in the late 20th and early 21st century in France. Piketty then showed that this French trend was older, stretching back to the late 19th century and going forward with one big exception—the 30 years after the Second World War. And from the mid-1970s on, increasing inequality was a worldwide trend, arising from the fact that in global and domestic markets, the return on capital exceeded the rate of economic growth. He expressed this finding in a snapshot formula: r > g. Historian Charles Maier succinctly explained why this formula was explosive: r > g meant that "capital must claim a greater share of national income over time, all the more so when the greater rate of saving (and thus returns on savings) among higher earners were calculated. Since the wealthy derived more of their income from capital than from work, inequality must increase."[27]

Not everyone followed Piketty's interpretation, but he found support from a source not usually aligned with the left. McKinsey's Global Institute analyzed income data on the world's 10 leading economies, holding 60 percent of the world's wealth. McKinsey showed that "At the level of the global economy, the historic link between the growth of wealth or net worth, and the value of economic flows such as GDP no longer holds."[28] Why did net worth grow more rapidly than GDP? Their answer is that price increases outstripped increases in investment. The descendants of Marx's capitalists were hoarding their ballooning wealth outside the production boundary of national income analysis.

Piketty's argument that profits and other kinds of income from capital grow faster than wage income let another cat out of the bag. Trade unions and Socialist parties resting on support from them had colluded unintentionally in this phenomenon by privileging efforts to maintain national economic growth over measures to promote income equality. Global capital closed factories in Britain, Belgium, or France and relocated them in Asia, where labor costs were lower. In Europe, the factory and the factory worker no longer dominated the economic landscape, and neither did the workers' representatives in the trade union movement.

Social democratic coalitions had led the reconstruction of Europe after 1945, and the brief exceptional period of diminishing inequality that followed the war. But 70 years later, their raison d'être had faded away. Structural inequality in wealth was impervious to legislative intervention in one country since it was global in character. Tax great wealth in France, and it will move with the touch of a cell phone to another more protected country. Reading Piketty, it was no longer evident that a vote for the parties of the traditional left would help reduce inequality, or help create jobs in a country stripped of them by global corporations.

A disturbing set of questions flowed from his work: the outlook of the 21st century left was out of date. No one had a good idea as to how to replace it. In France, the Socialist Party's share of the vote in national elections between 2012 and 2022 dropped like a stone in a deep pool of water. The party gained less than 2 percent of the vote in 2022.[29]

Structural inequality helped discredit the political parties of the traditional right in Europe too. For decades they had entered into coalitions with their social democratic adversaries in many European countries. After the global economic crisis of 2008, some felt that conservatives became not the solution but part of the problem of an economic system that gave to the very wealthy everything they asked for and left the rest to live with diminished hopes and incomes. Centrist parties of the right faced challenges over immigration and asylum seekers. If they could not "protect" the nation, new carriers of the torch of nation, race, and religion would do so.

The New Populist Challenge

Filling the political vacuum created by the atrophy of European parties of both the left and the right were a very mixed group of political movements generally known as "populists." They were there before the turn of the 21st century, but took on new life and vigor in recent years. There is no one term that can capture the allure of the coat of many colors of populism. Here we will present just three versions of populism.

One group is best known by its hostility to the European project: Euroskeptics. A second group are advocates of what may be termed "Nativism," a kind of terrified patriotism, fearful of an alien invasion made worse by declining birth rates among home-grown populations. A third kind of populist is obsessed with the "Conspiracy of the Experts," who are in the pay of the rich and the powerful, and who create or manipulate health crises to maximize their profit and control. Together, they cut right across the European political spectrum from left to right to create new spaces for angry oppositional politics. In each kind of populist politics, demographic issues become political hot potatoes, thrown around for effect rather than for serious discussion. Populists are masters of rhetorical distortion. Let us examine each of these breeds of populist politics in turn.

Euroskepticism

Euroskeptics are drawn to two kinds of opposition to the European Union. One focuses on its democratic deficit.[30] European Union Commissioners are appointed by political leaders. They are not elected by popular vote. They do the work of applying policy to the different member states of the EU. To be sure, there is a European Parliament, and a European Court of Human Rights, but the EU is not a federal state with a federal constitution, like Australia or the United States. It is not even a confederation, like Switzerland. The EU is a "partnership" among sovereign states, who sign a Treaty of Accession to become full members, and who fund the workings of the EU.

A second group of opponents to Europe argue that it undermines national sovereignty. Governments of states in the EU recognize that the judgments of the European Court of Human Rights take precedence over the judgments of their own supreme courts. This is a considerable sacrifice of national autonomy, and so is the acceptance by most members of the EU's free internal labor market. Those countries accepting the Schengen accords of 1985 and 1990—23 of the 27 member states—have no border controls within the EU. Citizens of any member state have a right to work and live in any other member state. In 2025 roughly 400 million people residing in the EU are eligible to do so.[31]

The balance between European identity and national, regional, and local identities is an uneasy one. The core states—France and Germany—believe the EU is an antidote to destructive nationalism. There are patriots in every member state who fear that EU policies corrode their national identity and undermine the freedom, security, and well-being of their citizens. The more power the EU has accrued, the more local patriots have felt diminished, marginalized, and ignored. Many of them are the "losers" in the "rigged" economic system Piketty described—rigged, that is, to make the rich richer. Others who oppose being in the European Union are well-off, but unprepared to pay the annual membership fee for being in the EU or to share their advantages with substantial numbers of immigrants. There is no inherent reason why people cannot feel comfortable with two collective identities, one European and one national. Especially at times of social tension, though, shedding or renegotiating the terms of European membership can appear to be a positive step,[32] seized by populists as their pathway to power.

Brexit

The best instance of this kind of populism was the Brexit campaign of 2016 that succeeded in capturing the anger of working-class communities in the north of England whose traditional industries were gone.[33] They came together with patriots throughout the country who never bought into the European idea in the first place, and cynical politicians who joined the bandwagon once it got rolling. On June 23, 2016, over 15 million people voted to leave the European Union; 12 million voted to stay.[34] The United Kingdom's days in Europe were over.

Demographer David Coleman provided in December 2016 a precise snapshot of what Brexit was all about. "The vote," he argued, "was about more than the economy, or even migration and specifically English resentments. It matched a mood shared with many industrial states: a disaffection with politics illustrated by falling turnouts and party membership, a dislike of rising inequality and insecurity, and a distrust of a political elite disconnected from popular contact and opinion."[35] Brexit was a populist victory, and at the heart of that success was worry about immigration. A reliable poll captured the issues that underlay the pro-Leave victory. Here is Coleman's summary of it: "For Leave supporters, sovereignty and autonomy were the most important considerations," and the only way that immigration could be controlled. "Few saw economic advantage in leaving." Of all referendum voters "66 percent believed that EU immigration to the UK would decrease if Britain left the EU; 44 percent even agreed that the government's annual net migration target of 'tens of thousands' . . . could be achieved following Brexit."[36]

What drove the Brexit campaign was concern over EU immigration: between 2000 and 2014 over 3 million EU immigrants came to the United Kingdom. Many were young workers from the Eastern European countries that had recently joined the EU. The inflow meant that migration accounted for roughly 85 percent of the population increase of the United Kingdom between 2001 and 2012. The total fertility of immigrants was higher than the native-born, though assimilation was likely to bring the two figures closer together over time.[37]

Coleman accounted for the link between demographic change and political outrage. What made EU immigration unacceptable to many was "First that it is driving population growth and size to highly unsustainable levels, and second that it is rapidly changing the composition of the population

Table 2.2 Change in the ethnic composition of the population of England and Wales, 1991–2011.

	1991	2001	2011
	Population (millions)		
Total population	49.9	52.0	56.1
White	46.9	47.5	48.2
White British	n/a	45.5	45.1
Other White	n/a	2.0	3.1
Non-White	3.0	4.5	7.9
	Population (percent)		
White	94.0	91.3	86.0
White British	n/a	87.5	80.5
Other White	n/a	3.8	5.5
Non-White	6.0	8.7	14.0

Source: Census 1991, 2001, 2011. David Coleman, "A Demographic Rationale for Brexit," *Population and Development Review* 44, no. 4 (December 2016): 682.

in ways highly unpopular and damaging to the social structure."[38] The new immigrants were bound to increase pressure on the nation's housing stock, on classroom size, and on the National Health Service.

There was a second element in the Brexit crisis. Immigration had effects on the ethnic composition of the British population. Coleman showed in tabular form the source of popular fears. In Table 2.2, the category "other White" is largely EU recent immigrants. Taken together with non-White immigrants, they constituted 12 percent of the British population in 2001, but almost 20 percent in 2011, and there were much higher proportions of "other White" and "non-White immigrants" in London and other major cities. This "alien invasion" triggered the shift in public opinion registered in the Brexit vote.

The political exploitation of these fears was open and unabashed. The United Kingdom Independence Party (UKIP) led by Nigel Farage organized a mobile campaign to rally the "Leave" vote. On the side of one of his bandwagons was a poster announcing "The Breaking Point: the EU has failed us all." In the background were thousands of Syrian refugees, fleeing the civil war in their country. The conclusion was clear. Those getting into the EU were sooner or later going to arrive in the United Kingdom. The unstated message was that they were Middle Eastern Muslims—definitely in the space between "other White" and "non-White." Were some of these people planning to form "sleeper cells" of terrorists in Britain? No one could be sure.[39]

The "Remain" camp cried foul, but the message could not be contained.[40] Its subliminal anti-Muslim message was picked up in other Leave posters.

And yet, to characterize all Leave voters as racists was a mistake. Some were racist, but others harbored deep anxieties over immigration of whatever race. The Archbishop of Canterbury, Justin Welby, was adamant on the point that fears over immigration were both endemic and understandable. They were not, he believed, racist in character:

> There is a tendency to say "those people are racist," which is just outrageous, absolutely outrageous [. . .]. Fear is a valid emotion at a time of such colossal crisis. This is one of the greatest movements of people in human history. Just enormous. And to be anxious about that is very reasonable. In fragile communities particularly [. . .] there is a genuine fear: what happens about housing? What happens about jobs? What happens about access to health services? There is a genuine fear.[41]

To be sure, there were other political factors that tipped the balance in the Brexit vote. The two mainstream British parties – Labour and Conservative – were divided internally over the issue of membership in the European Union. In addition, the tabloid press, more vulgar and garish than similar publications in other countries, played a central role in getting the Leave message across to both Labour and Conservative voters. The outpouring of anti-immigrant rhetoric that they orchestrated struck a chord in a population unhappy about the security of their country and the capacity of essential services to cope with increasing numbers.

AfD: The Alternative for Germany

Euroskepticism came late to Germany. While the majority still supported the EU, the Eurozone crisis of 2008–2012 shook German confidence in the capacity of European institutions to control the shock waves arising from the burden of debt in Greece, Portugal, Ireland, and Spain. Bailouts and other measures stabilized the banking sector, but at the cost of massive increases in unemployment in these countries. Germany was more fortunate; her unemployment rate remained below 5 percent, lower than all other European countries (and the United States too). And yet, given the political commitment of both mainstream German parties to the EU, there opened up a space for those in Germany who were fearful for her future.

The Alternative for Germany (AfD) was created in April 2013, and won seats in the European Parliament the following year. It secured a presence in 14 of the 16 state parliaments and won 94 of 709 seats in the election for the federal parliament in 2017. That number made it the third-largest party in Germany. Over time, the party took up an increasingly anti-EU stance, in particular on the subjects of the Euro and immigration. It has been subject to surveillance by the state offices for the protection of the Constitution. A series of court decisions confirmed that such surveillance was justified, determining that the AfD was engaged in extremist political campaigns. In 2021, the party registered 20 percent of the vote in the districts that were formerly in East Berlin. The party's strength nationally was greatest in Saxony and Thuringia, formerly regions of East Germany. In September 2024, the party won the largest number of seats in regional elections in Thuringia, outstripping both the Conservative and Socialist parties.[42] Then in the German federal elections of February 2025, the AfD became the second largest parliamentary party, supplanting the center-left Social Democratic party, by winning 30 percent of the popular vote, and 152 of the 630 seats available.

Muslim immigration to Germany is the issue on which the AfD's campaign rests. Thomas Meaney, a liberal observer in residence at Berlin's Einstein Forum, places this issue in the context of a broader sentiment among AfD backers that Germany's political elite has betrayed the population.[43] Here is his account of attending the AfD congress in 2017:

> In Stuttgart I was awoken by a large man outside my hotel window wearing a niqab. "I am the protest for the AfD/and that is totally ok!" went the hoarse refrain. It was the annual convention for the Alternative für Deutschland, Germany's no longer fledgling far-right party. More than four thousand of the faithful had converged in Stuttgart to make it the largest rally of its kind in Germany since the war. (Unlike other German political parties, which send delegates to conventions, the AfD leadership, true to its populist credo, had invited all members to attend.) For AfDers passing by, the niqab man from Pforzheim was a Charlie Hebdo caricature come alive: a bit of a chore for the media-relations department, perhaps, but nevertheless a rude emblem of the cause.[44]

Björn Höcke leads the party in Thuringia. He opposes Germany's asylum policy and "worries openly about the dilution of the ethnic German population due to the 'reproductive strategies' of Africans." He is prepared to tolerate street fighters like "Pegida" (Patriotic Europeans Against the Islamicization of the West). To garner press headlines, he uses old Nazi slogans in his speeches.

It would be a mistake, though, to label these people as neo-Nazis, who have been a marginal presence for decades. The new parties are more dangerous, in that they bring into the mainstream views that previously were discredited by contact with racist thinking. Like other populists, they use provocation to air their belief that Islam is a threat to Germany and to the West as a whole.

Other prominent figures in German public life have advanced such views. As we have noted in the Introduction, a Social Democrat and former board member of the German Bundesbank, Thilo Sarrazin, published a bestseller in 2010 called *Germany Abolishes Itself: How We Are Putting Our Country at Risk*. In it, he warned of Turkish immigrants' "innate mental deficiencies" and called for safeguarding the German Volk from "genetic contamination."[45] Closing down immigration for all but the most highly skilled is the remedy these people offer.

Professor of philosophy Peter Sloterdijk has helped spread the AfD message. In a popular monthly journal, he used the language of Nazi legal theorist Carl Schmitt to argue that in today's Germany it is the refugee, by crossing the nation's borders, and not the state, who defines German sovereignty. Schmitt famously defined the sovereign as he who takes decisive action and declares a state of exception when democracy no longer works, as Hitler did in 1933. When asked about immigration, Sloterdijk replied to Meaney, "no society has the moral obligation to self-destruct."[46] That is exactly what the AdF believes: immigration is a lethal threat to German society.

Sloterdijk bottles their message in catchy phrases. Social tension, he says, produces "rage banks" from which "rage entrepreneurs" draw their savage denunciations. Refugees release this rage, and so are enemies of the peace. Sloterdijk clearly enjoys shocking people, and his scattergun technique of universal denunciation manages to hit a real target or two. But he is less a populist than a kind of pilot fish swimming alongside the populist whale. He thrives on their power to frighten conventional people. With such popularizers, is it surprising that anti-immigrant and anti-asylum sentiment has gone mainstream in Germany?

Populism and Population in Hungary

The coming to power in 2010 of the Fidesz party and its president Victor Orbán presented another instance of the intersection of populist politics and demographic issues. This time, demographic regeneration was not a theme of a marginal group of extremists. It was at the center of the ideology and rhetoric of the regime and its ruling antiliberal party. Claiming to be the champion of family values, successive Orbán administrations have sketched out a Christian pronatalist program. The government was anti-immigration, in particular, during the refugee crisis of 2015. To Orbán and his followers migration should not be the driver of population growth. To the contrary, migration was a threat to the Hungarian nation.

We will survey a number of facets of this form of Hungarian biopolitics. Among them are the division of the nation into the native-born and the "other," conceived of as an irreconcilable split between friend and enemy. The term "enemy" has Christian-Muslim overtones and undertones, referring to Hungary's long conflict with the Ottoman empire and today's jihadi cells. Other enemies are outsiders, liberals and Jews, trying to manipulate Hungary from abroad. Hungarian-born American Jewish financier George Soros is enemy-in-chief.

Minorities, to Orbán and his followers, are a threat to the Hungarian nation, alongside Muslims, refugees, and immigrants. The nation's Roma population is a case in point; it numbers below 500,000, or 5 percent of a population of a little under 10 million. A recent court case brought out to what extent ethnic discrimination against Roma is at the heart of the Fidesz movement. As soon as Fidesz came to power in 2010 it moved against policies aimed at integrating Roma children in Hungarian schools. Families of children put in separate schools challenged this policy first in Hungary and then in the European Court of Human Rights in Strasbourg. This legal challenge is known as the "Gyöngyöspata case," named after a town in north Hungary. The plaintiffs won the case in Strasbourg. What stung Orbán was that the European Court said that the Hungarian government had an obligation to "undo a history of racial segregation."[47] Instead, they brought in new measures of what they called "benevolent segregation." The European Commission launched an infringement procedure against Hungary.

Here, we see all the pieces of this puzzle come together. The quarrel was over minority rights. The European Court found for the plaintiffs and put its law above that of Hungary. After losing the case, the Hungarian government was instructed by its own Court of Appeals to pay compensation to the Romani parents who brought the case.

It was at this point that Orbán had had enough. In a number of broadcasts, he said the Gyöngyöspata case "violated the people's sense of justice." He called the Roma "workshy" and their children unruly and violent. In classic populist language, he stood up for the real victims of the case—the Hungarian majority. "Non-Roma in Gyöngyöspata," he said, "began to feel that they had to back down and apologize, despite being the majority. They feel like they are in a hostile environment in their own homeland." He went further: "I am not from Gyöngyöspata, but if I were to live there, I would be asking how it is that, for some reason, members of an ethnically determined group living in a community with me, in a village, can receive significant sums of money without doing any work, while I work my butt off every day." The entire case was to Orbán a "provocation," set in motion by outsiders led by financier George Soros.

The "people" finally saw the faces of their enemies: minorities, liberals, refugees, outsiders, wealthy philanthropists, and (some) Jews. Orbán defended himself against accusations of anti-Semitism by citing his repeated statements of support for Israel. He didn't hate all Jews, just liberals. It is unlikely some of his supporters made the distinction, but what matters most here is the juxtaposition of Hungarian nationalism against both minorities and the European Commission.[48]

Orbán has gone even further. In two separate speeches he declared his allegiance to White, Christian "civilization." After the refugee crisis of 2015 and repeated acts of Islamist violence in Europe, he reached this conclusion in 2017:

> I find it very important that we should preserve our ethnic homogeneity. Nowadays, one can say such a thing, though a few years ago, one would have been executed for such a turn of phrase. But now, one can say things like that because life has confirmed that too much mixing causes trouble. We Hungarians are naturally heterogeneous in the sense that we are a European nation. If we just started reading the names of those present here today, they would reveal all sorts of nationalities: from Bunjevci to Swabian. But in ethnic terms, these fall within certain limits, and so there is still a certain ethnic homogeneity. We are from a single civilisation. Preserving this is a key issue.[49]

Five years later, in 2022, he made clear that "his" civilization was White European:

> There is a world in which European peoples are mixed together with those arriving from outside Europe. Now that is a mixed-race world. And there is our world, where people from within Europe mix with one another, move around, work, and relocate. So, for example, in the Carpathian Basin, we are not mixed-race: we are simply a mixture of peoples living in our own European homeland. And, given a favourable alignment of stars and a following wind, these peoples merge together in a kind of Hungaro-Pannonian sauce, creating their own new European culture. This is why we have always fought: we are willing to mix with one another, but we do not want to become peoples of mixed-race.[50]

Demographic Summit

On September 21–24, 2021, Orbán hosted what he called a European demographic summit to discuss the "Renewal of Europe." Attending it were the leaders of four Eastern European states—Hungary, the Czech Republic, Poland, and Slovakia—as well as former American vice president Mike Pence. This was the fourth such meeting, called to rally support for measures to increase national populations through a rise in the birth rate rather than through immigration, a threat to the "cultural identity" of each and all.[51] What they did not want for their countries was the "vast migratory nightmare" of Western Europe, where substantial Muslim immigrant communities threatened the "preservation of Europe's Christian culture." Unstated but in the air was the theory of "the Great Replacement" of White Christian populations by others.

The meeting issued a declaration based on the notion that "The vast majority of Europeans are family-centric" and that "family-friendly initiatives" work to improve demographic indicators. While "increasing the number of European children is essential to preserve Europe's Christian culture," immigration is not the right means to do so. The signatories also called for each country to enact measures consistent with its own traditions and for "the mainstreaming of demographic considerations in all EU policies."[52]

That last commitment seems uncontroversial, but it touched on the way demographic debates have exposed weaknesses within the structure of the

European Union itself. In its current form, the EU has adopted measures to strengthen its policy on clarifying and strengthening the way it handles all stages of asylum and migration management.[53] The EU also has a policy for "investing in children," outlining ways of supporting families and children, including those of first- and second-generation immigrants. At no point does the EU document indicate that migration is a less preferred option than an increase in the birth rate or that migration is a threat to the culture of the native-born.[54]

European populism is both inside Europe and a thorn in its eastern side. Orbán has cultivated the art of provocation, and regularly risks losing EU funding through violations of European law. Such acts seem to increase his support within the Hungarian voting public, producing a stand-off. How long such tensions can be contained is anybody's guess.

Populism and the Plague: COVID in Europe

Migrants and COVID Mortality

So far, we have focused on the multiple ways European political groups and leaders have made political capital out of trends in fertility, family formation, and the ethnic composition of the population. In similar ways, those in search of evidence to advance their political goals have seized on facets of the mortality crisis associated with the COVID epidemic of 2020–2022.

One striking feature of the first wave of COVID was the extent to which migrants living in but born outside of Europe both contracted the disease at significantly higher rates and suffered substantially higher mortality rates from the disease than did people born in Europe. This finding was even more striking when compared with the lower mortality rates such migrants registered in the years 2016–2019. This migrants' advantage was more than canceled out during COVID.[55]

The explanation seems to be that many such migrants, the bulk of whom are of working age, live in substandard housing in crowded urban centers, and may not have had access to testing, medical care, or vaccination during the pandemic. Many work in industries, such as healthcare, in which transmission rates of the virus are high. Together, these factors account for higher morbidity and mortality rates due to COVID, especially in the first wave of the pandemic. French, Spanish, Portuguese, Norwegian, Italian, and Swedish data support this conclusion.[56] What is true for migrants is also true for poor people among the native-born populations. COVID deepened the health disadvantages of social inequality worldwide.[57]

The Hidden Hand: Populism and the Conspiracy of the "Experts"

The remarkable development and distribution of an effective vaccine against COVID saved lives in Europe as it did in other parts of the world. But the rapid arrival of vaccines stimulated a form of populism we have yet to discuss in this chapter. It is the populism of conspiracy theorists, those who turned the COVID emergency into a vast money-making operation on behalf of sinister and shadowy elites.

One variety of populism juxtaposes the good sense of "the people" against the arrogance and corruption of elites and their experts. During the COVID epidemic we heard the argument that medical and scientific knowledge is being manipulated by Big Pharma. Critics claimed that the rot is so deep that state campaigns to vaccinate everyone in the midst of the COVID pandemic were a sinister response to a fabricated medical crisis, intended to make fortunes for the companies producing the vaccines. Who knows, some speculated further, whether other chemicals or even microchips were also being injected into an ignorant and docile public? Suspicion of experts of all kinds underlay doubts about the credentials of scientific and medical "experts," funded by public and private interests suspected of corruption or worse.[58]

Conspiracy theories are almost always the product of febrile imaginations rather than of systematic study. But it is important to see the extent to which some anti-vaxxers expressed an argument that is not so easily brushed aside. To sociologist Ulrich Beck, writing in 2000, to doubt the voice of "experts" was an inevitable response to problems built into the nature of the advanced industrial societies in which we live. Why did the "experts" not foresee the 2008 economic crisis?

Indeed, Beck went on, in our private lives, none of us can calculate accurately the increasing risks we face in building our families or our careers. Under conditions of uncertainty, we construct and try to adapt to what he termed "risk societies."[59] Consequently, risk-averse behavior of various kinds makes sense to large sections of the population. Some refuse to risk parenthood, since marriage is an unstable institution, and responsibility for childcare for single parents lands disproportionately on the backs of mothers rather than fathers. If a woman wants both a fulfilling family life and a rich professional life, she may have to curtail the first to achieve the second. Risk-averse professional women will have fewer children than did their mothers, who were not so troubled by risk. Thus, declining fertility is in part a response to the prevalence of divorce under conditions of patriarchy, meaning a set of values placing primary responsibility for childcare on the shoulders of women.[60]

The level of risk we all faced rose exponentially when the COVID epidemic broke out in March 2020. At that point, shock, fear, and disbelief combined in many circles to produce wild stories about the origins of the pandemic. Was it the product of a leak in a Chinese lab, as some Westerners said?[61] Or was it a leak from a US Army lab, as the Chinese retorted? We may never know its origins, just as we do not have a clear idea about the origins of the influenza pandemic a century ago. In 1918–1919, there was no effective treatment for what was called the Spanish Flu. In contrast, and with dizzying speed, an effective COVID vaccine was developed and became available in late 2020. Some studies claim that vaccination between December 2020 and December 2021 saved between 15 and 20 million lives.[62]

One of the costs of this staggering achievement was what some called the arrival of the "pandemic surveillance state."[63] It was evident that tools developed to track patterns of viral infection could be used for other purposes. Furthermore, the privacy of individual medical files seemed to vanish when a public health emergency broke out. Parallels emerged between COVID exposure and the transmission of sexual diseases; both are dangerous and require invasions of privacy to stop the spread of infection. In Europe, mobile phones and bank cards have been surveyed to track the movement of carriers of COVID. Contact tracing platforms are powerful tools almost impossible to control once made commercially available. Those who fear the shadow of Big Brother on our freedoms were quick to see the threat. These worries were not about imaginary dangers, but real ones.

But for others, the global effort to contain the COVID pandemic quickly turned into the stuff from which wild conspiracy theories were born. Even before an effective vaccine emerged, and information technology was applied to tracing those infected by the virus, the question of vaccination was hijacked by those convinced that both the disease and its treatment were artificially created by sinister elites. These shady elites, never explicitly identified, were supposedly the authors of a vast conspiracy both to make staggering fortunes and to control the world's population. Social media made the viral circulation of these claims possible and their refutation very difficult. Those who get their information online and only online were vulnerable to conspiracy theories posted one moment and shared by thousands or more, minutes later.

What may be termed "biological populism" was born during the pandemic. Some refused to be vaccinated on the grounds that they did not trust the companies or political leaders of countries producing the vaccines. No matter that unvaccinated people risked contracting COVID themselves, and even worse, risked infecting the elderly or other people with medical conditions that made them vulnerable to severe forms of the disease. Those who resisted vaccination distrusted the state and its experts, who told everyone to get vaccinated and penalized those who refused.

Anti-vax populists distrusted mainstream political parties as either naive or part of a conspiracy to defraud the public. In a distortion of the content of the World Economic Forum's June 2020 call for "the Great Reset" of economies after COVID, right-wing conspiracy theorists saw vaccination and national mandates for limiting the pandemic as steps leading to the control of the global economy by sinister, shadowy forces.[64] Some linked vaccination to the Great Replacement theory by claiming that those vaccinated would become infertile. In this febrile atmosphere, vaccination was a form of "White genocide," a term bandied about among conspiracy theorists who popped up in every European country.[65]

We should not be surprised that a pandemic that took between 3 and 7 million lives, 2 million of them in Europe,[66] and infected 700 million people created in its wake an ideological firestorm of accusation, counteraccusation, and sheer nonsense.[67] For those unable to follow Albert Camus's sage advice in his allegorical novel *The Plague*—that the best way to confront an epidemic is to go about your life with dignity—fantasy and paranoia shaped a populist nightmare. Unfortunately, there are no vaccines available to inoculate people against the urge to invent conspiracies. When epidemic disease is at issue, paranoia or just plain foolishness can be lethal.

Putin's Plague: The War in Ukraine

The exception to the rule of caution on admitting refugees has been the European response to the outflow of between 5 and 7 million Ukrainians after Putin launched his invasion of their country in February 2022. In contrast to the tensions observed when Syrian refugees fled the civil war in 2015 only seven years later, there was an upsurge of support both moral and material for Ukrainian victims of war. In part, there was genuine shock that Putin had brought the full weight of the Russian army to bear on the Ukrainian people. As in Syria, and before that in Chechnya, Russian tactics included targeting civilians and their neighborhoods, schools, hospitals, and maternity homes. Children and families in the occupied east of the country were moved to new homes in Russia and given new Russian identities. Once the Ukrainian army stopped the initial onslaught, European support for the Ukrainian people at home or in exile was significant. To be sure, Ukrainians were unlike Middle Eastern refugees. They were Christian, and, so the logic went, not under suspicion of unwittingly harboring terrorists in their ranks.

As of 2025 this wall of European solidarity with Ukraine still stands, though cracks have appeared in it here and there. Viktor Orbán has staked out a position of neutrality as between Moscow and Kiev. His argument is that Russia cannot lose the war, due to its massive material advantage in the conflict; hence a negotiated settlement is the only way out. Donald Trump has weighed in to say that European nations who don't pay their share of the costs of NATO deserve to be attacked by Russia. His provocations captured headlines, as they were intended to do.[68] There are protests on the part of Polish farmers over the "dumping" of low-priced farm produce from Ukraine across their common border. As always, waging war by alliance is an unstable matter, and it is too soon to tell what will be the position of European public opinion or of Europe's populists should the war drag on for years.

What we can say is that Ukrainians do not threaten the ethnic—meaning White—composition of European populations. So far, Ukrainians have not triggered discomfort similar to that Brexiteers felt about the presence of Polish plumbers competing with their British brethren. Refugees are not the same as migrants seeking better-paid jobs. Furthermore, Poles are on the front line of this war of drones and missiles targeting civilians, and they share a visceral sense of vulnerability with their Ukrainian neighbors. And yet, who knows if the tide of European sympathy for them will turn into a trickle or disappear altogether? Given the upsurge in violence in the Gaza strip starting in 2023, and the war between Israel and Iran that followed in 2025, the attention of Europe's leaders and people is less focused on the war in Ukraine than it was at the moment in 2022 when Putin's forces invaded the country.

The choices faced by the combatants are starker still. Both Russia and Ukraine have faced population decline over the last 30 years. In the current war, both have suffered from heightened male mortality and outmigration of young adults in the population. The Russian outflow may reflect unwillingness to serve in the military, or a general disenchantment with their life chances should they remain in Russia. Ukraine, too, has paid a demographic price for staying the course in the war. Its total fertility rate before the invasion was about 1.14, a figure significantly lower than Russia's 1.4 in 2021. Internal and international displacement, family separation, and military service have probably lowered both figures. War has always been the enemy of family life, and this conflict is no exception.[69]

No one would call Putin a populist, since his power does not rest with the people, nor does he fight against corrupt and conspiring elites, most of whom he controls. But in very cruel and cynical ways he does play the numbers game as well as any populist. Just as Viktor Orbán dreams of the times when Hungary was a great nation, so does Putin conjure reveries about the Russian past. Ukraine is an intrinsic and inseparable province of Russia, he claims, confusing a shared history and cultural affinities with citizenship. By invading the country, he has managed to create the very monster he fears—a fiercely distinct Ukrainian national identity.[70] At the same time, he has revitalized NATO and brought into the fold erstwhile neutrals. In 2023 Finland formally joined NATO, and a year later Sweden followed suit, reinforcing the enduring truth that those who open Pandora's box almost always lose control of their future.

From the vantage point of 2025, how far we have come from 1945! It is true that war has returned to the European continent, but the European world east and west bears hardly any resemblance to that rising from the ruins of 1945. And yet, some facets of political conflict remain strikingly similar. Then as now political leaders view population questions through ideological lenses that almost always distort them. Most still believe that declining numbers mean diminished power and prestige. They still like to hear their native language spoken and admired in the world. They still prefer homogeneous to ethnically mixed populations. Racial tensions are still there. They feel that migrants are usually a headache, although occasionally they are treated like cousins in temporary difficulties.

In Europe as elsewhere, fertility, nuptiality, mortality, and migration are not just measures of human behavior but matters invested with values, emotions, traditions, and beliefs. As such they fuel heated and occasionally explosive political discussions and debates. Demography is indeed about the past and the present, about people's lives and hopes. It is also about the fire next time.

PART II
THE UNITED STATES

3

Demographic Transformations and Political Realignments, 1945–1990

The Allied victory over the Axis Powers in 1945 was followed by at least 45 years of momentous changes in both international and domestic politics, many of which were neither anticipated nor desired by the victorious powers. Over this period the United States experienced robust economic growth and prosperity, as one of the few countries actively engaged in the war that did not experience severe damage to its infrastructure and territory. The period also proved to be one of unprecedented demographic changes, occurring at tempos that for the most part had not been anticipated. These political, economic, and population trends were interlinked, and in many ways the trajectories they followed in the United States were similar to those in Europe (see chapter 1).

Domestic Politics

From roughly 1945 to 1965, domestic public policies of the New Deal and the political ascendancy of the Democratic Party that began during the 1930s were consolidated and became firmly institutionalized. Economic growth during this period accelerated and was sustained, notwithstanding several recessions and downturns. And higher fertility and population growth rates reappeared and accelerated as well. Between roughly 1965–1990, domestic US politics became more contentious and fractious, but per capita economic growth continued (net of inflation, as measured by real GNP per capita) despite occasional economic downturns.

Toxic Demography. Jennifer D. Sciubba, Michael S. Teitelbaum, and Jay Winter, Oxford University Press.

DOI: 10.1093/oso/9780197745038.003.0004

The Politics of Demographic Trends, 1945–1990

As can be seen in Fig. 3.1, overall US population growth was substantial in the decades following World War II. The total US population increased by nearly two-thirds, from around 154 million in 1950 to around 252 million in 1990. Annual population growth rates fluctuated considerably over this period, initially rising to over 1.7 percent during the late 1950s and early 1960s, then decelerating to below 1 percent by the end of the 1980s.[1]

Fertility: Boom and Bust

The driving force of the high postwar US population growth was a sustained and unprecedented "baby boom," in which the total fertility rate rose from the 1940 level of 2.1 to a 1969 peak of about 3.7—an increase of nearly 75 percent in less than two decades. To better place this postwar baby boom in its historical context, Fig. 3.2 provides an overview of US fertility trends over the long term, from shortly after the founding of the republic to 1990.

As may be seen, the total fertility rate has been steadily declining from the very early days of the new republic in 1800, when it was about 7 children per woman, to more recent levels of under 2. This fertility decline became steeper during the Great Depression of the 1930s.

But the most notable anomaly of this very long-term fertility decline was the baby boom that occurred during the 3–4 decades after World War II. By the standards of the prior 150 years, these few decades experienced

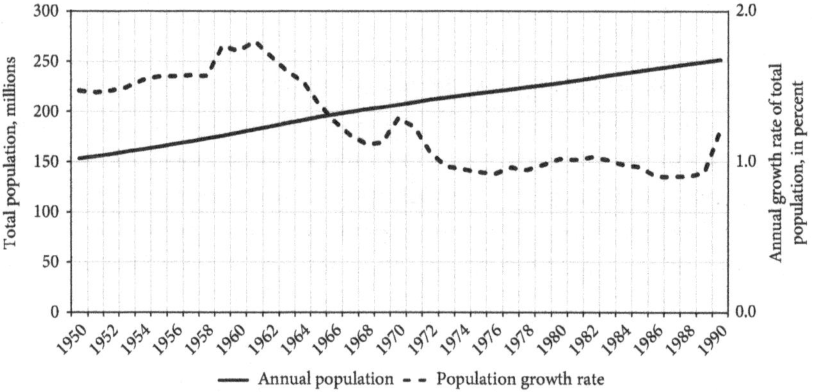

Fig. 3.1 Total population and annual growth rate, United States.
Source: UN *World Population Prospects, 2024 Revision.*

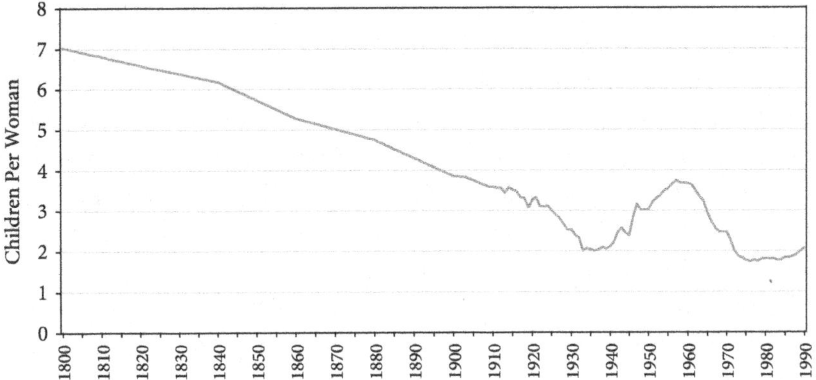

Fig. 3.2 Total fertility rate in the United States, 1800–1989.

Source: Data compiled by Gapminder, various sources http://www.gapminder.org/data/documentation/gd008/.

unusually rapid—one might even say dramatic—fertility increases and subsequent fertility decreases. The upward surge in fertility was not limited to a few years of postwar demobilization, but instead was sustained for nearly two decades. As may be seen more clearly in Fig. 3.2, this upward surge was followed by an abrupt reversal that some call the "baby bust"—fertility declines that began in the early 1960s and accelerated through the 1970s to reach an interim low in the mid-1970s.

While many who write of this period in Europe and other developed countries also refer to their "postwar baby booms," these fertility increases would more accurately be described as short-term "boomlets" for a few years immediately following the war, when fertility rose sharply but then reversed directions and declined to far more moderate levels. There are a few, though not many, exceptions of countries that experienced large and sustained postwar baby booms similar to that of the United States. In general, these were developed countries that, though involved in the war, were located outside war-torn Europe, most notably Canada, Australia, and New Zealand.

The causes of the multidecade postwar cycle of upward and downward fertility experienced in the United States has been a topic of extensive research, which we can only summarize here. Part of the postwar fertility increase was indeed driven by "catch-up" as in Europe and other developed regions—additional births that had been deferred during the war years, due both to the marital separations and deferments caused by military mobilization as well as to the many economic uncertainties and challenges that prevail in a time of global war. There were other factors at play as well. During this multidecade period of welcome peace and a return to "normalcy," the average age at marriage became younger, while a large army of demobilized male soldiers returned to jobs that had been filled by women during the wartime emergency. Marriage and family norms reverted to prewar norms, while broad measures of living standards adjusted for inflation (as measured by real gross national product per capita) improved steadily and substantially, as can be seen in Fig. 3.3.

As traditional marriage patterns and related childbearing became more prevalent and earlier, births that otherwise might have occurred in subsequent years were recorded earlier.

Political and Other Effects of the Baby Boom/Bust Cycle

This multidecade "boom-bust" fertility cycle experienced in the United States engendered long-term echoes over subsequent decades that had significant implications—social, economic, and political—as the trajectory of rapid and sustained fertility increases followed by rapid and sustained declines translated into birth cohorts that initially more than doubled in size over the two decades of the 1950s and 1960s—and then rapidly reversed course. With understandable delays as newborns gradually aged into childhood and then adulthood, the boom-bust cycle first led to sharp increases in the size of key age cohorts such as those entering school, higher education,

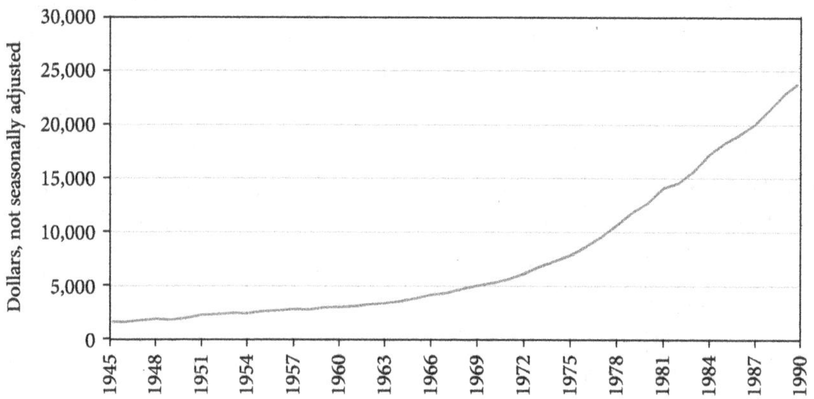

Fig. 3.3 Gross national product per capita, United States, 1945–1990.

Source: US Bureau of Economic Analysis, *Gross national product per capita* [A791RC0A052NBEA], retrieved from FRED, Federal Reserve Bank of St. Louis; https://fred.stlouisfed.org/series/A791RC0A052NBEA (accessed November 23, 2024).

the labor force, marriage, family formation, and retirement, followed within 2–3 decades by substantial declines in the size of such age-defined categories.

These in turn produced a series of social and political challenges that were both disruptive and costly for age-related social institutions such as education, health, and labor markets. Political responses had lagged well behind the fertility upsurge. Because fertility data are collected at the state level, national compilations usually become available at least 1–2 years later, and in any case, it was hard to know if the reported trends would last for a few or many years. By the mid-1950s, however, it became clear that the baby boom would persist.

In response, public and private decisions at both national and local levels mobilized to expand capacity to meet rapid growth in the age groups they served, initially in maternity facilities, then in primary and secondary education, and then in higher education. These expansions were understandably slow, because they required years to plan, finance, and implement. Indeed, by the time some of these expanded resources became available, the sharply higher fertility rates to which they were responding had begun to moderate.

During the decades of the baby boom, and facilitated in part by federal political decisions such as low-cost mortgages for World War II veterans under the 1944 Servicemen's Readjustment Act (almost universally known as "the GI Bill") and later from the Veterans' Administration and Federal Housing Administration, rural areas on the outskirts of cities were rapidly transformed into suburban housing developments that offered affordable and more spacious single-family homes suitable for larger families. Meanwhile, large government investments in a new Interstate Highway system made suburban housing more accessible, while car ownership proliferated as factories previously converted to produce military equipment reverted to consumer products.

By the 1960s other unrelated factors began to emerge that tended toward deceleration and then reversal of the postwar fertility increases. Modern methods of contraception, such as oral contraceptives and intrauterine devices (IUDs), became available and proved more attractive and effective than older methods of voluntary fertility regulation. The first oral contraceptives received regulatory approval in 1960, and experienced enthusiastic reception and rapid adoption by many women; two years later over 1 million US women were using oral contraceptives. In 1965 the US Supreme Court struck down laws in some states that had limited the use of contraception by married couples (*Griswold v. Connecticut*), and during the same decade a few US states led by Hawaii and New York liberalized state laws that had long prohibited abortion.[2]

In 1973 the US Supreme Court declared most state laws prohibiting or unduly restricting abortion to be unconstitutional (*Roe v. Wade*). Over the ensuing two decades there were substantial increases in the number of reported legal abortions. The best data have been collected separately by two unrelated organizations: the governmental US Centers for Disease Control (CDC), and the nonprofit think tank Guttmacher Institute. These two data sources use somewhat different definitions and data collection methodologies, and the absolute numbers reported by the CDC generally are lower. However, the time series from both sources show similar trends following the 1973 Supreme Court decision: substantial increases from between 615,000 (CDC) and 744,000 (Guttmacher) in 1973 to peaks of between 1.4 million (CDC) and 1.6 million (Guttmacher) in 1990, that is, increases of 127 percent and 115 percent respectively. Both time series then show substantial declines over the ensuing two decades, by between 65 percent (CDC for 2021) and 42 percent (Guttmacher for 2020). The Guttmacher Institute data also suggest modest increases after 2020, whereas the CDC data show an end to previous declines but no increase.[3]

In effect, the up-and-down fertility cycle from 1945–1990 produced a kind of demographic whipsaw. At considerable cost, the major age-related institutions—most notably those in education and health—expanded to meet surging demand during the 1950s–1970s. But by the 1980s these expanded capacities began to be in surplus when subsequent but unanticipated fertility declines led to declining demand and to projections of continuing future declines. Unfortunately, many local school boards misinterpreted such projections as credible forecasts, and moved to shrink the educational capacity they had been expanding over the prior 2–3 decades. Sometimes they did so in ways that were difficult to reverse, by reducing teaching staff and closing or selling schools, actions that later were seen as unwise as enrollment plateaued and then began to rise again.[4]

During the same period, aspirations for additional education were on the rise among young American women, and coupled with the effects of new antidiscrimination laws and regulations women's educational attainment and labor force participation began to increase rapidly. This development was one factor underlying increases in age at first marriage, as more and more young women chose to enter higher education and/or the workforce rather than the earlier marriage and childbearing patterns of the immediate postwar decades.

Though the direction of causation is unclear, and indeed is likely to be reciprocal, the availability of modern contraception and legal abortion coincided with the emergence of the "Second Wave of Feminism"[5] (also called "The Women's Liberation Movement") that ultimately became one of the most successful social and cultural movements in US history. This development is discussed below.

Immigration Boom, 1945–1990

Over the same period as these rapid shifts took place in US fertility, there were also dramatic changes underway in both the policies and trends in international migration. The US had long been one of a small number of "traditional countries of immigration"—a list similar to that for countries with sustained postwar baby booms, including Canada, Australia, and New Zealand, and a few others (such as Argentina and Brazil). Most of these relatively new and sparsely populated countries had long been actively recruiting immigrants to populate their expansive territories and to expand their workforces and economies.

To inform the discussion that follows, Fig. 3.4 provides a useful long-term overview of the number of US immigrants and their share of the total US population over the period from 1850 to 2023.

From Numerically Unlimited Legal Immigration to Restrictions by National Origin

During the 19th century there had been no numerical limits nor visa requirements for immigration to the United States. To the contrary, there was active immigrant recruitment—especially by manufacturing employers concentrated in the US Northeast and Midwest, which recruited immigrant labor in Southern and Eastern European countries with low wages and high levels of unemployment and/or social tensions, and by railroad and mining companies of the then sparsely populated American West recruiting labor in Mexico and southern China. In the middle of the 19th century, the California Gold Rush attracted large numbers of would-be miners from many parts of the world followed by even larger numbers of other migrants attracted by rising wealth and demand for services. The growth of long-distance

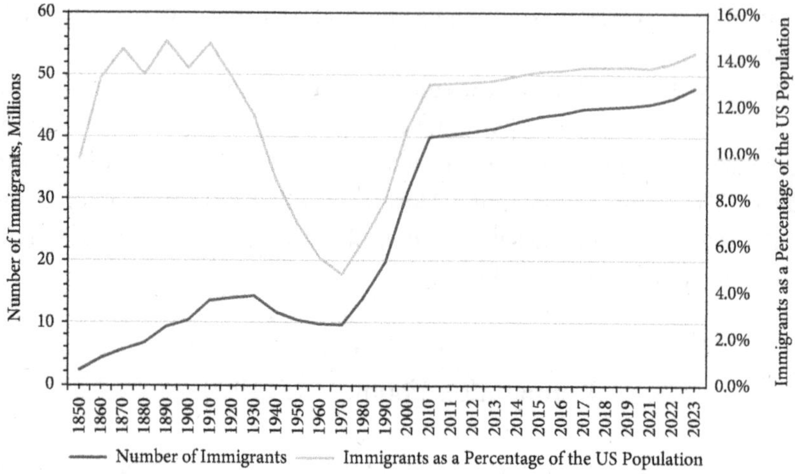

Fig. 3.4 Number of immigrants and their share of the total US population, 1850–2023.

Source: Migration Policy Institute (MPI) tabulation of data from US Census Bureau, 2010–2023 American Community Surveys (ACS), and 2000 Decennial Census. All other data are from Campbell J. Gibson and Emily Lennon, "Historical Census Statistics on the Foreign-Born Population of the United States: 1850 to 1990" (Working Paper no. 29., US Census Bureau, Washington, DC, 1999).

migration also was powerfully facilitated by the development of steam power, which transformed expensive, arduous, and dangerous movement by sea and land into relatively rapid, safe, and cheap options.

Political Opposition to Increased Immigration

Over time, this surge of immigration aroused domestic political opposition, emerging first in California and leading to national legislation known as the Chinese Exclusion Act of 1882. The politics of such restrictions were driven in part by flagrant racism against Asian immigrants, but also by mobilization of US workers and unions against employers' efforts to recruit immigrant workers with far lower wage expectations and greater reluctance to join growing unions. By the turn of the 20th century, Asian immigration to the United States had been sharply curtailed by legislation and enforcement. However, immigration from Eastern and Southern Europe was not curtailed and continued to expand rapidly through the second half of the 19th and into the 20th century, until it ended with a bang as the onset of World War I disrupted transatlantic passenger travel. Political opposition against rising immigration from Eastern and Southern Europe had also been on the rise, again propelled by both prejudice and the rising struggle led by organized labor against employers' recruitment of lower-wage workforces from abroad.

Public support for enhanced restrictions on Eastern and Southern European immigration was also deeply intertwined with the domestic politics related to World War I, in what came to be known as the first "Red Scare" in the United States.[6] The "Red" here refers to the Bolshevik Revolution of October 1917 in Russia, but such fears were also linked to perceived domestic threats from surging agitation and violence by radical and anarchist groups, of which some of the most visible leaders were immigrants from European countries such as Germany, Italy, and Russia.

During World War I, a triad of new laws were rapidly enacted to address such concerns—the Espionage Act of 1917, the Sedition Act of 1918,[7] and the Immigration Act of 1918. In 1919, a series of letter bombs were sent to prominent Americans including millionaires, a Supreme Court Justice, and then attorney general Alexander Palmer.[8] Two months later simultaneous bombs exploded in eight US cities, and in 1920 a large bomb in the New York financial district killed 38 and injured more than 100. Such bombings were widely attributed to anarchist groups linked to immigrants from Southern and Eastern Europe.[9]

In this fraught political context, a new "Emergency Quota Act" was enacted in 1921 with broad-based political support. It established the first, though temporary, numerical quotas that sharply limited future immigration from Southern and Eastern Europe while allowing far higher quotas for immigration from Western and Northern Europe. The successor Immigration Act of 1924 modified and reduced the 1921 Act's quotas, and made them permanent. It also effectively banned nearly all immigration from much of Asia, but did not impose numerical limits on immigration from sparsely populated Latin America. In the opinion of the Office of the Historian of the US Department of State, the goal of this legislation was "to preserve the ideal of U.S. homogeneity."[10]

For our purposes it is important to understand that most of the measures originally adopted during the 1910s and early 1920s continued in force for an extended period stretching over 40 years, well into the period that is the focus of this book. The key immigration policies adopted during the early 1920s were not repealed until 1965, as we shall see. As may be seen in Fig. 3.4, by then the share of the total US population represented by immigrants had declined from nearly 15 percent during the earlier 40-year period of the late 1800s through the early 1900s to about 5 percent by 1965.

Internal Migration Trends

As noted earlier, during the 1950s and 1960s US economic growth was robust, notwithstanding episodes of economic difficulty and recession. Strong consumer demand and manufacturing prowess produced a large and prosperous middle class that for a variety of reasons chose to migrate into newly developing suburban neighborhoods surrounding major cities such as New York, Detroit, and Chicago. Although large fractions of these middle-class workers had only limited educational attainment, in the robust economy of the period most were able to find employment offering very attractive earnings and benefits in burgeoning and heavily unionized manufacturing occupations, most notably in the then-dynamic US auto and aerospace industries. Such work was concentrated in the Northeast, Midwest, and to a lesser extent on the West Coast, and over time attracted substantial numbers of internal migrants, both White and Black, from the primarily agrarian, far poorer, and segregationist states of the American South.

The Politics of Immigration Reform in the 1960s

While the national origins quota system that originated toward the end of World War I had been sustained for more than four decades, by the 1960s it had become a political and diplomatic embarrassment for the United States. This was the most dynamic period of the domestic civil rights movement, the goals of which were clearly incompatible with those of the national origins quota system.

The 1960s was also a period of rapid decolonization and independence for numerous colonies of waning European empires (British, French, Belgian, Portuguese, Dutch), mostly located in Africa, Asia, and the Caribbean. In this context the continuing national origins quota system, with its heavy preferences for would-be immigrants from Western and Northern Europe, was not only domestically unacceptable but posed vexing diplomatic embarrassments for the US during its global Cold War competition with the USSR. In a June 1963 speech, then president John F. Kennedy termed the national origins system "intolerable."

After President Kennedy was assassinated five months later, the torch for immigration reform was passed to his two younger brothers, then attorney general Robert F. Kennedy and senator Ted Kennedy. Both worked closely with President Lyndon B. Johnson as energetic proponents of legislation that was adopted in 1965 as the Immigration and Nationality Act (INA) of 1965.[11] Perhaps the central feature of this legislation was its rapid phase-out of explicit immigration preferences by national origin (and hence also by racial and ethnic categories). This legislation can best be understood as deeply entwined with the politics of both the dynamic civil rights movement and the Cold War of that period. Three landmark Acts were adopted during a period of only 15 months—the Immigration and Nationality Act of 1965, Civil Rights Act of 1964, and Voting Rights Act of 1965—and all three initiated far-reaching shifts in long-standing national policies.

The Unintended Effects of the 1965 Immigration Reforms

The Immigration and Nationality Act of 1965 has been described accurately as a transformational shift away from US immigration policies that had originated in the late 19th and early 20th centuries. It is often forgotten, however, that during debate about the proposed reforms many of the Act's supporters were at pains to assure their fellow legislators that these legislative changes would have only modest demographic impacts, and certainly would not result in large increases in overall immigration nor in dramatic shifts in the characteristics of future immigration flows.

For this reason, an overall numerical cap of 120,000 immigrants per year was applied for the first time to immigration from Latin America, by then experiencing rapid population increases. More importantly however, the 1965 legislation allocated overwhelming immigration preferences to family members of US citizens. These provisions enabled reform proponents to assure their skeptical colleagues that most future immigrants would need to have close relatives who were US citizens. This requirement, they declared, would ensure that the national-origins composition of future immigrants under the new law would be similar to that of past immigration, while allowing repeal of the embarrassing near-exclusion of Asian migrants and the national origins quota system from the 1920s. In particular, there would be no large-scale increase in immigration from Asia, Latin America, and Africa because few would-be immigrants from these regions would have close relatives with US citizenship. One prominent Asian American proponent, Senator Hiram Fong (Republican, Hawaii), offered these specific quantitative assurances during the Senate hearings on the bill:

> Asians represent six-tenths of 1 percent of the population of the United States . . . with respect to Japan, we estimate that there will be a total for the first 5 years of some 5,391 . . . the people from that part of the world will

> never reach 1 percent of the population.... Our cultural pattern will never be changed as far as America is concerned.[12]

Similarly, in his 1964 remarks to the House Subcommittee on Immigration, Attorney General Robert F. Kennedy also promised that the legislation he was urging would lead to only small increases in immigration from Asia:

> [A]pproximately 5,000, Mr. Chairman, after which immigration from that source would virtually disappear; 5,000 immigrants would come in the first year, but we do not expect that there would be any great influx after that.[13]

In testimony the following year, Kennedy's successor, Attorney General Nicholas Katzenbach, forecast a similarly small number of 6,000 additional immigrants from Asia.[14] In the words of Senator Ted Kennedy during the Senate floor debate,

> [O]ur cities will not be flooded with a million immigrants annually. . . . Secondly, the ethnic mix of this country will not be upset.[15]

Activist groups that had long demanded repeal of the national origins visa system apparently agreed with such forecasts, which in some cases actually led them to oppose the proposed legislation. The Japanese American Citizens League (JACL) testified in Senate hearings that

> although the immigration bill eliminated race as a matter of principle, in actual operation immigration will still be controlled by the now discredited national origins system and the general pattern of immigration which exists today will continue for many years yet to come.[16]

Subsequent developments proved such promises and forecasts to have been wildly incorrect or misleading, as US immigration numbers surged and came to be heavily dominated by migration from Asia and Latin America. Indeed, some leading historians of US immigration conclude that the 1965 Immigration Act turned out to be an "unintended reform" that led to radical effects over the ensuing decades that surprised and confounded both its supporters and opponents.[17]

However, the arguments of the bill's proponents prevailed, and the legislation was passed by large and bipartisan majorities. The bill was signed by President Lyndon Johnson at a ceremony specially organized at the base of the Statue of Liberty in New York Harbor in October 1965. The consequences—both intended and unintended—of this legislation is itself a fascinating political story, to which we shall return.

International and Domestic Politics, 1945–1990

From Hot War Alliance to Cold War Conflict

From the end of World War II to around 1970, international politics evolved in ways very different from the hoped-for postwar elimination of conflicts and antagonisms. To the contrary, deep fissures appeared rather quickly in the victorious wartime alliance between West and East, as tensions rose over interventions by the Soviet Union to create allied "People's Republic" governments in Soviet-occupied Eastern Europe.[18] Within a two-month period in 1946 alone, two prominent speeches by Josef Stalin and Winston Churchill, along with an equally well-known strategic analysis by the US chargé d'affaires in Moscow, George Kennan, introduced what was to become a half century of "Cold War" confrontation between a bloc of Western liberal democracies led by the United States (formalized in the NATO Treaty of 1949) and a bloc of socialist states in Eastern and Southern Europe dominated by the Soviet Union (formalized by the Warsaw Pact in 1955). During the 1950s this Cold War standoff contributed greatly to the onset of two brutal proxy wars in Asia: the Korean War of 1950–1953, and the protracted Vietnam War of 1954–1975.

In the ideological political context of this Cold War, the Soviet Union's successful launch of the first earth-orbiting satellite in 1957—Sputnik I—produced a multiyear panic in US domestic politics[19] that bolstered prior claims that the Eisenhower administration had allowed the emergence of a strategic "missile gap" with the Soviet Union. During the 1960 presidential campaign, Democratic Senator John F. Kennedy deployed such claims effectively in his successful campaign against Eisenhower's vice president Richard Nixon, though these claims later proved to have been unfounded.[20]

Only a few months after his inauguration in January 1961 President Kennedy approved implementation of plans that had been developed during the Eisenhower administration for a US-supported invasion of Soviet-supported Cuba by anti-Castro Cuban expatriates. This proxy military invasion at the Bay of Pigs was a spectacular failure that did serious political damage to the new Kennedy administration in both domestic and international terms. Perhaps more importantly, within a year of the failed invasion the governments of Cuba and the Soviet Union agreed to the clandestine shipment and installation of Soviet medium- and intermediate-range nuclear missiles in Cuban bases within range of the US mainland. In October 1962, US surveillance planes acquired clear photographic evidence of these nuclear missile installations, and almost immediately what came to be known as the Cuban Missile Crisis erupted.[21] The Kennedy administration called for an emergency UN Security Council meeting at which it released the revealing surveillance images, demanded that Soviet missiles and any nuclear weapons already on the island be removed, and announced a naval blockade or quarantine of Cuba to prevent additional shipments. The ensuing Cuban Missile Crisis lasted for 35 days and was described by the American historian and Kennedy biographer Arthur M. Schlesinger Jr. as "the most dangerous moment in human history."[22]

Ideological conflict continued between Cuba and the United States, and in 1966 the US Congress passed the Cuban Adjustment Act[23] defining Cuban natives and citizens able to migrate from Cuba to the United States as "refugees," and providing special exemptions from immigration restrictions by guaranteeing them permanent residence and other benefits after one year of residence in the United States. Nearly 15 years later, in 1980, these provisions were exploited by Cuban President Fidel Castro to engineer what came to be called the Mariel Boatlift, a chaotic migration of what Castro termed "undesirables" in which hundreds of US-based boats and Cuban fishing vessels transported some 125,000 Cubans from Mariel Harbor to Florida. Among them were family members of Cubans already resident in the United States; Cuban political prisoners and dissidents; and inmates from Cuban prisons and mental institutions.[24]

In 1962 and 1963 Kennedy also greatly expanded the small contingent of US military advisors that had been sent earlier to Vietnam by President Dwight Eisenhower. The mission was to assist the pro-Western government of South Vietnam in its foundering war efforts against a long-standing guerrilla war supported by the pro-Soviet government of North Vietnam. When Kennedy had taken office in January 1961 there were 700 such advisors; by the end of 1963 the number had risen to 16,000.[25]

Kennedy was assassinated in late 1963. His successor, the former vice president Lyndon Johnson, continued the expansion of US military involvement in what was to become a full-throated proxy war of the Cold War. In 1964 he sought and received Congressional authorization to deploy US forces in direct military operations, and subsequently Johnson continued to increase the scale of US military involvement. By 1969 the number of US military combat forces in Vietnam had escalated to 543,000, up from the 16,000 in military advisory roles in 1963.[26]

While US military involvement in the war was expanding rapidly during the 1960s, a national antiwar movement emerged that eventually was to fracture Johnson's Democratic Party coalition. As the 1968 presidential election loomed in 1967, Johnson announced that he would not seek the presidential nomination of his party. Divisive Democratic primaries ensued, and the Democratic Party convention in August 1968 was disrupted by sometimes violent antiwar protests and policing. In the end, Johnson's vice president, Hubert Humphrey, won the nomination to face Republican nominee Richard Nixon, the same politician who by a narrow margin had lost the 1960 presidential election to Kennedy. In the 1968 election Nixon was able to win an equally narrow victory over Humphrey. Opposition to Humphrey as a defender of Johnson's still-expanding US involvement in the Vietnam War was one source of this defeat. In addition, the election revealed a further deep split in the New Deal Democratic coalition, as George Wallace, the former Democratic governor of Alabama, ran a third-party campaign defending Southern racial segregation on a "states' rights" platform. Wallace received nearly 10 million votes, or 13.5 percent of the total vote count. His supporters were located disproportionately in the formerly "Solid South" that had since the 1930s been a solid base of support for Democratic Party presidential candidates.

Domestic Politics—Consolidation of the New Deal, but with Fault Lines

In domestic US political terms, the emergence of this Cold War during the late 1940s—exacerbated by suspicions that Soviet agents within the United States had expedited the surprisingly rapid development of nuclear weapons by the USSR—spilled over into domestic politics in the form of the acrimonious Second Red Scare characterized by strident accusations of espionage, subversion, and treason.[27] This domestic political convulsion was energized by Senator Joseph McCarthy, whose name became memorialized in a new pejorative noun, "McCarthyism." The net effect was a years-long period of divisive domestic political rhetoric and the spread of suspicion widely among American institutions, including within the internal counsels of the US Government itself.

Notwithstanding these divisive domestic clashes related to the Cold War, the period 1945–1970 saw successful consolidation of major US domestic programs (known collectively as the New Deal) that had been adopted within the first few years after the 1932 election of President Franklin Roosevelt. Some of the short-term New Deal measures were intended to be temporary and were allowed to lapse, but others had been designed for the longer term and were institutionalized: legislation creating new federal institutions to regulate the banking system and stock markets that had precipitated the Depression; new measures to guarantee the right of unions to organize; and creation of a social insurance program called Social Security to provide pensions for retirees and other dependent persons such as widows and orphans.

In strictly political terms, these long-term New Deal programs attracted widespread public support. Roosevelt was able to assemble a broad if tenuous Democratic Party coalition that brought together otherwise dissimilar constituencies: organized labor and its largely white "blue collar" members; large majorities of African Americans and other underrepresented minorities; liberal/left-wing intellectuals and professionals; and conservative segregationist Southern white voters reflecting the collective memory that Abraham Lincoln was a Republican.

This otherwise anomalous New Deal coalition held together to dominate US Congressional politics from the 1930s through much of the 1945–1970 period. Indeed, the Democratic Party had a virtual "lock" on the US Congress over this 35-year period, during which Republicans held control of Congress for only four—1947–1948 and 1953–1954—and their 1947–1948 majority was constrained by the veto power of a Democratic president (Truman).[28]

While at the time this appeared to be an unbeatable political coalition, it harbored deep fault lines that eventually ruptured and came apart during the 1960s and 1970s. While most Congressional Democrats from other than the South were politically "liberal"[29] or moderate, their party's Congressional majorities depended on a substantial number of conservative Democrats elected from the "Solid South"—solid in the sense that repression of Black voting power meant that it could be relied on to elect heavy majorities of mostly White Democratic members of Congress, many of whom supported conservative social and economic policies and did not oppose the Southern system of racial segregation that emerged during the late 19th century. Moreover, because the Republican Party was very weak in most of the states of the American South—these states were essentially single-party entities—Democratic members of Congress from the South benefited from the power of incumbency and thereby held disproportionate Congressional power due to the decisive role played by seniority in the allocation of party and committee leadership positions.

This meant that even during periods of unified Democratic Party control of the presidency and both houses of Congress during the 1940s and 1950s, most legislative efforts to prohibit the segregation laws of 17 Southern states and to strengthen protections for civil and voting rights were stymied—even though they were supported by a majority of Democrats from other regions and those Southern Democrats opposed to segregation, and by substantial numbers of moderate and liberal Republicans. The resulting political stalemate in a Congress long controlled by Democrats was an underlying factor in the US Supreme Court's cautious and initially divided deliberations about whether it should overrule long-standing precedent from its 1896 decision in *Plessey v. Ferguson* that declared "separate but equal" school systems to be constitutional. Although most of the sitting Justices had been appointed by Democratic presidents Roosevelt and Truman, the Court deliberated for two years before reaching its unanimous landmark ruling in 1954 reversing its Plessey ruling and declaring segregation in public education unconstitutional (*Brown v. Board of Education*).[30]

The 1960s and 1970s, however, proved to be very different—both were decades of political ferment and change, in which domestic and international political developments were closely intertwined. These decades saw the flowering of at least the following important US political movements, most of which can be viewed through a demographic lens: civil rights; women's rights; immigration reform; pro-life and pro-choice; environmental; and antiwar. Most of these political movements continue to be active and influential well into the 21st century.

The Civil Rights Movement

In particular the US civil rights movement built on its success in *Brown v. Board of Education* and flowered into an increasingly powerful political force.[31] President Kennedy had offered his support, though cautiously and hesitantly given the still-potent influence of Southern segregationists in the Democratic Party coalition. The assassination of Kennedy in 1963 evoked national and bipartisan revulsion that enabled his successor, Lyndon Johnson, to deploy his considerable political skills to finally gain Congressional majorities for what became the landmark Civil Rights Act of 1964 and the Voting Rights Act of 1965, reforms that been languishing in a stalemated Congress for many years.

During the same two-year period, the surge of national political support for civil rights strengthened advocates for long-standing but stalemated proposals to transform US immigration law, enabling them to finally achieve passage of a package of such measures in the Immigration Act of 1965. This Act, as we shall see below, produced significant demographic effects that apparently were neither expected nor desired by many of its Congressional sponsors and supporters.

The Women's Movement

A re-energized women's movement, often called Second Wave Feminism, also flowered during this period. Leaders of this movement focused on a variety of issues of special concern to women of that period, including reproductive rights and health; women's sexual liberation; equal opportunities in education and employment; revised laws surrounding divorce and child custody; and measures to reduce violence against women. Books embodying second-wave feminist sensibilities, such as Betty Friedan's *The Feminine Mystique* (1963), became best sellers, and also stimulated expanded attention to earlier books such as Simone de Beauvoir's *The Second Sex*, which a decade earlier had been translated from French into English. New feminist groups were formed, the most prominent of which was the National Organization for Women (NOW), an organization cofounded by Betty Friedan in 1966 that became widely known through substantial and largely supportive coverage in the mass media. Meanwhile, women's magazines, many of which had been focused on homemaking and childrearing, began to include more feminist perspectives, while new and more activist magazines such as *Ms. Magazine* appeared (1972) and gained traction.

This influential new women's movement engaged in sustained and effective lobbying efforts for adoption of the Equal Rights Amendment (ERA) to the US Constitution, originally proposed in 1923 but still languishing a half-century later. Initial victory was achieved in 1972 with Congressional passage of the Amendment by the US Congress, but like all Constitutional Amendments the ERA required ratification by the legislatures of three-quarters of the US states. Effective opposition quickly emerged, especially that led by the lawyer and conservative antifeminist Phyllis Schlafly, who in that same year founded the group Stop ERA, later renamed Eagle Forum.[32] Ultimately the campaign for the Equal Rights Amendment's final adoption collapsed in 1979 after it failed to obtain ratification in a sufficient number of State legislatures.

Pro-Life and Pro-Choice Movements

Meanwhile, a campaign focused on the courts rather than the Congress did achieve success in overcoming another long-standing Congressional stalemate about the prohibition of voluntary abortion in many US states. In its 1973 decision (*Roe v. Wade*), the Supreme Court declared abortion during the first 24 weeks of pregnancy to be a woman's right guaranteed under the US Constitution.

This Court decision, however, also mobilized a new "Right to Life" political movement, with strong financial, political, and moral support from the Catholic Church. This movement, later renamed "Pro-life," stimulated decades of political activism among social conservatives and religious activists determined to reduce what they saw as the prevailing liberal/center-left majority on the (unelected) Supreme Court. The *Roe v. Wade* decision also stimulated creation of the Federalist Society, a conservative legal society established in 1982 by students at Yale University, Harvard University, and the University of Chicago based on the principles "that the state exists to preserve freedom, that the separation of governmental powers is central to our Constitution, and that it is emphatically the province and duty of the judiciary to say what the law is, not what it should be."[33]

This organization later was to become an influential actor in disputes about the role of the courts, including subsequent litigation about abortion. In response, supporters of legalized abortion created "Pro-choice" groups that defended the *Roe v. Wade* decision and opposed numerous proposed restrictions on access to abortion.

In 1987 political polarization of judicial appointments exploded when President Reagan nominated a prominent conservative jurist, Robert Bork, who had long expressed questions about the validity of the *Roe v. Wade* decision.[34] Bork was a prominent advocate of "original intent" or "originalism" in Constitutional interpretation, and argued that the *Roe v. Wade* decision was based weakly on an argued constitutionally protected right of privacy that was nowhere mentioned in the Constitution but instead was deemed by more progressive US jurists to be implicitly guaranteed.[35]

Bork's views on constitutional interpretation were anathema to the more progressive members of the Democratic Party. Only a few hours after his nomination was announced, Senator Ted Kennedy went to the Senate floor to express strong condemnation of the nominee. The obituary of Kennedy in *The New York Times*, a longtime media supporter of Kennedy's legislative efforts, described this speech as "an attack that even friendly commentators called demagogic." In its obituary of Mr. Kennedy, the *Economist* commented, "'There was not a line in that speech that was accurate,' wailed Judge Bork afterwards. He was right. But it worked."[36]

There ensued a highly politicized set of confirmation hearings on the Bork nomination before the Senate Judiciary Committee, then chaired by Senator Joe Biden. The hearings evoked passionate opposition to Bork's nomination, to which Bork responded in kind with forceful and sometimes undiplomatic restatements of his long-standing views on constitutional interpretation and jurisprudence.

In the end, Bork's nomination was rejected by the full Senate by a vote of 42–58. This 1987 confirmation battle is often described as the origin of subsequent highly politicized controversies about Supreme Court nominations, during which most nominees have chosen not to offer clear responses to questions about their constitutional perspectives and about how they would rule on hypothetical cases. In the words of Tom Goldstein, publisher of SCOTUSblog, a widely cited blog on the Supreme Court:

> The [Bork] nomination changed everything, maybe forever. . . . Republicans nominated this brilliant guy to move the law in this dramatically more conservative direction. Liberal groups turned around and blocked him precisely because of those views. Their fight legitimized scorched-earth ideological wars over nominations at the Supreme Court, and to this day both sides remain completely convinced they were right. The upshot is that we have this ridiculous system now where nominees shut up and don't say anything that might signal what they really think.[37]

In addition to transforming the nomination and confirmation process for federal judges, the Bork episode enhanced the growth and influence of the aforementioned Federalist Society, established by law school students five years earlier, which over the ensuing decades was to become one of the most influential legal organizations in the United States. In particular, the Society became a key source of advice for Republican presidents regarding judicial appointments, and played an important role in the establishment of a conservative majority on the US Supreme Court.[38]

Bork's surname even evolved into an American slang verb, as in "to bork" and "to have been borked," for example:

> To defame or vilify (a person) systematically, esp. in the mass media, usually to prevent his or her appointment to public office; to obstruct or thwart (a person) in this way. (*Oxford English Dictionary*)
>
> To attack or defeat (a nominee or candidate for public office) unfairly through an organized campaign of harsh public criticism or vilification. (*Merriam-Webster Dictionary*)

The Environmental Movement

Another political movement also emerged during this period, focused on protecting the environment. Once again, best-selling publications of the 1960s such as Rachel Carson's *Silent Spring* (1962) and Paul Ehrlich's *The Population Bomb* (1968) gave scientific impetus to activist claims. Initially, many environmental activists focused on the environmental and other threats they saw in the "population explosion" that emerged from the 1950s on. Eventually, as high fertility rates began to wane in much of the world during the 1970s and beyond, references to population growth declined as a focus of the environmental movement, which later evolved into today's influential international activism about global climate change. A shift toward a rights-based approach to population was marked by the 1994 International Conference on Population and Development in Cairo.

The Antiwar Movement

Finally, the antiwar movement emerged during this same period, and was powerfully energized by the Johnson administration's decisions in the mid-1960s to greatly expand direct US military involvement in the festering Vietnam War. Initially the antiwar movement focused on international issues of war and peace, but ultimately it had influential and concrete impacts on domestic US politics. Indeed, it was rising sentiment against the Vietnam War that proved to be perhaps the major factor in President Johnson's decision not to seek re-election in 1968, culminating in the election of conservative Republican Richard Nixon.

During Nixon's nearly 6 years in office, he and many Republican politicians supported some of the movements just outlined above. This was particularly the case for the environmental movement—it was Nixon who proposed the Environmental Protection Act in 1970 and the Clean Water Act in 1972. There was also substantial bipartisan support for the civil and voting rights movement, for changes in immigration policy, for public provision of family planning services, for some of the goals of the women's movement, and in some cases for the antiwar movement. Ultimately, however, the Nixon administration lost public support and eventually collapsed as opposition rose to Nixon's continuation of the US military intervention in Vietnam and especially during the Watergate scandals, which forced him to resign in 1974 despite his large re-election victory only two years earlier.

The Troubled and Single-Term Presidency of Jimmy Carter

Nixon was succeeded by his vice president, Gerald R. Ford, who himself lost public support by issuing a prospective pardon for Nixon for any subsequent criminal convictions. Ford sought reelection in the next presidential election in 1976, but ultimately was defeated by relatively small margins by the progressive Democrat Jimmy Carter, the former governor of Georgia who ran as an "outsider" critical of both the Republicans and of "establishment" Democrats in Washington.

Carter's presidency proved to be a troubled one, buffeted by energy crises and "stagflation"—slow economic growth, high inflation, high interest rates, and high unemployment. As if this combination was not challenging enough, his efforts were stymied by conflicts with both Democrats and Republicans in Congress, by his initial appointment of an "outsider" White House staff lacking in Washington experience, by disruptive shortages and price increases for gasoline, and by foreign policy crises including the Soviet invasion of Afghanistan and Carter's ineffective responses after revolutionary students in Iran took 52 US Embassy personnel hostage in 1979.

To be fair, Carter had inherited the inflation and unemployment problems from his Democratic and Republican predecessors, Johnson, Nixon, and Ford. The center-left Democratic administration of Lyndon Johnson had sown the seeds by the decision to finance expansion of the Vietnam War with deficit financing rather than tax increases, while at the same time greatly expanding government spending on a portfolio of progressive domestic policies known collectively as the Great Society. The burgeoning budgetary deficits that followed were accommodated by a compliant Federal Reserve

Board which embraced a variety of expansionary but ultimately inflationary monetary policies to finance the growing Federal debt.

Moreover, the inflationary surge during Carter's presidency was driven in part by a reprise in 1979–1980 of the energy crises that had bedeviled Nixon in 1973. Beginning in 1978, global petroleum markets were disrupted by revolutionary changes underway in Iran, while expansion of domestic petroleum supplies was constrained by the price controls imposed during the 1973 energy crisis and still in effect. International oil prices doubled, with gasoline price increases not far behind. There were also perceived shortages of gasoline and fears of possible rationing that contributed to hoarding behaviors and widely publicized long waits at fueling stations, though in retrospect the actual declines in global petroleum supplies were smaller than many at the time thought.

In this setting of political controversy about a perceived energy crisis, Carter in July 1979 delivered a widely anticipated and nationally televised address in which he began by pointing to what he called a "fundamental threat to American democracy"—a national "Crisis of Confidence." Indeed, this was the title he chose for this national address.

Most of Carter's policy prescriptions to deal with the concerns he described failed to win Congressional support, and continuing high inflation and unemployment rates were politically damaging. Later in 1979 the damage was amplified by unrelated political decisions that together proved toxic. In early 1979 the Iranian government, ruled at least since the 1950s by the autocratic modernizer and pro-Western shah Mohammad Reza Shah Pahlavi, had been overthrown by followers of his longtime Islamist opponent Ayatollah Ruhollah Khomeini. The shah fled into exile, but in the autumn of 1979 his health deteriorated, leading a number of his influential American supporters to claim that effective treatment could be obtained only in the United States.[39]

The US ambassador and chargé d'affaires to Iran and other State Department experts on Iran advised strongly against granting the shah a US entry visa for medical care, on grounds this likely would reverse their diplomatic efforts to build better relations with the new but unstable provisional government of Iran, would strengthen religious fundamentalist forces against secularist Iranian moderates, and put the US Embassy in Iran and its staff at risk of violent action by active revolutionary groups. Though President Carter had previously expressed strong reservations about granting US admission to the shah under these circumstances, in October 1979 he approved temporary admission of the shah for cancer treatment in New York.[40]

As forecast by US diplomats, this US decision infuriated the shah's Islamist revolutionary opponents in Iran, culminating in early November in a violent assault on the US Embassy in Tehran and the taking of diplomatic hostages. Lengthy US diplomatic efforts seeking their release proved ineffective, as did economic sanctions. In April 1980, after more than a year of fruitless negotiations with the Iranian government and as the US presidential election in November 1980 loomed larger, Carter approved an armed hostage recovery mission designed by the US military, but only after insisting that its size and scope be sharply reduced. In the event Carter's police action failed in the Iranian desert, and in spectacular fashion, culminating in the deaths of eight US service members whose bodies were paraded on Iranian television. Carter's secretary of state, Cyrus Vance, resigned.

In November 1980, Ronald Reagan defeated Carter by a margin of nearly 10 percent, winning a majority of the votes cast in 44 of the 50 US states and a large majority in the Electoral College (489–49). As he began to implement the policies he had promised, the independent Federal Reserve (led by Chairman Paul Volcker, appointed in August 1979 by President Carter) sought to contain inflation—which by 1980 had risen to nearly 14 percent (see Fig. 3.5)—by reversing the accommodative monetary policies that the Federal Reserve had embraced since the late 1960s.

US short-term interest rates rose sharply, peaking at 20 percent in 1981, while 30-year mortgage rates rose above 18 percent (see Fig. 3.6). The US

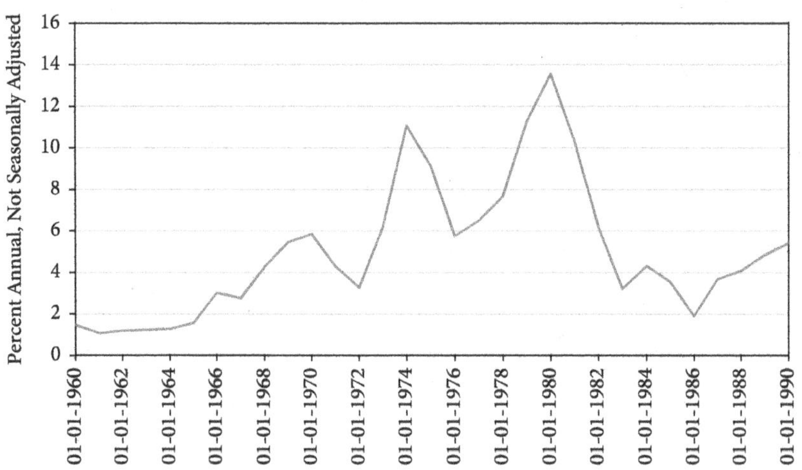

Fig. 3.5 US inflation, consumer prices for the United States, 1960–1990.

Source: World Bank, *Inflation, consumer prices for the United States* [FPCPITOTLZGUSA], retrieved from FRED, Federal Reserve Bank of St. Louis; https://fred.stlouisfed.org/series/FPCPITOTLZGUSA (accessed November 23, 2024).

economy quickly fell into a deep and painful economic recession that increased unemployment to double-digit levels early in the 1980s (see Fig. 3.7), followed within a few years by rapid declines in the rates of inflation, interest, and unemployment rates.

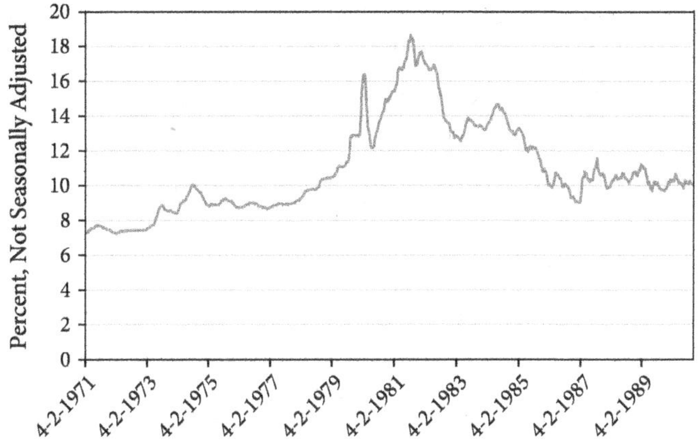

Fig. 3.6 30-year fixed rate mortgage average in the United States, 1971–1990.

Source: Freddie Mac, *30-year fixed rate mortgage average in the United States* [MORTGAGE30US], retrieved from FRED, Federal Reserve Bank of St. Louis; https://fred.stlouisfed.org/series/MORTGAGE30US (accessed November 23, 2024).

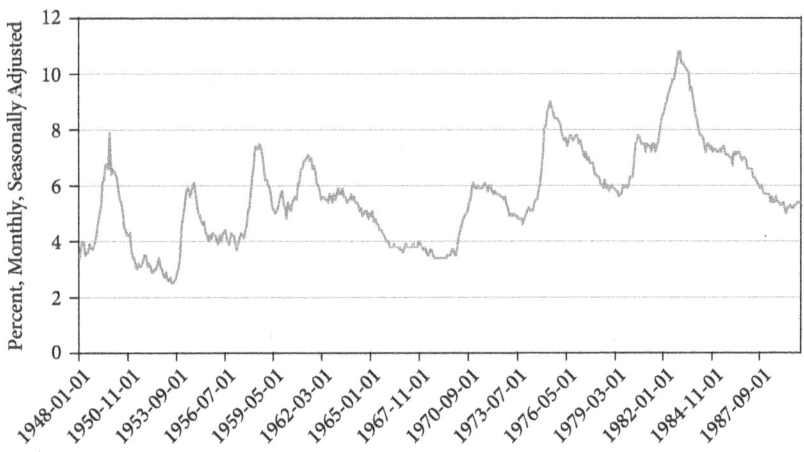

Fig. 3.7 US unemployment rate, 1948–1987.

Source: US Bureau of Labor Statistics, *Unemployment rate* [UNRATE], retrieved from FRED, Federal Reserve Bank of St. Louis; https://fred.stlouisfed.org/series/UNRATE (accessed November 23, 2024).

During Reagan's two terms as president from 1981 to 1988, the demographic realignment of electoral politics that began during the 1960s accelerated. As forecast in 1969 by Kevin Phillips (see chapter 4), the "Solid South" that had provided such critical and reliable support for the Democratic Party since Franklin Roosevelt's New Deal gradually became less solid as electoral support for Democratic candidates weakened. By the 1990s the region had been transformed into a *new* Solid South that served as an equally reliable political bastion—but for the Republican Party.

4
Demographic Shifts and Political Polarization, 1990–2024

By 1990, as the 45-year-long Cold War was unexpectedly ending, very different patterns of demographic change and related political and economic perspectives were emerging in the United States. From 1990, US total fertility rates approximated replacement level for nearly two decades until the "Global Financial Crisis" and "Great Recession" that began in 2007/2008, after which they gradually declined further. Other demographic variables saw more substantial shifts than fertility. Mortality rates as measured by life expectancy at birth continued to improve until around 2010, but then stagnated until the mortality surge that began in 2020 with the appearance of the deadly COVID-19 pandemic. In some respects, the most dramatic demographic changes after 1990 were those related to immigration. We will address each of these in turn.

Fertility

As may be seen in Fig. 4.1, for nearly two decades after 1990 there were no dramatic changes in the total fertility rate, which had previously peaked around 1960 at 3.7 during the postwar baby boom. During the 1960s and early 1970s this fertility measure had declined rapidly, before stabilizing and then fluctuating within a narrow range of 1.8 (about 15–20 percent below the "replacement" level of 2.1) until the late 1980s. By 1990 the fertility decline had reversed and risen modestly, back up to 2.1 but not any higher, and then declined again to levels somewhat lower than those recorded in the late 1970s.

As noted in chapter 3, US fertility rates appear to have declined further during the disruptive pandemic years of 2020–2023, back down to about 1.66 and 1.67 in 2021 and 2022, and slightly further to 1.62 in 2023 and 1.63

Toxic Demography. Jennifer D. Sciubba, Michael S. Teitelbaum, and Jay Winter, Oxford University Press.

DOI: 10.1093/oso/9780197745038.003.0005

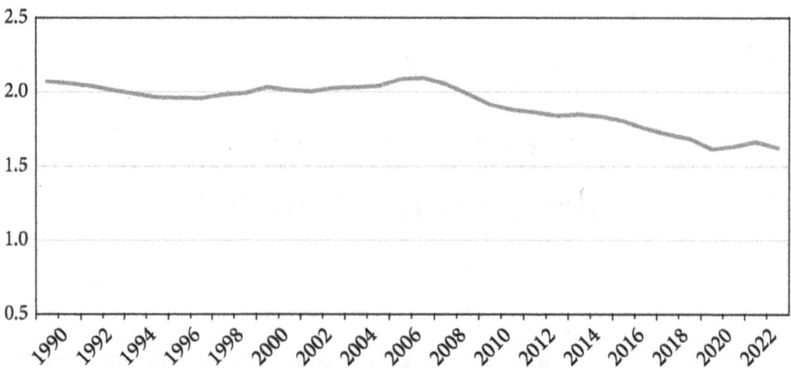

Fig. 4.1 Total fertility rate, United States, 1990–2022.
Source: UN *World Population Prospects, 2024 Revision.*

in 2024.[1] Over the coming decade or so we will be able to judge if these further declines during the early 2020s represented a return to earlier trends of slow decline during the years following the 2008 financial crisis, as seen in many US peers and as many demographers anticipate, or instead prove to be temporary downward blips driven by deferment of births during a period of chaotic and disorienting pandemic and economic emergencies.

Unfortunately, there is no methodologically acceptable way to predict whether declines over recent years in period total fertility rates, and especially those during the years of the 2008 Global Financial Crisis and Great Recession and the 2020 pandemic emergency, will be sustained and hence be reflected in comparable measures of cumulative fertility over the reproductive lifetime. In a recent comprehensive study of this set of issues, Wu and Mark note that the fundamental scientific challenge is that recent period fertility declines have been concentrated among younger cohorts—especially those born between 1988 and 2010 and hence aged 12–34 in 2022. Large proportions of these cohorts currently are 1–3 decades younger than the ages at which they will have completed their ultimate fertility, while fertility rates among older cohorts of US women have been increasing. Wu and Mark attempt to project the ultimate cumulative fertility for those younger cohorts, and these projection efforts suggest their cumulative lifetime fertility rates are likely to be below replacement. However, they immediately caution that

> the projections for these younger cohorts rest on implicit assumptions that we regard as increasingly problematic when projecting further and further

into the future, as is needed when estimating the lifetime fertility of the very youngest cohorts of US women.[2]

One conclusion of this careful study is that at present it is impossible to know whether the recent declines in the US period total fertility primarily reflect downward shifts in future completed fertility of these cohorts, or instead represent downward distortions due to delayed births that demographers have long recognized may substantially bias period fertility measures during periods when shifts are underway in the timing or tempo of fertility. As they say,

> [T]he answer for the youngest cohorts of US women is that it is simply too early to tell. These cohorts—those in their teens and early 20s—have only begun their childbearing, but what their future fertility will be can be monitored by following them over time. . . . Similar clues for these cohorts can be obtained by monitoring their future fertility intentions and desires, which to date continue to follow a two-child norm and thus closely resemble those in older cohorts. . . . Data over the next decade can thus be used to provide a more concrete sense regarding the degree to which the lower fertility at early ages currently observed in these cohorts will or will not be offset by fertility increases at older ages.[3]

Mortality

As may be seen in Fig. 4.2, the long-standing improvements in mortality conditions (as indicated by rising expectation of life at birth) continued until after 2010, then stagnated before turning sharply downward before 2020—a new trajectory often attributed to excess deaths from drug overdoses including opioids such as OxyContin and later fentanyl. Then, beginning in early 2020, a convulsive pandemic caused by the novel COVID-19 virus led to a dramatic surge of excess mortality. Fig. 4.2 clearly shows substantial increases in life expectancy at birth that continued from 1990 until after 2010, and then the stagnation that followed before life expectancy declined sharply during the years surrounding 2020.

Preliminary analysis suggests that overall US life expectancy between prepandemic 2019 and 2021 experienced the most significant decline over such a short period in about a century, declining by some 2.7 years, from 78.9 in 2019 to 76.4 in 2021. Moreover, as can be seen in Fig. 4.3, these negative

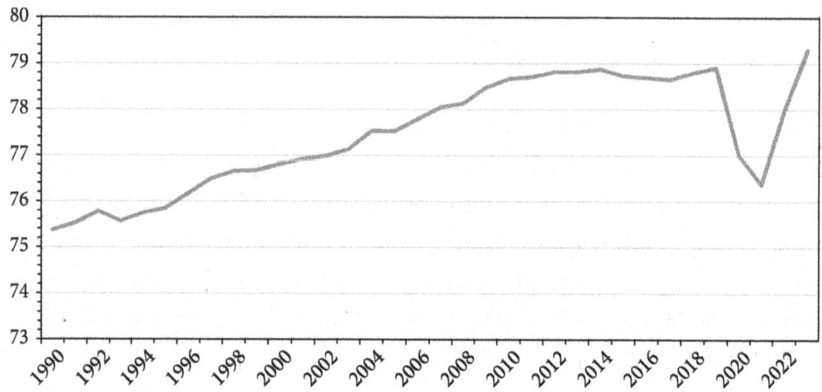

Fig. 4.2 Life expectancy at birth, United States, 1990–2022.
Source: UN *World Population Prospects, 2024 Revision.*

mortality effects disproportionately affected racial and ethnic minorities: life expectancy among "American Indian and Alaskan Native" (AIAN) people, already the lowest among such categories in 2019, declined by 6.6 years. Life expectancy for the "Hispanic" category declined by 4.2 years (from relatively high prior levels), and by 4 years from the lower levels of the "Black" category. Comparable declines for the "White" and "Asian" categories, with the highest life expectancies in 2019, were smaller though still substantial, at 2.4 years and 2.1 years respectively. Most of these declines in life expectancy appear to be related to the direct mortality impacts of the COVID-19 pandemic itself, along with indirect mortality surges related to upturns in alcohol and drug use, violent crimes, and "deaths of despair" suggested by increases in suicide.[4]

Immigration

Mortality changes over the past few years have been substantial, at least by the slow-changing norms of this demographic driver, but the most dynamic US demographic change after 1990 has been that in immigration. Although official data on immigration are less robust and credible than those on fertility and mortality, it appears that net international migration to the United States (i.e., the difference between the number of international migrants arriving versus leaving) was on the increase at least until 2016. After the inauguration of Donald Trump as president in early 2016, this trend of rising immigration reversed, due initially to the new administration's policies

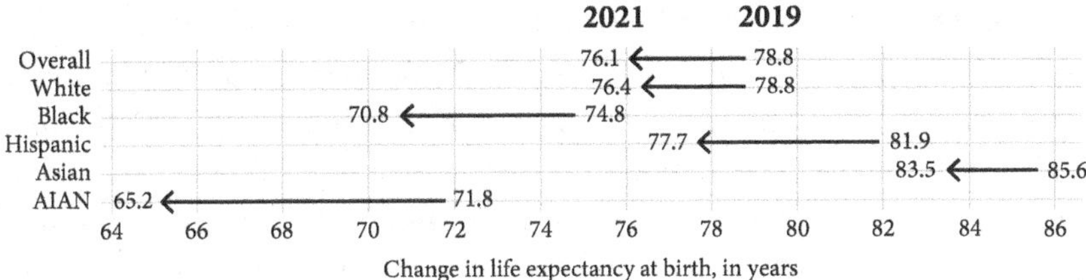

Fig. 4.3 Change in life expectancy at birth between 2019 and 2021, by race and ethnicity, United States.

Source: KFF, "Recent Widening of Racial Disparities in U.S. Life Expectancy Was Largely Driven by COVID-19 Mortality," 2, https://www.kff.org/racial-equity-and-health-policy/press-release/recent-widening-of-racial-disparities-in-u-s-life-expectancy-was-largely-driven-by-covid-19-mortality/

related to irregular migration, asylum, and refugees. These initial declines accelerated from early 2020 on, as both international travel and US economic activity were substantially restricted during the COVID-19 pandemic emergency.[5]

There is a wide range of estimates of the net demographic effect of international migration on US population change. In part this is due to long-standing deficiencies of official US data on international migration, which means that much depends on estimation procedures that are subject to considerable uncertainties. In addition, there are conceptual disagreements about whether, and if so how, to include the demographic effects of births taking place in the United States among its subpopulation of recent international migrants, leading to differences among analysts that in some cases seem to reflect differing ideological perspectives.

Consider, for example, whether such estimates of demographic impacts of immigration should (or should not) include children born in the United States to irregular migrants recently arrived in the United States (e.g., within the past five years). What about births to naturalized immigrants who arrived 20 years earlier—should such births be excluded from estimates of the demographic effects of immigration because they are US citizens, or does this lead to substantial underestimates of the true demographic impact of international migration?

However such decisions are made, there is little doubt that net international migration has become a major factor in US demographic change, due to the convergence of two largely unrelated trends: continuing, though gradual, declines in fertility among the US-born population, accompanied by rising net international migration. Both trends have been underway for decades, but immigration has reflected far more erratic consequences of US political and economic policies. If analysts choose to include births to immigrants in the United States as an effect of immigration—on grounds that these births otherwise would not have occurred in the United States—then net international migration over the past two decades would have accounted for between two-thirds and just over three-fourths of US population growth. If other analysts prefer instead to exclude all such births, immigration still would account for between one-third and 45 percent of US population growth.[6]

As may be seen in Fig. 4.4, if only legal immigration is considered, this continued to increase substantially after 1990 to more than 1 million per year, more than doubling from the previous decades. This increase was due in the first instance to the delayed impacts of the unexpected growth of legal immigration due to provisions of immigration legislation adopted in 1965 (see chapter 3).

In addition, irregular/unlawful/illegal/undocumented migration also increased substantially over the same period due to the inadequacies of US immigration law and its enforcement. Two decades after the 1965 immigration act, after a multiyear debate involving much lobbying by a multitude of interest groups, the Immigration Reform and Control Act (IRCA) of 1986 sought to restrain growing unlawful migration with a "three-legged stool" approach: strengthening enforcement of existing laws regarding lawful entry and visa abuse; for the first time making it unlawful for employers to knowingly employ undocumented migrants (known as "employer sanctions"),

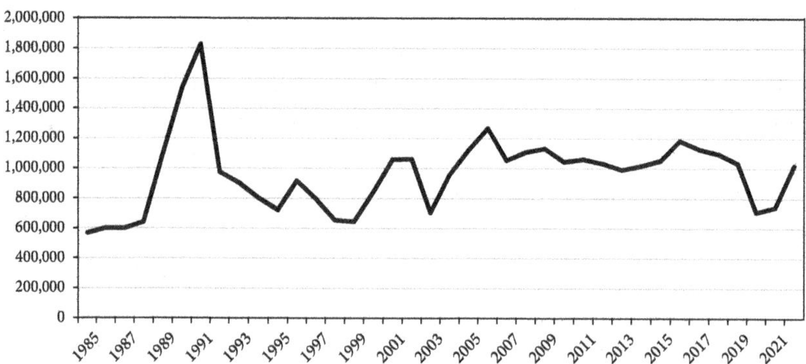

Fig. 4.4 Number of legal permanent residence visas issued, United States, 1985–2022.

Source: Migration Policy Institute tabulations of US Department of Homeland Security, Office of Immigration Statistics, *Yearbook of Immigration Statistics* (various years), www.dhs.gov/files/statistics/publications/yearbook.shtm.

while authorizing a new temporary worker program for agricultural employers; and legalization of large numbers of persons who had been unlawfully resident since before 1982.

The 1986 Act is generally agreed to have failed to achieve its goals, primarily for three reasons: inadequate follow-up funding provided by Congress for the Act's enhanced immigration enforcement, accompanied by unenthusiastic enforcement efforts by Executive Branch agencies; failure of the Act's employer sanction provisions due to political compromises that enabled widespread use of fraudulent documents; and the unanticipated legalization of far larger numbers of undocumented migrants than anticipated, due both to incorrect or misleading official estimates of the eligible population and to apparently widespread fraud and abuse in the legalization process. Indeed, the extraordinarily high spike in legal immigration during the early 1990s that can be seen in Fig. 4.4 is due to the legalization in that period of more than 3 million unauthorized migrants under IRCA's provisions.[7]

During the same decade of the 1990s, and notwithstanding bipartisan promises to constrain it, irregular/unlawful/illegal/undocumented migration rose even more rapidly than legal immigration (see Fig. 4.5). This surge was due to the convergence of political compromises embodied in the immigration acts of 1965 and 1986, other political actions both national and local, and judicial decisions that rendered ineffectual many legal provisions intended to enhance immigration enforcement.

Developing credible data about clandestine demographic events is methodologically challenging, hence such estimates are subject to substantial uncertainties. The estimates presented in Fig. 4.5 are produced by researchers at the Pew Research Center and are widely accepted.[8] They indicate that the midyear unauthorized immigrant population in the United States more than tripled during the 17 years between July 1990 and 2007, surging from about 3.5 million to 12.2 million. This large increase was followed by a slow decline to 10.2 million by July 2020, as the number of new irregular entries declined while some in this category departed, died, or obtained a legal status. This slow decline ended after 2020, with the estimated numbers rising back to 11.0 million in the two years ending in July 2022.

It is important to note here that the widely reported surges of irregular migration experienced since 2022 are not included in the estimates summarized in Fig. 4.5, as the official US Census Bureau data needed to produce such estimates for July 2023 were not available until late 2024. In a note

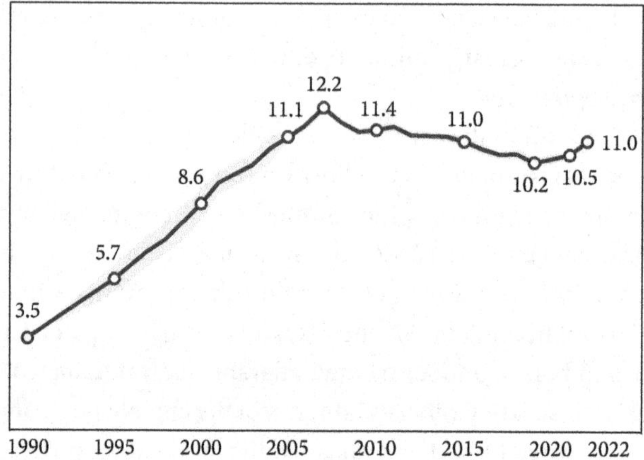

Fig.4.5 Unauthorized immigrant population in the United States, 1990–2022 (in millions).

Source: Pew Research Center, "What We Know about Unauthorized Immigrants Living in the U.S."

included in their report, Passel and Krogstad indicate that other immigration data indicate that the Biden administration issued protection from deportation for a large number (some 1.5 million) of irregular migrants since then, but cautioned that there are too many unknowns to derive a July 2023 estimate by simply adding this number to their 2022 estimate.[9]

The US Census Bureau makes regular estimates of changes in the size of the US population that are widely cited and used. In recent years the Census Bureau has acknowledged that its past estimates of net international migration, a major factor in US demographic change, have proven to be serious underestimates, and it has endeavored to develop improved estimating methods. Based on these new estimation techniques, in 2022 the Census Bureau released much higher alternative estimates, and then in late 2024 again revised its estimates sharply upward. One of its key conclusions from these revised estimates is that in the three years 2022, 2023, and 2024 net international migration to the United States was accelerating rapidly, rising to a total of 6.77 million (and with 2.79 million in 2024 alone).[10] Using these and other Census data, the Center for Immigration Studies, a Washington immigration think tank critical of US immigration policy, concluded that during the four year term (2021–2025) of President Biden the US foreign-born population increased by 8.3 million, of which about two-thirds or 5.4 million were in an irregular or illegal status.[11]

All such estimates must be understood to be preliminary and subject to adjustment as improved data becomes available over time. But few would doubt that the volume of the net flow of irregular/unlawful/illegal/undocumented migrants to the United States has been increasing substantially in recent years.

There also have been substantial increases in the number of lawfully resident "nonimmigrants."[12] This category, which does not include tourists and short-term visitors, is described as a "temporary" status but one that can last for many years. The numbers involved expanded after legislation adopted in 1990 created additional large categories of temporary but multi-year and extendable work visas. The official data are limited and difficult to analyze, but the US Government reports for example that there were 1.83 million residents in this category in 2008 and 3.19 million in 2019.[13] The numerically most important such visas include the large H-1B program for so-called specialty workers.

The 1990 legislation also created a new category of Temporary Protected Status (TPS), provided for nationals of certain countries experiencing political crises or natural disasters. Over the ensuing decades, additional countries have been included, and the time limits of many of these recipients of "temporary" protection have been extended—some have held TPS status for two decades or more. During the Biden administration, the scope and scale of TPS programs were expanded substantially, such that by 2024 the numbers either eligible for or already receiving TPS had grown to about 1.2 million from 16 countries: Afghanistan, Cameroon, El Salvador, Ethiopia, Haiti, Honduras, Myanmar, Nepal, Nicaragua, Somalia, Sudan, South Sudan, Syria, Ukraine, Venezuela, and Yemen.[14] The Biden administration also implemented a parallel program of "advance humanitarian parole" that by late 2024 had admitted and provided two-year residence and work permits to over 530,000 migrants authorized to fly directly to the US from four countries (including three of those eligible for TPS): Cuba, Haiti, Nicaragua, and Venezuela (hence commonly described as the CHNV program).[15] During 2025, the Trump administration issued executive orders terminating some TPS designations and extensions, as well as the Biden administration's CHNV program, but these orders were quickly challenged by lawsuits filed by political opponents and migration advocates. Hence, the ultimate effects upon current numbers in these categories depend on pending judicial determinations that cannot be predicted.

During the 1990s the problematic asylum system inherited from the 1980 Refugee Act was restructured and reformed by the Clinton administration, leading to more prompt adjudications and to declines in dubious, weakly founded, or frivolous claims for asylum. Between 1997 and 2014, the number of asylum claims remained fairly constant at approximately 50,000 per year. However, this stability was not to last. Between 2014 and 2017 the numbers tripled to about 150,000, then declined back to around 60,000 by 2021. And then, in a remarkable surge that overwhelmed the US asylum system, the number of such claims increased by over sevenfold between 2021 and 2023—from about 60,000 to nearly 440,000. Most of those claiming asylum were new arrivals filing "affirmative" asylum claims, but "defensive" asylum claims by persons who were already subject to removal also increased, to a lesser degree though still substantially.[16]

All of these demographic changes have been related reciprocally to domestic political trends underway in recent decades in the United States that included:

- growing political and regional polarization,
- the rise in extreme and populist movements on both the right and the left,
- and important shifts in the demographic perspectives that had long prevailed within the two dominant political parties.

These ideological and political trends came to the forefront during the 2024 presidential campaigns by Republican nominee Donald Trump and Democratic nominees Joe Biden and Kamala Harris. In his campaign, Trump focused heavily on what he alleged were the failures of the Biden-Harris administration's immigration and asylum policies, and the issues involved are widely seen as having played an important role in his election victory in November 2024.

The End of the Cold War ("The End of History"?), ca. 1990

The Cold War that had dominated international relations since 1945 came to an unexpected end between 1989 and 1991, first with the fall of the Berlin Wall in 1989 and the ensuing collapse of the Soviet-led Warsaw Pact, and culminating in 1991 with the dissolution of the Soviet Union itself. The end of this 45-year confrontation, with the risks of nuclear war that it had posed most notably in the Cuban Missile Crisis, was enthusiastically welcomed by most in Western liberal democracies. At last, it would be possible to avoid not only the risk of nuclear disaster but also costly arms races and future Cold War proxy wars such as those in Korea, Indochina, and Afghanistan. Military budgets of NATO countries could be reduced, with funding to be reallocated toward economic and social policies to resolve long-standing social challenges of economic inequality and poverty, homelessness, drug abuse, and the financing of increasingly costly healthcare and public pensions.

Some Cold Warriors expressed triumphalist claims of "victory over Communism." Other less ideological analysts also wrote with considerable optimism about the implications. In an influential essay predating by a few months the 1989 fall of the Berlin Wall, and in a 1992 book-length expansion of his ideas, Francis Fukuyama revived in modified form the idea of "the end of history," long associated with Hegel. In Fukuyama's formulation, during the decades between 1945 and 1990 the Western liberal democracies that combined legitimate popular elections, parliamentary democratic institutions, and regulated market economies had demonstrated the stability, dynamism, flexibility, and creativity necessary to withstand challenges from the autocratic political systems and government-controlled economies of both fascism and communism:

> What we may be witnessing is not just the end of the Cold War, or the passing of a particular period of postwar history, but the end of history as such: that is, the end point of mankind's ideological evolution and the universalization of Western liberal democracy as the final form of human government.[17]

His historical argument was essentially that of an evolutionary process, in which the comparative advantages demonstrated by Western liberal democratic structures since World War II would over time lead many other states to move in that direction. Over the long term, liberal democracies would become more prevalent, though not necessarily universal.

The Bipartisan Embrace of "Free Trade," Including with China

These and other optimistic forecasts were embraced by political movements from center-left to center-right. Some argued that the forecasted spread of liberal democracy and market economies would, at last, lead to the realization of the benefits they believed would accrue to all from ambitious liberalization of remaining impediments to international trade—toward what they termed "free trade."

With bipartisan support, the presidential administrations of Republican George H. W. Bush and his successor, Democrat Bill Clinton, formed common cause in promoting a new free trade agreement with Mexico and Canada, brought to fruition by the Clinton administration in 1992 as the North American Free Trade Agreement (NAFTA). Democratic and Republican leaders joined the Mexican president in energetically assuring skeptical legislators that the proposed NAFTA agreement would be the most effective way to restrain unauthorized migration by improving employment and wages in Mexico. During the multiyear debate about NAFTA, the president of Mexico, Carlos Salinas Gortari, regularly promised that adoption of NAFTA would mean that Mexico would "export goods, not people." President Clinton and Attorney General Janet Reno[18] made similarly enthusiastic claims, and with equal assurance. In Reno's words,

> We will not reduce the flow of illegal immigrants until these immigrants find decent jobs, at decent wages, in Mexico. Our best chance to reduce illegal immigration is sustained, robust Mexican economic growth. NAFTA will create jobs in Mexico—jobs for Mexican workers who might otherwise cross illegally into America.[19]

Most large US manufacturers lobbied strongly for NAFTA, and after it was implemented they accelerated direct investment and shifted production to new manufacturing facilities in northern Mexico to take advantage of its far less costly wage rates and environmental regulations, combined with its favorable geographical contiguity to US markets and transportation infrastructure.

Meanwhile some of the same advocates and interests began a more ambitious campaign to disseminate the virtues they saw in free trade on a truly global scale. In effect they revived a plan originally proposed during the formative postwar years of the late 1940s for a full-fledged multilateral organization to promote such free trade. The 1940s proposal had urged creation of a new International Trade Organization (ITO), which was to be the third of a proposed trio of multilateral economic organizations that included the International Monetary Fund (IMF) and the World Bank. In the end only the proposed ITO failed to garner sufficient support, due in part to the onset of the Cold War and the problems inherent in free trade between market and directed economies.

Yet, over the ensuing half century the flame of the free trade ideal had been kept alive by a provisional and semi-institutionalized multilateral treaty regime known as the General Agreement on Tariffs and Trade (GATT). In the bipartisan enthusiasm for ambitious free trade and economic globalization during the 1990s, the Clinton administration embraced free trade efforts initiated by his predecessor George H. W. Bush. In April 1994 it joined 122 other states in signing the Marrakesh Agreement to create a new World Trade Organization (WTO), which was established in 1995 as a more powerful successor to the semi-institutionalized GATT.

Here the matter might have rested, as trade restrictions were gradually liberalized among the hoped-for growing numbers of liberal democracies embracing market economies. But such was the political optimism of the moment that bipartisan voices began to argue also for the expedited admission of China to the (still quite new) WTO. No one claimed that China suddenly had been transformed from an autocratic Communist Party state into a liberal democracy with a functioning market economy, which normally would have been required to qualify for WTO admission. Instead advocates argued almost the opposite: that rapid admission of China to the WTO would accelerate Chinese economic development and thereby would empower a growing Chinese middle class who—over time—would insist on political liberalization and genuinely democratic institutions. The argument for China was that free trade would engender and enhance a transition to market economics and liberal democracy.

The hotly contested US presidential election of 2000 ended with confirmation of the Republican candidate (and son of the elder Bush) George W. Bush to succeed the Democratic president Bill Clinton. Though the younger Bush opposed many of the Clinton administration's initiatives, he embraced its efforts (which in turn had drawn on his father's) to greatly expand trade relations with China. In an important presidential campaign speech, the younger Bush had argued that "This is not a Republican or Democratic concern. It is an American concern. This trade agreement is the work of 13 years and three administrations. We cannot let that work be undone."[20]

In December 2000, shortly before leaving office, President Clinton granted China "most favored nation" (MFN) status (later reframed as "permanent normal trade relations" [PNTR]).[21] A year later, President George W. Bush succeeded in gaining agreement in the WTO for the admission of China as a full member state. The bipartisan optimism of the preceding decade about the virtues of globalization had succeeded in political terms.

Over time, however, concerns began to arise about the domestic benefits and costs involved, as China continued to pursue a government-incentivized and exports-led strategy that greatly stretched the boundaries of the WTO rubric. Increasing numbers of US and other Western political leaders and critics—including some of those who earlier had advocated for China's expedited integration into the global trading system via the WTO—began to argue that China's economic and trade policies had proven to be predatory and incompatible with the obligations it had undertaken to follow the norms-based international trade regime embodied in the WTO.

Such arguments were by no means universal—some Western advocates for Chinese membership in the WTO may have had second thoughts about the outcomes, but initially seemed reluctant to challenge these Chinese economic and trade strategies. By around 2020, however, the bipartisan consensus had shifted, as it became widely accepted in US political and economic circles that the assurances from NAFTA and WTO advocates that expanded globalization and "free trade" would benefit the entire world—including the United States—had not proven true. The economies of both Mexico and China had indeed prospered. In particular, the Chinese government's industrial and trade policies operating under the WTO umbrella succeeded in achieving remarkably high rates of Chinese economic growth and in establishing China as a dominant factor in global manufacturing.

However, it also became apparent that in important parts of the US economy the new policies were doing real damage. This was most obvious in manufacturing, where employment had been among the best-paid and most unionized. Critics pointed to a "hollowing out" of the large US middle class as manufacturing employment and hence private-sector unionization declined, to devastation of "rust belt" manufacturing regions concentrated in the Northeast and Midwest, and more broadly to intensification of US inequalities in income and wealth. To some degree US manufacturing would have changed due to ongoing technological change, but in this view the new and powerful forces that began around 1990 were the creation of NAFTA and then the WTO, followed by the US Government decision on a bipartisan basis to grant "permanent normal trade relations" with China and then to promote its admission to the global World Trade Organization.

These revised views, coupled with concerns about Chinese human rights violations and its government's increasingly aggressive foreign and military policies especially with respect to Taiwan and the South China Sea, produced a new bipartisan consensus that China should be viewed as a strategic competitor rather than a mutually beneficial trading partner. During the Trump and Biden administrations (2017-2025), multiple measures embodying such perspectives were adopted with bipartisan support, including substantial tariffs on Chinese exports, the Infrastructure Investment and Jobs Act of 2021, and the CHIPS and Science Act of 2022.[22]

While broadly bipartisan, some revised views were not universal. Some credible observers criticized subsequent costly efforts by the US and other Western governments to incentivize "re-shoring" of manufacturing employment, arguing that the large public subsidies being provided might prove inefficient and that in any case employment conditions in manufacturing are no longer superior to those in the services sector.[23]

The Rise of Modern US Populism

These trends in turn gave birth to rising US political movements now commonly described as "populist," especially in key "rust belt" regions that had experienced deep economic declines in manufacturing industries that had long employed well-paid and highly unionized workforces. Populist anger was directed against political and economic elites of both mainstream parties, and was skillfully exploited by a number of political candidates, most notably by Donald Trump in his unlikely but successful 2016 presidential campaign.

In his primary campaign for the Republican Party nomination, Trump directed concerted attacks on the long-dominant "corporate" and "internationalist/globalist" wings of the Republican Party, which he described as controlled by economic and political "elites." He accused them of energetically promoting policies that enriched elites but harmed the bulk of the nonelite US population. His primary focus was on policies that had promoted free trade, economic globalization including China, and "out-of-control" immigration. One of his favorite targets was the then-frontrunner for the Republican nomination: Jeb Bush, George W. Bush's brother and former governor of Florida. Nearly a dozen other mainstream candidates also sought the Republican nomination. Most targeted both the mainstream frontrunner Jeb Bush and the "outsider" populist challenger Trump, but ultimately, they split mainstream Republican voters and left Trump as the last Republican candidate standing.

After his nomination, Trump focused his criticisms on his mainstream Democratic opponent Hilary Clinton, a former US senator and secretary of state, and the wife of Bill Clinton, whom Trump criticized as having led the charge for these policies while he was president from 1993 to 2001.

To the surprise of most mainstream pollsters and pundits in politics, media, finance, corporations, and thinktanks, Trump was able to win the 2016 presidential election. After taking office Trump initiated numerous challenges to the bipartisan consensus about the virtues of free trade, globalization, "permanent normal trade" status for China, and expansive immigration policies. Trump's personal behavior and presidential style offended many Americans who supported both the Republican and Democratic mainstream parties, but his populist attacks and his aggressive revisions of policies related to these issues proved to be popular with large numbers of voters.

Trump lost his reelection bid in 2020, but most observers now agree that opposition to the past (bipartisan) consensus on globalization and free trade, and especially about the trade practices of the Chinese government, had become broad-based and bipartisan. According to *The Economist*, a respected British publication focused on economic policy, during this period there were dramatic shifts in perspective about economic policy, both on the left and the right:

> The populist era marked by Donald Trump's ascension has been tumultuous for economic policy on both the American left and right. What was once heterodox has quickly become orthodox . . .
>
> The diagnoses from the new right and new left of what ails America are strikingly similar. Both sides agree that the old order that prized expertise, free markets and free trade—"neoliberalism," usually invoked as a pejorative—was a rotten deal for America. Corporations were too immoral; elites too feckless, globalisation too costly; inequality too unchecked; the invisible hand too prone to error.[24]

It would appear that over the course of the past 2–3 decades there has been a broad-based shift away from the widely shared US support for maximizing free trade, globalization, and related enthusiasms that had emerged since the end of the Cold War around 1990.

Changes in the Politics of US Demographic Trends

US Political Parties Trade Places on Immigration

After 1990, US immigration policy also became attractive fodder for political campaigns. As the topic rose as a political issue, many leaders and advisors of the mainstream Republican and Democratic parties also began to trade places on the issues involved.

Until the 1980s, most Republican politicians had been highly responsive to the lobbying of economic interest groups (especially employers) seeking expansive legal immigration as a means to restrain wage increases and unionization while enabling enhanced international recruitment of both high- and low-skilled labor. Most supported increases in permanent immigration, as well as in nominally "temporary" worker programs—initially for low-skill agricultural labor, and later for "high-skill" workers as in the H-1B visa program. Many expressed opposition to irregular/unlawful/illegal/undocumented migration, but opposed efforts (often led by organized labor) to increase the effectiveness of immigration enforcement.

By the 1990s however, some Republican strategists had begun to express concern about the political effects of the lagged but by then rapid growth in both legal and illegal immigration that had been set in motion by immigration reform legislation in the 1960s and 1980s—much of which had been adopted with bipartisan sponsorship and support. The rapid increases in immigration of all types, they argued, coupled with declining fertility among US-born voters, was driving momentous shifts in the "demographics" of US politics. Harbingers of the future could be seen in the electoral transformation underway in California—the leading immigration state—from reliably Republican to reliably Democratic. Others expressed alarm about rising "identity politics," which they saw as amplified by immigration trends, as factionalizing the electorate into voting blocs based on ethnicity, national origin, race, language, gender, and religion. Still others claimed that ineffective enforcement of immigration laws was discrediting legal immigration and contributing to increases in rising criminality, terrorism, homelessness, drug abuse, and human trafficking.

Meanwhile, elements of the Democratic coalition were also moving toward major shifts in their longtime views. Organized labor, led by the

AFL-CIO union federation that had long been a powerful force in the Democratic coalition, had for decades been demanding (mostly without success) more effective enforcement of immigration laws and sharp limits on temporary visas for workers whose wage expectations were lower than US workers and were less likely to join unions. But as unionization rates in the private sector declined with the globalization of highly unionized manufacturing occupations, so too did the influence of leading manufacturing sector unions such as the United Auto Workers (UAW). Other unions such as the Service Employees International Union (SEIU) took up the slack in the labor movement, rapidly expanding their memberships by organizing lower-wage service workers in healthcare and building services. Indeed, the SEIU had grown to become the largest union in the AFL-CIO, and in 1995 its president, John Sweeney, was elected president of the AFL-CIO federation.

Given the low-wage service occupations organized by the SEIU, an unusually large fraction of its membership were of immigrant background, including many in irregular/unlawful/illegal/undocumented status. Over time, the union formed alliances with activist and employer groups committed to even more expansive immigration policies, and began to advocate strongly against organized labor's long-standing concerns about the effects of large-scale immigration on US workers. Instead, the SEIU began to support relaxation of immigration limits and legalization of many of the estimated 10–11 million irregular migrants, a category that included many of its own members. Advocacy from the SEIU was taken seriously in the Democratic Party, in part because the union had become one of the 10 largest sources of financial and in-kind contributions to candidates in federal elections, nearly all in support of Democratic Party candidates.[25]

Meanwhile some leading Democratic advisors and analysts were seeing partisan advantage in the ongoing demographic changes increasingly dominated by immigration. Some began to claim that the combination of the demographic and economic trends underway would lead ineluctably to a permanent Democratic majority. The most influential of these arguments appeared in a 2002 book by John B. Judis and Ruy Teixeira titled, appropriately enough, *The Emerging Democratic Majority*.[26] Its core argument was that rising percentages of immigrant and other Democratic-leaning "demographics" were favorable for Democrats at a national level. Moreover, they were increasingly concentrated in politically critical metropolitan areas of densely populated US regions, especially the Northeast, upper Midwest, and West Coast. In ethnic terms these included rising percentages of

Hispanic and Asian residents resulting from the expansion and transformation of US immigration produced by immigration legislation adopted in 1965, 1986, and 1990, and enhanced in occupational terms by growing numbers of professional and technical employees in rising postindustrial fields (computing, semiconductors, pharmaceuticals, media, entertainment, fashion, design, advertising, business services, etc.). Taken together, they concluded, the geographical regions experiencing rapid growth in these Democratic-leaning "demographics" accounted for 260 electoral votes, only 10 short of the majority needed in presidential elections.[27]

Forecasts such as those by Judis and Teixeira now appear to have been overly confident, as Hispanic voters (and especially Hispanic men) have proved to be a less reliable Democratic voting bloc than the forecasters had been assuming. To their credit, they recently have publicly raised doubts about their 2002 forecast that demographic changes would lead ineluctably to an "emerging Democratic majority" (see further discussion below).[28]

Other voices, led by some religious leaders, human rights advocates, and immigration lawyers often aligned with the Democratic Party, argued that both theological principles and international and domestic law require that all who are able to present themselves at US borders have a basic human right to be admitted in order to claim asylum, and to remain in the United States pending adjudication of their asylum claims, even if this process often took many years. Others went further, asserting that international human rights principles guarantee to all the right to migrate internationally to improve their life prospects, and especially so for people of color from countries with histories of imperialism, neoimperialism, and globalization.

During the first Trump administration from 2017 to 2021, the controversial and often harsh immigration enforcement policies adopted did seem to modulate the rising volumes of irregular/unlawful/illegal/undocumented immigration that had been underway since 1990. In 2020, the disruptions and spiking unemployment caused by the pandemic emergency dramatically lowered nearly all categories of international movement, including immigration. Trump's immigration policies became a major focal point of criticism from his many outraged critics in both mainstream parties and in the media, and the reversal of his immigration policies emerged as a central campaign issue for his Democratic opponent Joe Biden in 2020.

Following Biden's electoral victory over Trump in the 2020 election, the new administration fulfilled its campaign promises by moving almost immediately to reverse or sharply modify most of Trump's immigration and asylum policies. Though it is difficult to know for sure, subsequent events suggest that those involved in implementing these policy shifts may not have fully anticipated the surge of millions of irregular migrants and asylum seekers that ensued. Indeed, after Biden's election in November 2020 but before his inauguration in January 2021, large numbers of migrants had already trekked northward across Mexico from Central America under difficult and dangerous conditions, and shortly after Biden took office began to cross the border into the United States without permission. A large proportion claimed asylum once inside US territory, guided by advice provided by nongovernmental organizations (NGOs), immigration lawyers, and smuggler networks and disseminated widely via social media, that this strategy would enable them to reside and work in the United States for lengthy periods if not permanently.

This advice was correct. The US asylum system had been designed to adjudicate individual claims with a quasi-judicial process characterized by limited capacity and lengthy delays. When a surge of many hundreds of thousands of claims appeared, the asylum system designed for individual reviews was quickly overwhelmed, creating multiyear backlogs. In response the Biden administration began to invoke the president's "parole" authority on a mass scale, admitting hundreds of thousands who had crossed the border without authorization in order to claim asylum. Adjudication of the asylum claims of those so paroled was deferred due to the multiyear backlogs in the asylum adjudication system.

The cumulative numbers so admitted since Biden's inauguration are murky. Data made available by the Department of Homeland Security are convoluted and confusing, leading to estimates that vary widely, even wildly. But all such estimates are in the multiple millions. According to one necessarily crude estimate by FactCheck.org,[29] over a 32-month period from February 2021 through October 2023, there were some 6.5 million "encounters" of this type at the US-Mexico border. Of these 6.5 million persons encountered, some 2.5 million were released into the country by federal border agencies, and another 1 million-plus (including 367,000 unaccompanied minors) were transferred to other federal agencies but with outcomes that FactCheck.org was unable to determine. FactCheck.org also reported that the Department of Homeland Security had declined to provide them with any estimates of the numbers who entered the country successfully by avoiding contact with the border authorities ("getaways"), but had offered assurances that the apprehension rate was identical to the prior administration's estimate of some 1.6 million in this category over the same 32-month period.

Taken together, over these 32 months these categories totaled on the order of 3.5 to 5 million persons who under the Biden administration's new policies had been legally admitted to the United States or who had successfully evaded contact with border agencies. Other widely cited estimates were considerably higher, but no one should assume that even this wide range of estimates correctly reflects the actual numbers. The circumstances at the border over this period were too chaotic to allow accurate data collection, and the data made available by the US government too limited and ambiguous to allow accurate independent assessment. All that can be concluded is that the volumes involved were large, most likely in the multiple millions, though most likely not in the tens of million as alleged by some critics.

A cacophony of political turmoil and even theatrics accompanied these chaotic migratory movements, especially so in Texas, the US state with the longest (1,241 miles, over 2,000 kilometers) border with Mexico across which the largest number of such asylum claimants entered. The Texas state government, dominated by Republicans, announced that Texas cities and counties were being overwhelmed by the migration surge that followed Biden's 2021 inauguration and called on the federal government to strengthen immigration enforcement. When enhanced enforcement was not forthcoming, the state government deployed units of its own National Guard and state police to the border, and took other actions aimed at slowing the migratory flow. The Biden administration responded with lawsuits in federal courts seeking to reverse such state-level policies as infringing on federal control over immigration.

Later, the Republican-controlled state governments of Texas and Florida began offering newly-arrived migrants allowed by federal agencies to remain in the country the option of subsidized transportation by bus or plane to states further north. The destinations offered were mostly cities controlled by Democrats, with special emphasis on those that previously had declared themselves to be "sanctuaries" for undocumented migrants or had prohibited local cooperation with federal immigration enforcement agencies. These destinations included New York City; Washington, DC; Los Angeles; Chicago; Denver; and even the small and wealthy vacation island of Martha's Vineyard, Massachusetts. Critics in turn denounced these state-subsidized trips by bus and plane as deceptive, theatrical, and inhumane, and lawsuits were filed seeking to halt future free transportation offers of this type.

In the end, the (mostly Democratic) political elites of sanctuary cities and states found it difficult to accommodate the surging flows of migrants, and soon began to criticize the admissions and release policies of the Biden administration and to demand that it provide them with large-scale financial assistance to compensate for what they claimed were the large costs they incurred as a result. These unprecedented policies, counterpolicies and political cacophony illustrate how very politically fractious and partisan immigration debates in the United States became during the second and third decades of the 21st century. That they had significant impacts on the 2024 election cannot be doubted, but the ultimate outcomes of such debates remain to be seen.

In addition to its border policies, the Biden administration announced a new policy providing direct admission of a total of 30,000 asylum seekers each month, that is, 360,000 per year, from four countries: Cuba, Haiti, Nicaragua, and Venezuela. Under this special "advance humanitarian parole" program, asylum seekers could apply online from their home countries rather than after traveling to the US border. Their online application would have to identify a financial sponsor in the United States, who could be a family member or unrelated person, and such applications would be subject to a vetting process described as capable of identifying those inadmissible on grounds of criminal records, terrorist associations, or other disqualifying conditions. Once approved, parolees would be authorized to fly directly from their home countries to a US airport and would be granted two years' legal residence with a work permit. A federal lawsuit challenging this program was filed by 21 Republican-led states. It was dismissed at the initial stage on grounds that the states had not demonstrated legal "standing," that is, that they had suffered financial harm from this policy.[30] An extended series of appeals to higher courts seems likely.

In February 2024, the US House of Representatives impeached Alejandro Mayorkas, the Secretary of Homeland Security who was the Cabinet member primarily responsible for implementation of the Biden administration's immigration and asylum policies.[31] The formal grounds of this Congressional action were that Mayorkas had allegedly "willfully and systematically refused to comply with Federal immigration laws," and then "breached the public trust" by falsely testifying under oath before

Congress and obstructing Congressional investigation into the actions of his Department.[32] Mayorkas thus became only the second cabinet secretary in US history to be impeached.[33]

The attempt to impeach Secretary Mayorkas illustrated once again just how partisan US immigration and asylum policy had become. The February impeachment vote in the Republican-majority House followed party lines and was adopted by a razor-thin majority of one vote. Two months later the Democratic-controlled Senate conducted pro forma procedural votes that terminated the impeachment process.

As the Mayorkas impeachment process was proceeding, Donald Trump's presidential campaign focused heavy criticism on the immigration and asylum policies that the Biden-Harris administration had promulgated within days of taking office in January 2021—the very policies that were implemented by Secretary Mayorkas over the ensuing 3½ years. Most US media reported polling evidence that immigration was one of the two leading issues in the election—second only to the economy and inflation. Most reported immigration and border issues as Trump's "signature issue" (*Wall Street Journal*) and a "key reason" for his unexpectedly strong performance (*Newsweek*).[34] As if to highlight the importance of immigration as a factor in Biden's lagging poll numbers, in early June 2024, six weeks after the termination of the Mayorkas impeachment trial in the Senate and five months before the pending November election, President Biden suddenly reversed many of these policies. But it was apparently too late. Shortly thereafter Biden withdrew from his campaign and endorsed Vice President Harris to succeed him as the presidential candidate of the Democratic Party.

Almost all US news media of all political orientations attributed the administration's volte-face on its immigration and border policies to the national elections then looming five months hence, noting that nearly all opinion polls showed likely voters considered immigration issues to be one of the two most important election issues and that large majorities expressed strong criticism of these Biden/Mayorkas policies. The highest-quality and most in-depth survey of public opinion, conducted by the Pew Research Center in February 2024, concluded that about 80 percent of respondents indicated that "the U.S. Government is doing a bad job handling the migrant influx," but also expressed a wide range of views that divided along partisan lines about what new measures should be taken.[35]

Trump shifted his campaign focus to attack the new Democratic candidate for the roles she had played in the administration's immigration and asylum policies, describing her as Biden's "border czar."[36] He promised that if elected he would reverse policies that he argued had stimulated the disorderly migration of millions of people into the United States during the prior 3½ years, and would mobilize an energetic "mass deportation" campaign to remove "millions" of those unlawfully resident.

Most election polling proved to have seriously underestimated voters' support for Trump. Postelection evidence indicated that immigration, asylum, and border issues had continued to be an important factor in the unexpectedly strong performance of Republican candidates, as they took control of the presidency and of both houses of Congress.[37]

Under such circumstances the issues involved seem almost certain to continue as prominent elements of US political debate over the coming years. In this respect US political trends appear to be similar to those underway in other liberal democracies, especially in European countries including Germany, Austria, Hungary, France, Italy, Netherlands, Sweden, Denmark, the United Kingdom, and others. In most of these cases relatively new "populist" parties on the political right that espouse opposition to recent immigration and asylum policies have begun to pose serious challenges to long-dominant mainstream center-left and center-right parties. Politics in Germany have been roiled by one such party since at least 2015, the Alternative for Germany (AfD), and more recently a new left-wing anti-immigration party (Sahra Wagenknecht Alliance—BSW) has been gaining public support (see chapter 2).

Contraception and Abortion

From the 1990s to the present, both pro-life and pro-choice activism became more partisan, vociferous and visible. Debate increased about federal "Title X" support for Planned Parenthood, the largest provider of contraceptive and abortion services.[38] The distinction between contraception and abortion seemed to have become blurred or forgotten as abortion rights became more partisan, with some abortion opponents arguing that IUDs and other modern contraceptives actually cause abortions.[39]

As noted in chapter 3, in the aftermath of the 1973 *Roe v. Wade* decision that declared a constitutional right to abortion up to the 24th week of pregnancy, and later of the highly partisan 1987 Senate vote rejecting confirmation of Robert Bork as a Supreme Court Justice, subsequent judicial nominations also became openly partisan and politicized—especially so for nominations to the Supreme Court. Choices of nominees by Republican presidents were increasingly influenced by the recommendations of a relatively new conservative legal association, the Federalist Society,[40] and by assessments of nominees' likely views for or against *Roe v. Wade.* Although that 1973 Supreme Court decision had been authored by Justice Henry Blackmun, a Republican jurist nominated by President Reagan, by 1987 abortion had become a partisan battleground, with most Republicans opposed to the *Roe v. Wade* decision and most Democrats supportive.

In his campaign for the 2016 presidential election, Donald Trump openly promised that he would nominate conservative jurists likely to challenge earlier Supreme Court rulings such as *Roe v. Wade.* During his presidency (2017–2021) he nominated three candidates for the Supreme Court. All were confirmed by the US Senate, though only after highly partisan and often-bitter confirmation hearings and floor debates in which abortion issues loomed large. These confirmations shifted the Court from a 9-member body narrowly divided 5–4 between center-right and center-left to one with a new 6-3 center-right majority.

In its 2022 decision *Dobbs v. Jackson Women's Health Organization*, the Supreme Court overruled the earlier Court's 1973 *Roe v. Wade* precedent, thereby returning to the 50 states the power to regulate the availability of legal abortion. In subsequent state-level legislation and judicial decisions, legislators in only a few states have sought to ban abortion entirely, though a number have substantially limited access in a variety of ways—most notably by limiting abortion after 15 or even 6 weeks of gestation as compared with the 24-week limit that was a central feature of the *Roe v. Wade* decision. There were also efforts in a few states to constrain access to abortion services available in other states, including by prohibiting the mailing of medications widely used to induce early abortion such as mifepristone. Most of these restrictions have subsequently been challenged in state and Federal courts, and litigation and legislative efforts continue to evolve.

The issues in conflict are now so highly politicized and contentious that they seem likely to continue to resonate for many years to come. Democratic politicians now see abortion rights as a core campaign issue, and opposition to the *Dobbs* decision (along with other matters related to the environment, affirmative action, and diversity, equity and inclusion (DEI)) has further animated the trend toward political polarization that had been underway since the 1980s. Some mostly Democratic politicians and advocates have responded to the Supreme Court decisions by promoting legislation that would increase the number of Supreme Court Justices whom they hope would be nominated by Democratic presidents (denounced by opponents as "Court-packing"); the imposition of term or age limits on Supreme Court Justices (which would require a Constitutional amendment); and a variety of other actions that would increase Congressional influence and limit the independence of the federal judiciary.

Once again, these divisions have tended to be partisan, polarized, and driven by disagreements about abortion. It may be that these Democratic politicians have been overly confident that opposition to abortion restrictions, like opposition to immigration enforcement, would deliver electoral victories to Democratic candidates. Only time will tell.

Demographic Changes and Political Controversies, Postpandemic

Though no one can know for sure that the deadly assault on humanity by the COVID-19 pandemic is now permanently under control, the relaxation of pandemic emergency measures already has been followed by political debates with significant demographic elements. As noted earlier, US fertility rates before the pandemic were already moderately low but stable at levels modestly below the replacement level of 2.1 children per woman. However, during the pandemic years 2021–2023 US fertility rates declined further to 1.62 (see Fig. 4.1), and there is no way to accurately predict whether they will bounce back to prepandemic levels in the coming years, remain at these lower levels, or decline further.

Some advocates and analysts have asserted that pandemic fertility rates would have trended even lower had it not been for the temporary federal child payments of $3,000 to $3,600 per year for children up to age 17 that were included in the Biden administration's $1.9 trillion emergency stimulus legislation known as American Rescue Plan Act of 2021.[41] Center-left advocates have argued that these payments not only kept fertility from dropping even further but also reduced child poverty rates, and have called for them to be made permanent.[42] Some center-right Republicans, including the former Republican presidential nominee Senator Mitt Romney, proposed child payment plans that differed from those from the center-left, but which Romney described as both family-friendly and addressing America's falling birth rate.[43]

Others pointed to the inflationary effects of tight labor markets (usually called "labor shortages" by advocates) and rising wages that followed the reopening of the US economy after the lengthy pandemic closures, and argued that these could be addressed by expanding admissions of immigrants and temporary workers.[44]

Meanwhile, some progressive Democratic strategists and advisors began to raise questions about earlier assumptions that the demographic changes underway would lead ineluctably to Democratic majorities.[45] As noted, these earlier forecasts had assumed that the most rapidly expanding "demographics," namely, Hispanics and Asian Americans, would continue to tilt strongly Democratic. But what if these assumptions were also to prove incorrect, like those about globalization and "free trade"?

Indeed, growing evidence from polls and elections suggested that Hispanic voters might not continue to be a reliable source of large Democratic majorities, and new skepticism had been emerging among some leading Democratic Party strategists. Perhaps the most prominent were Judis and Teixeira, who as noted earlier were coauthors of an influential 2002 book predicting the emergence of a permanent Democratic majority driven by demographic change. By 2023 they were publicly expressing concerns that the opposite was happening, due to the "culture wars" led by the progressive wing of the Democratic Party that proved controversial among some of the same expanding demographic groups their book had assumed would continue to vote Democratic by huge margins. These topics included "affirmative action" and related policies that favored African American and Hispanic applicants to selective secondary schools and universities, but allegedly disadvantaged Asian American applicants;[46] controversies about LGBTQ+ rights (and especially "trans" rights and gender transition treatments), which polling suggested were not supported by many African American and Hispanic voters; concerns about increasing crime rates attributed to progressive efforts to "defund the police" and reduce prosecution and imprisonment for unlawful behavior such as shoplifting, burglary, and car theft; and opposition among many Hispanics and Asian Americans to the Biden administration's immigration policies.

A year later these concerns seem to have been validated by the results of the 2024 presidential elections. According to a joint assessment by the Americas Society (AS) and the Council of the Americas, both respected nongovernmental organizations focused on Latin America and the Caribbean region, the Democratic candidate Kamala Harris had received majority support among Hispanic voters, but by far smaller margins than in prior elections, 14 percentage points in 2024, compared to a margin of 34 points in favor of Biden in 2020.[47]

In short, for decades now, party strategists—both Democratic and Republican—have been applying demographic projection methods to predict that policies affecting demographic change would lead to permanent electoral majorities for their party. Both predictions could not be valid in a two-party system. As is true of all projections, the predictive value of such claims is only as good as the validity of the assumptions built into the projection model, which in this case includes assumptions about the degree to which past political orientations among voting "demographics" (ethnic, racial, linguistic, national origin, etc.) will continue into the long-range future.

In Dante's *Inferno*, there is a special place in the 8th Circle of Hell reserved for those who seek to forecast the future. In Dante's imaginings, their heads are to be rotated 180 degrees on their necks, so that they are forced to "walk backwards for all of eternity." Those who seek to make long-term forecasts of the voting behavior of demographic groups may wish to take note, as the relationship between demography and destiny is more complex than most assume.[48]

Official Concepts and Statistics on "Race"

Official "race" categories in US census data have played formative roles since at least the 18th century. These categories have been created by political decisions made by both the legislative and executive branches.

The origins of official US racial classifications go back to the politics surrounding the 18th century founding of the United States as a novel federal republic. As part of the Great Compromise that was required to reach agreement among the 13 founding colonies, the United States Constitution that was adopted in 1788 required the nascent federal republic to implement a national census every 10 years, on the basis of which important elements of political power would be reallocated to reflect population change. This mandate to allocate seats in the House of Representatives based on a decennial census—the first of its kind—provided an automatic mechanism for states with larger populations to hold more such Congressional seats than smaller states, with these seats to be reapportioned every decade as state population sizes changed at different rates. The same census data would be used to ensure that any additional states that might in the future be admitted to the federal republic would automatically be allocated seats on the same demographic basis. Meanwhile each state would be allocated an unchanging two seats in the Senate.

This Great Compromise about the allocation and reallocation of political power was a core element, without which agreement on a new Constitution would have been impossible among the 13 sovereign and disparate former colonies. However, some of the required compromises sowed the seeds of three-quarters of a century of persistent political conflict over slavery, ultimately leading to a brutal civil war in the 1860s. About half the original 13 colonies (including Virginia, the largest and most influential colony in the framing of the new constitution) were located in the south, with agrarian economies based on the forced labor of African slaves. Meanwhile there was strong opposition to slavery on moral and religious grounds in many of the northern colonies, most of which had more diversified economies in which slavery or the slave trade was banned.

Once the Constitutional Convention had agreed that the proposed new House of Representatives was to be apportioned on the basis of a census count collected every 10 years of all "persons," a fundamental disagreement quickly emerged about how the large number of African slaves in the southern colonies were to be treated in this allocation process. Southern delegates insisted that their slaves had to be included in the enumeration for purposes of apportionment; without this there could be no union. Northerners insisted that since Southern states treated slaves as chattel and excluded them from political life, their inclusion in the reapportionment count would unacceptably magnify the political power of Southern states and their White populations.[49]

A bitter political stalemate ensued, so deep that it threatened to destroy efforts to unify the 13 colonies. After extended debate and negotiation, the framers of the Constitution reached a reluctant and arbitrary compromise that ended the stalemate but later was to prove portentous: slaves would indeed be enumerated in the mandated decennial census, but for purposes of apportionment of the new House of Representatives their numbers would be reduced by two-fifths. Alexander Hamilton and Gouverneur Morris, both Northern cosigners of the Constitution and reluctant supporters of the Compromise, observed that (in Hamilton's words), "Without this indulgence, no union could possibly have been formed."[50] The Compromise was portentous as it allowed strong disagreements about slavery to fester and deepen for 75 years, until Abraham Lincoln's 1862 Preliminary Emancipation Proclamation during the throes of the disastrous Civil War that had been precipitated in substantial part by unresolved disputes over slavery.

The 1790 census enumeration required by the new US Constitution adopted in 1787 in Philadelphia embodied a racial classification that effectively divided the population into three categories: White persons, free; Other than White persons, free; Slaves (most Blacks).[51]

Racial classifications since then have changed substantially, and yet have continued to be central elements of the US Census and other US national statistics over the ensuing period of more than 235 years. If anything, attention to racial classification increased with the later rise of "race science" among 19th-century scientists, coupled with the adoption of official racial segregation and antimiscegenation laws in Southern states after the Civil War.

During the first part of the 20th century enthusiasm about scientific theories based on emerging Darwinian and genetic concepts were transformed into political and social ideologies (Social Darwinism, eugenics) in which racial classifications played a central role. In 1904, the eminent Cornell University statistician Walter Willcox[52] observed that "there is no country in which statistical investigation of race questions is so highly developed . . . as in the United States."[53]

Political controversies and actions led to numerous modifications of official US "race" classifications in both the Census and government policy. During the first two decades of the 20th century, political opposition grew against numerically unlimited and rapidly increasing immigration from Eastern and Southern Europe. Large numbers of Italians, Jews, Poles, Russians, and others from these regions initially were seen as fitting poorly within the long-established 19th-century "White" race category that had been based on groups from Northern Europe.[54] By then, however, perspectives drawn from the burgeoning social sciences (especially anthropology and sociology) had "largely displaced nineteenth century *race* science."[55] The shift from "race science" to social science meant that in the eyes of many "The northern, southern, and eastern Europeans could each be racially white yet differ radically in their fitness for membership in American society."[56]

After much controversy, between 1917 and 1924 these social science concepts of national origins became central components of a succession of new legislative limits ("quotas") on immigration from Eastern and Southern Europe that previously had been subject to no numerical limits. These provisions combined national origin with the existing racial classification system, and regulated much of US immigration policy for the ensuing 40 years, until they were ended by 1965 legislation. However national origin has continued to be a core component of US Census "race" classifications to the present day, as may be seen in Figures 4.6 and 4.7.

In his thoughtful analysis on the evolution and utility of official US classifications of "race," Prewitt argues that current US racial classifications are a hodge-podge created by more than two centuries of political decisions driven by advocacy about slavery, the "race science" and "Jim Crow" of the 19th century, and debates about immigration, civil rights, and affirmative action in the 20th century.

Prewitt concludes that current official classifications of "race" are not based on a "coherent definition of race" at all, but instead an incoherent mixture of "categories based on color with categories based on ancestry or national origin." He advises that the current "race" classification be reconfigured in a way that is more coherent and better reflects current concepts of race. He also argues that to make its use in policy terms more effective, the collection of data on "race" categories should be shifted from the US

→ **NOTE: Please answer BOTH Question 8 about Hispanic origin and Question 9 about race. For this census, Hispanic origins are not races.**

8. Is Person 1 of Hispanic, Latino, or Spanish origin?

☐ **No,** not of Hispanic, Latino, or Spanish origin

☐ Yes, Mexican, Mexican Am., Chicano

☐ Yes, Puerto Rican

☐ Yes, Cuban

☐ Yes, another Hispanic,Latino, or Spanish origin - *Print, for example, Salvadoran, Dominican, Colombian, Guatemalan, Spaniard, Ecuadorian, etc.*

Fig. 4.6 2020 US Census questions on Hispanic origin.

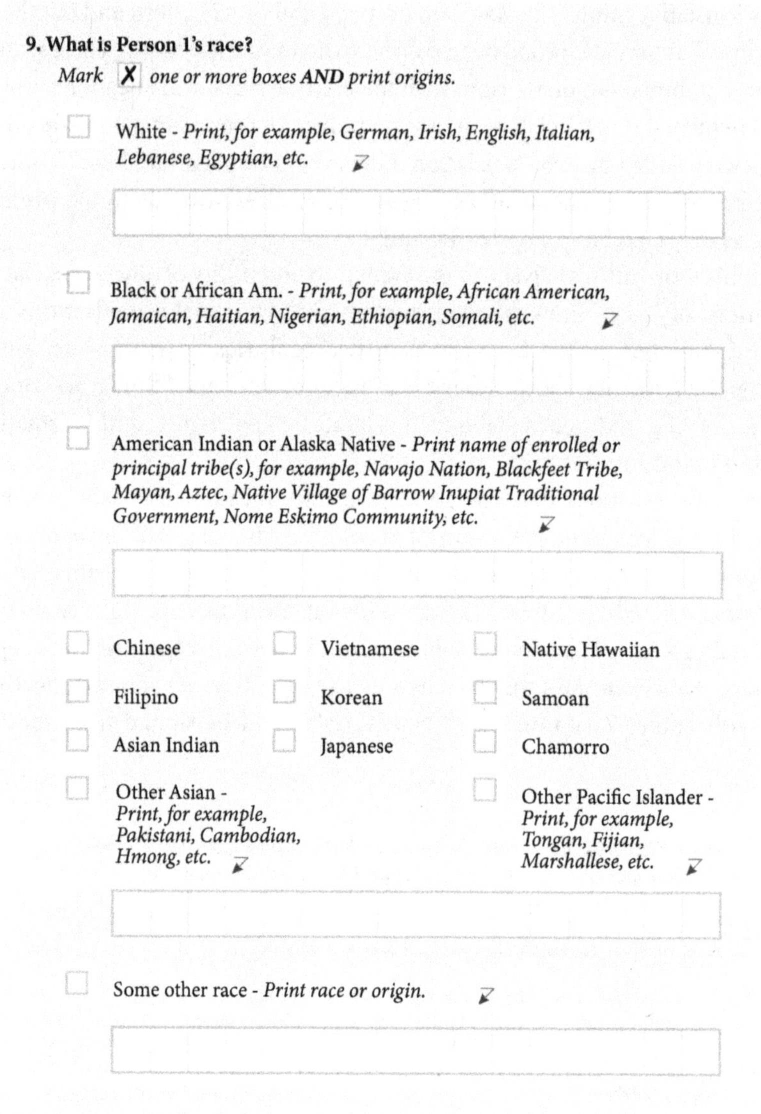

9. What is Person 1's race?
Mark **X** *one or more boxes* ***AND*** *print origins.*

☐ White - *Print, for example, German, Irish, English, Italian, Lebanese, Egyptian, etc.*

☐ Black or African Am. - *Print, for example, African American, Jamaican, Haitian, Nigerian, Ethiopian, Somali, etc.*

☐ American Indian or Alaska Native - *Print name of enrolled or principal tribe(s), for example, Navajo Nation, Blackfeet Tribe, Mayan, Aztec, Native Village of Barrow Inupiat Traditional Government, Nome Eskimo Community, etc.*

☐ Chinese ☐ Vietnamese ☐ Native Hawaiian
☐ Filipino ☐ Korean ☐ Samoan
☐ Asian Indian ☐ Japanese ☐ Chamorro

☐ Other Asian - *Print, for example, Pakistani, Cambodian, Hmong, etc.*

☐ Other Pacific Islander - *Print, for example, Tongan, Fijian, Marshallese, etc.*

☐ Some other race - *Print race or origin.*

Fig. 4.7 2020 US Census question on "race."

Census itself (conducted only once every 10 years) to the large American Community Survey, for which data is collected on a continuous basis.[57]

In March 2024, the Biden administration issued formal revisions to the Statistical Policy Directive No. 15 (SPD 15): Standards for Maintaining,

Collecting, and Presenting Federal Data on Race and Ethnicity that established the official "race" categories used by the Federal Government. These changes included:[58]

- using a single combined race and ethnicity question, allowing multiple responses;
- add Middle Eastern or North African (MENA) as a minimum reporting category, separate and distinct from the White category;
- require the collection of more detail beyond the minimum race and ethnicity reporting categories . . .;
- update terminology in SPD 15;
- and require agency Action Plans on Race and Ethnicity Data and timely compliance with this revision to SPD 15.

Unless these changes are challenged or modified, these revisions presumably will be implemented in the 2030 US Census and in all other official reporting on "race" categories in the United States during the 2030s. The historical development of the official US Census "race" classifications from the initial 1790 census to the 2020 census is a truly winding road with no end in sight—its categories and political controversies appear unlikely to ever be settled. Rather, the contours of this history trace the influence of ideologies of identity and demonstrate the inextricable links between population and politics.

PART III
EAST ASIA

5

Engineering a New Future

Demographic Distortion in Asia, 1945–1990

Introduction

The peace that ended World War II did not spell the end of political upheaval for China, Japan, Singapore, and South Korea. In China, civil war resulted in the victory of Mao's Chinese Communist Party in 1949 and the retreat to Taiwan by Chiang Kai-Shek's Nationalist government. Japan's imperial power in the region had been upended by its defeat and surrender to the Allied powers in 1945, a year that saw them go from occupier of much of Asia to a country occupied by US allied forces. The Korean peninsula, too, would be ripped apart along ideological lines in the form of a brutal war between 1950 and 1953, the aftermath of which would leave a permanent division between the north and south. Singapore faced its own political and geographic divisions in the post–World War II era, first as it was liberated from Japanese occupation and returned to British control as a crown colony in 1946, then as it gained independence from the British in 1963 and, after only a two-year flirtation with a Malaysian merger, decided to form its own independent state. Thus, as all four of these Asian states were still rending and forming after 1945, there was a deep sense of national trauma and economic crisis. With the conclusion of the Second World War, a new global order was dawning. The question was: What role would these Asian states get to play in this new order? How quickly could they heal from war, occupation, and internal division?

Population, for all four, would be one of the keys to unlock a new and better future in the eyes of their elites, who sought to shape a population that would be ideal in size, age structure, and ethnic composition. Appropriate population policies, they expected, could help drive the engine of economic growth and secure stability for their regimes. The ideological biases these elites carried distorted how they viewed demographic data and population dynamics. Space limitations preclude covering every distortion

Toxic Demography. Jennifer D. Sciubba, Michael S. Teitelbaum, and Jay Winter, Oxford University Press.

DOI: 10.1093/oso/9780197745038.003.0006

in each of these four countries, but the examples in this chapter are sufficient to demonstrate a few key generalizations.

One takeaway is that these states' leaders shared a common view of what an ideal population would look like and why it was important to pursue this goal through government policy. An ideal population would grow more slowly than it had in prior decades, but still supply a robust workforce—and many shared a sense of urgency about this. Asia in general was seen as a region of "too many births" after World War II, both internally by political elites concerned about economic recovery and growth, and by some in other regions who saw continuing rapid population growth as contributing to a future of poverty, hunger, and thus susceptibility to communism. The Chinese Communist revolutionary leader Mao Zedong vacillated between portraying a growing Chinese population as a source of national strength and asserting that slower population growth would strengthen the revolution. Mao's episodic support for expanding the Chinese population was the exception rather than the rule, even within China, which like South Korea adopted national population limitation policies early in the second half of the 20th century.

Overall, what we might call "ideologies of modernization" shaped strong state-sponsored efforts to moderate population growth in the name of economic prosperity and national security in all four Asian states. As political leaders in each state debated how to prioritize national goals, efforts to maximize economic growth bubbled to the top time and again. As their rapid rates of population growth declined during the 1945 to 1990 period, Singapore and South Korea experienced robust economic growth that created a foundation for continued economic success in the subsequent decades. China's surge of economic growth came later, but in general these governments placed high value on increasing economic growth and moderating population growth, in some cases by methods that infringed on individual rights.

To all four of these Asian states, an ideal population would also be ethnically harmonious. Ideologies of identity had a strong influence on the discussion of population in the public arena, and each state embraced strong efforts to realize its vision of ethnic harmony. In Singapore's case, that meant maintaining demographic balance among its several ethnic groups, with the government adopting a host of policies designed to manage ethnic identity in the service of a cohesive national identity. In South Korea, ethnic harmony was articulated as ethnic homogeneity, a goal that successive governments pursued through marriage, citizenship, and adoption policies.

An ideal population was to be undergirded by the ideal family. Gender dynamics are key to the story, as during this period women—and some men—began to reject rigid social structures that conditioned work practices and family dynamics. Throughout these four states from 1945 onward, marriage rates fell while average marriage ages increased, and fertility rates declined apace. Each country would see the effects of these changes more clearly after 1990.

But while the focus here is on elite-level politics, the story of demographic distortion in Asia is not one in which citizens stood by passively—another commonality among the four countries. Governments may have put policies in place to help them achieve what they defined as ideal demographic dynamics, from urbanization in China (particularly more recently), to fertility-related policies in all four, but these policies were contested by some groups within civil society. While civil society groups were not as influential in some of these states as perhaps in others, we still see individuals exercising their choices in ways independent of—and sometimes antithetical to—the goals of the various nations' leaders, particularly once individuals had greater control over their reproduction. For example, China's total fertility rate was trending sharply downward during its experiment with a "later-longer-fewer" policy implemented well before the introduction of its narrower and more coercive One-Child Policy. Enforcement also varied among China's regions and between its large rural and growing urban populations, in part because fertility rates in urban areas were generally lower than national targets. In Japan and Singapore, despite exhortations to have more babies that began in this time period and intensified in the following one, fertility rates continued to decline as many women across Asia increasingly opted out of prescribed family roles, often to the chagrin of their governments.

A fourth commonality is how the particularly strong central governments of each state during this time period from 1945 to 1990 facilitated their efforts at demographic engineering. While population politics is alive and well in all the cases and time periods covered in this book, the central governments of these four Asian states have had generally a tighter grip on power than have governments in the US or Europe. With far less alternation of power between political parties—none in China or Singapore, for example, and only rarely in Japan, given the dominance of the Liberal Democratic Party—policies relating to fertility were under less of a threat of electoral reversal in the Asian region than in much of the rest of the world.

While the governments of these four countries may have started the period 1945–1990 in the midst of serious economic and political challenges, they achieved tremendous gains in economic strength by the time the global order shifted with the end of the Cold War. Of course, they also ended it with radically different population dynamics.

Population Trends Overview

China, Japan, Singapore, and South Korea followed distinct paths in the post–World War II period as they shifted from high fertility combined with high mortality to low fertility and low mortality, a process long summarized as "the demographic transition." In each, some hard-to-estimate combination of state family planning policy, use of modern contraceptive technology, education, and economic modernization played a role in driving their transition. Modernization played the strongest role in Japan and Singapore, whereby rising education, income levels, and growing labor force participation rates among women drove fertility and mortality lower. In China, state policy accelerated fertility declines, and South Korea's transition was driven by more of a mix, with state policy somewhat accelerating the demographic transition in the context of strong economic modernization. During the 1945–1990 period these states also had unique experiences with mortality. For example, while the life expectancy at birth for Japanese females rose to the highest in the world during this time, the Chinese population suffered several catastrophic mortality events, including mass starvation driven by state-imposed policies of agricultural collectivization during the Great Leap Forward from 1958 to 1962. Finally, while immigration policies were more powerful in shaping the population of Singapore than any of the other states, there were also large-scale population exchanges between Japan and South Korea and between North and South Korea to reunite co-ethnics displaced by colonization or war.

Mortality

The gains in life expectancy at birth in East Asia were so rapid during the 1960s and 1970s that the region had narrowed the gap with European life expectancy from greater than 20 years in 1950 to less than three years by

1990.[1] The mortality transition in Japan was smoothest among this set of countries, with the crude death rate sharply decreasing by over 50 percent in less than a decade, from 17.6 per thousand in 1946 to 7.8 per thousand in 1955. Public health measures, including vaccination campaigns, were responsible for much of the gain.[2] Of course World War II, particularly the war's final year, brought about a sharp decline in Japanese life expectancy to around 24 years, but this deterioration of mortality conditions is best viewed as an interruption along what was otherwise a smooth and steep curve toward increasing life expectancy, as Fig. 5.2 shows. Japanese life expectancy at birth had been only 37 years in 1900, but had already increased to 48 years by 1935 and by the late 1940s was approaching 60 years.[3] While initial improvements were in infant and young adult mortality, later in this period gains in life expectancy were mostly made at the upper ends of the age scale, meaning those over 65 years. In Singapore, as in Japan, life expectancy in the mid-20th century was already higher than that in many states in the region and in the two decades prior to Singapore's independence in 1965, death rates had fallen 75 percent. Over that time, noncommunicable diseases, such as cancer and stroke, replaced infectious diseases as leading causes of death.[4]

South Korea and China did not see such impressive improvements as early as Japan did, and gains were especially slow in South Korea due to the Korean War, which spiked the death rate to a record high of 33 deaths per 1,000 in 1955.[5] The Korean War had long-lasting effects on marital status composition and family structures in South Korea due to high mortality among males aged 20–34 combined with the historically low remarriage rate conditioned by Korean cultural norms.[6] While life expectancy at birth was dismal in the early 1950s, as Fig. 5.1 shows, after the end of the Korean War in July 1953 it began to improve dramatically, quickly eclipsing China and rocketing to over age 70 by 1990—a remarkable gain of 50 years in life expectancy at birth over that period. Broad socioeconomic development, including the transition from an agrarian to an industrialized and urbanized population, was an important factor in the mortality transition. However, South Korea reduced mortality earlier than would be expected given its then-low level of economic development, demonstrating the influence of the centralized state in leading the mortality transition, particularly government efforts at infectious disease prevention such as compulsory inoculation, rather than improvements in living standards driving slower mortality gains.[7] The expansion of health and medical

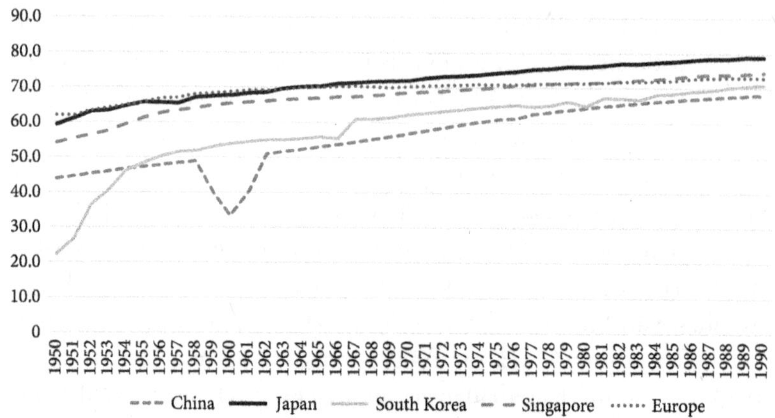

Fig. 5.1 Life expectancy at birth in selected nations of East Asia and Europe, 1950–1990.

facilities, improving nutritional standards and voluntary but well-organized family planning programs contributed to a continuous decline in mortality after 1960.[8]

With its victory in 1949, the Chinese Communist Party gained political control of the most populous country on the planet. During the first two decades of its rule, the population of China grew almost 50 percent, in part from reductions in infant and child mortality. Before the Communist victory over the Nationalist Kuomintang, the predominantly peasant population of China had very high mortality, and estimates of China's life expectancy at birth in 1930 range from under 25 years to the low 30s.[9] The catastrophic Great Famine of 1959–1961 during Mao's Great Leap Forward reduced China's population by 30 million during a time when most countries were still experiencing major population booms.[10] Despite that tragedy, the country saw remarkable life expectancy increases from around 35 to 40 years in 1950 to 65.5 years in 1980, mostly from significant expansion of education and public health campaigns. Gains were particularly rapid in the 1950s as Mao launched his "Patriotic Health Campaigns" early in that decade. These first focused on improved sanitation and infectious disease reduction through pest control, and later included programs such as midwife training, "barefoot doctors," campaigns against malnutrition, or promoting immunization. After the Great Famine, life expectancy improved, driven in part by social and economic disruptions of the Cultural Revolution.[11]

Fertility

While each of these four countries reached below-replacement fertility at different times—earliest in Japan in the 1950s and latest in China in the early 1990s—they all ended the period at a similarly low point, as Fig. 5.2 shows.

In the region, Japan was the first to experience a sharp decrease in fertility rates after their short post–World War II baby boom—and experienced the greatest drop among industrialized economies. Fertility rates in Japan dropped below replacement level early in the postwar era, dipping below 2.1 children per woman in 1958, then hovering around replacement until a slower but steadier decline began after 1975. In China the fertility rates of both rural and urban areas were cut in half between 1970–71 and 1978–79, from approximately 6.0 to 3.0 in rural areas and from 3.3 to 1.5 in urban areas.[12] In Korea, the Korean War caused a decline of about 15 percent in live births between 1950 and 1953.[13] Still, fertility rates there were high; the average number of children per woman fell to 5.6 according to some estimates during the Korean war from 1950 to 1953, after which it rose to 6.3 from the period 1955–1960, a period when the annual population growth rate peaked at 2.9 percent.[14] Leaving aside this exceptional wartime period, South Korea's rapid and dramatic fertility decline after 1945 generally was driven by changes in family formation, especially later marriage—significant because of the rarity of Korean births outside of wedlock—while there were also changes in preferences toward much smaller family sizes among married couples.

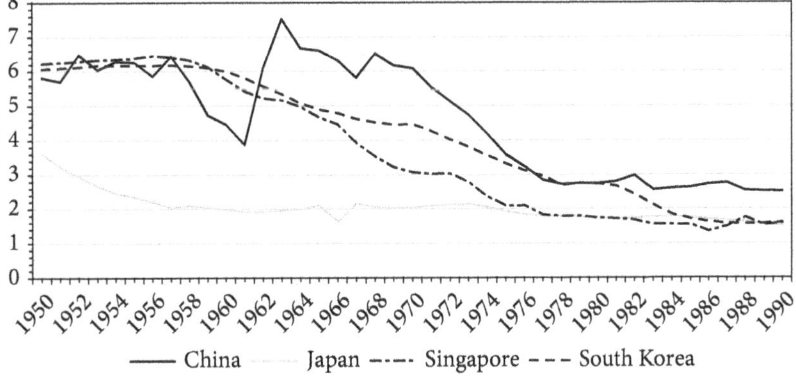

Fig. 5.2 Total fertility rate in China, Japan, Singapore, and South Korea, 1950–1990.

In response to record-setting fertility levels during the late 1950s, Korea's first five-year economic plan, adopted in 1962, called for a nationwide family planning program. It began with a rural campaign that focused on reducing desired family size from 5 to 3 through community-based education efforts provided to Korean women by family planning workers. It was well received and led to rapid fertility declines in these rural areas. The plan also abolished laws prohibiting importation and production of contraceptives, and emphasized temporary methods of family planning, including IUDs. As important as the government program was, demographers point out that it clearly was not the only reason for South Korea's initial fertility decline, which started in the early 1960s, because the program did not start until 1962 and did not operate nationwide until 1965.[15] A desire for smaller families was already starting to spread around 1960 before the government stepped in. Later marriage played a role as well over this period; the 35–39 age group had the highest number of births during 1960–2000.[16] Korea's fertility peaked in 1959, but generally its fertility rate was high from the 1953 end of the Korean War to 1983, when it then fell below replacement level.[17] There is much more to say about fertility trends over time in the region, but that lengthier discussion is reserved for the section on ideologies of modernization.

Migration

As in Europe, part of the upheaval of the end of World War II in Asia was the extensive relocation and exchanges of populations as occupying forces and colonial settlers were repatriated and new governments were established. Imperial Japan, for example, had sent many of its own citizens abroad as colonial settlers, and 200,000 Japanese per month were repatriated during the first months after the war ended, adding up to 4.9 million repatriates by the end of 1947.[18] With the victory of the Communist Revolution in 1949, the Nationalists relocated their seat of government to Taiwan, along with around 1.2 million Chinese supporters who migrated to Taiwan throughout the late 1940s and early 1950s.[19]

It was during this 1945–1990 period that Singapore formed into the contemporary version of the city-state that we see today. From the early days of British settlement in Malaya and Singapore, British colonial labor policies had imported massive inflows of workers from China, India, and Java and concentrated them by ethnicity in what some have called a "racialized division of labor."[20] After Singapore's independence from the British in 1959, the population grew quickly, as it did during this same period in China, Japan, and South Korea, but in Singapore's case immigration and high fertility boosted Singapore's annual population growth rate to 4–5 percent around the time of independence in 1959 to the early 1960s.[21]

Korea was ruled by the Japanese Empire from 1910 to 1945, during which period many Koreans had migrated to Manchuria and Japan. Japanese rule ended in 1945, and then the political division of the Korean Peninsula and the ensuing war led to a massive influx of Korean repatriates and returnees from Japan and China and of Korean refugees from North to South Korea. And massive it was. From 1945 to 1949, Korean migrants (re)entering the country numbered 2.6 million, or 12 percent of the 1949 population. Their influx reshaped the distribution of Korea's population, which had heretofore been mostly rural, as most returnees went to cities, not to native villages, and contributed to an urban population explosion.[22] Nearly 2 million people also fled abroad during the Korean War and 290,000 citizens migrated to North Korea. That number excludes the 646,000 North Korean refugees who went to the south during the war, mostly during the two-month period between December 1950 and January 1951, a time immediately preceding the Chinese intervention and the retreat of United Nations forces from North Korean territory.[23]

Upon the end of the Korean War, the sudden influx of war refugees from the north into the few southern cities that had not experienced the North Korean military invasion led to strained living arrangements, economic hardship, and uneasy intergroup relations, which produced antagonistic attitudes and exacerbated regional prejudices.[24] The large-scale settlement of North Korean refugees in South Korean urban areas and rural–urban migration streams in the southern provinces were turning points in the urbanization and modernization of South Korea.[25] Between 1966 and 1970, net migration from rural areas constituted 73.2 percent of urban population growth. Worried about rapid population growth in Seoul, the government encouraged growth outside of Seoul by constructing satellite cities starting after 1975.[26]

Ideologies of Modernization

The global discourse around modernization in the post–World War II era was closely associated with efforts to lower high rates of population growth to more moderate levels. In line with that discourse as the decades went on all four of these Asian states eventually perceived slowing population growth as a key to boosting economic growth and living standards, in China's case particularly as a source of geopolitical influence. Their ability to control their populations varied, but they all tried. None went so far in pursuing this goal as the Chinese Communist Party toward the end of and following Mao's lifetime, which in many cases limited Chinese citizens' right to determine the size of their own families. In Singapore, the tight grip of the government—what many political scientists refer to as a "managed democracy" or "illiberal democracy"—and the small population size (3 million in 1990) facilitated demographic and social engineering that sought to balance "the needs of the economy for more and better-qualified workers and such social and political considerations as the size of the dependent population and ethnic balance," as one scholar frames it.[27]

It is all the more striking that these East Asian countries' efforts to encourage or incentivize reductions in family size, coupled with their success in accelerating economic growth, resulted in continuing fertility declines to the point that fertility eventually became "too low" in leaders' minds. This shifting perspective was already visible toward the end of this 1945–1990 period and particularly so in the following years, but whether perceiving births as "too many" or eventually "too few," views about the role of population policy as a contributor to economic growth and modernization remained consistent.

Both global discourses and local contexts, including historical and cultural nuances, shaped national views about population and actual population dynamics. As we will see, alongside economic goals, eugenic ideas had an important influence on views about demographic issues in these Asian states, as they had previously in Europe and North America. Much of this was homegrown, but global influences mattered, too. For example, the American family planning advocate Margaret Sanger visited Japan and China in 1922 and her visit contributed to discussions of birth control in both countries; there were multiple translations of the works of Sanger and of British birth control campaigner Marie Stopes in Chinese news and intellectual circles.[28]

Modernization at All Costs in China

The idea that a strong, healthy population was the foundation of a modern, economically and politically competitive state was common among both

Chinese Nationalists and Communists, both of whom saw population as a central element in ensuring China's sovereignty and preventing further encroachment by foreign powers. After the humiliation of occupation by empires based in Europe and Asia, scientific rationality became one strategy to strengthen China's global position. As Sarah Mellors Rodriguez states, China's "intelligentsia envisaged citizens' bodies to be microcosms of the nation, [and] therefore creating a healthier citizenry would logically force a stronger nation."[29] That, of course, included governing reproduction. Frank Dikötter argues that racialized discourse had long been present in China. The scientific language of biological determinism, including the eugenics movement that was spreading around the globe in the decades prior to World War II, further legitimated those Chinese ideas.[30] The desire for "quality" births continued to find expression in public policy throughout this period of 1945–1990. China's 1980 marriage law, for example, stated that marriage was not permitted "Where one party is suffering from leprosy, a cure not having been effected, or from any other disease which is regarded by medical science as rendering a person unfit for marriage."[31]

Eugenics was one source of views about population; neo-Malthusianism was another. In China, elites throughout this post-1945 period to the present have attempted to manage the population in their pursuit of economic ascendancy, with the goal of realizing China's destiny as a global power. There was no unified view on what form that management should take, however. The Nationalist government limited abortion and birth control through World War II and the Chinese civil war.[32] Communists began their period of rule with the same approach, and CCP leadership after 1949 initially viewed China's large and growing population as a strength, a vast labor source that could help China produce its way into prosperity. But those who produce also consume, and worries among some of the Chinese elite over the demands of a young and rapidly growing population soon overwhelmed their optimism. While birth "control" was controversial in Marxist-Leninist circles, who saw it as reeking of bourgeois capitalist views about the poor, birth "planning" was permissible as yet another extension of long-term state planning under communism—planning that could be either pro- or antinatalist depending on circumstances.

As Chinese centralized planning began in earnest in the 1950s, the state initiated some meager voluntary birth planning campaigns. The results of the first national census in 1954, however, spurred worry at how rapidly China's population was growing.[33] The CCP liberalized abortion and birth control out of fears of mass starvation, fears that mounted as the decade went on. A second birth planning program, which mostly took the form of a public information campaign, was launched out of such alarm.

Concerns that population growth was still too rapid ultimately led birth planning to take on a more coercive tone in the 1970s. The Chinese leadership established an expert team to research the effect China's projected population might have on the national economy. Their computerized population models indicated that China had to adopt a policy of "a single child for each couple" or face significant economic ramifications.[34] Thus began a decade of three key birth planning campaigns. The "one is not too many, two is just right, three is too much" campaign launched in 1971, and the "later, longer, fewer" birth planning campaign began in 1973. The latter raised the legal age of marriage to 23 for women and 25 for men, encouraged parents to wait three years between births, and limited the total number of children to two.[35] Government efforts consolidated around the Fourth Five-Year Plan, when China's leaders carried out a campaign between 1973 and 1975 promoting sterilizations, IUD insertions, and abortions.[36] With these campaigns, plus changing norms and preferences around family size, fertility rates in urban China fell from 3.3 children in 1970 to 1.5 by 1978 and in rural areas from 6 children per woman on average to 3 between 1971 and 1979.[37]

Despite these declines, Deng Xiaoping, who took Mao's place as Party leader in 1978, continued to feel that high population growth would hold China back. In his March 30, 1979, speech to the CCP's Theory of Work Conference, Deng said:

> [W]e have a large population but not enough arable land. Of China's population of more than 900 million, 80 percent are peasants. While there are advantages to having a large population, there are disadvantages as well. When production is insufficiently developed, [a large population] poses serious problems with regard to food, education, and employment. We must greatly increase our efforts in [birth] planning.[38]

And thus, toward the end of the 1970s the CCP saw fit to institute what would become the hallmark of its birth planning efforts, the One-Child Policy. The role of the One-Child Policy in pressuring fertility rates lower should not be unduly minimized, but all of China's fertility rate declines cannot be properly attributed to that one policy, nor indeed to any government policy. Chinese individuals and couples began to limit their own family sizes before the One-Child Policy, and have continued to do so even after these restrictions have been lifted.

Despite the excesses of the One-Child Policy, at the beginning of the Sixth Five-Year Plan period (1981–1985) rural birth rates were still higher than the party preferred, and 28 percent of births in 1981 were third or higher-order births.[39] This period was marked by two key fissures: one between rural and urban areas; and one within the Chinese Communist Party itself, between the left and right. Central Document 7 (CD7) was the most important *diktat* about population during this time and used population to address those two fissures. Remarkably, this document was produced in the context of extremely strained relations between the Party and the people, which were actually caused in part by the coercion and crackdown on reproduction in the early part of the 6th Five Year Plan, just after the One-Child Policy had been introduced. Preceding the document, the CCP undertook another mass sterilization campaign in 1983. This turned out to be a huge political misstep, as it led to backlash against the regime. In response, Central Document 7 marked a new approach, one that would be more flexible overall, increase voluntary birth planning, and suit individual cases and localities.[40]

Rural-urban politics, in particular, drove the Party to devise and release Central Document 7, as it was rural communities who had been most resistant to and affected by the mass sterilization campaign of 1983. The leniency described in CD7 was the idea of "opening a small hole to close up a large one," or allowing a small percentage of rural couples to have a second child because they were probably going to do so anyway, with the result that there would be less resentment against the CCP for its policies.[41] This tactic worked. Complaints and individual petitions were down in 1984 compared to the previous year.[42] CD7 was also remarkable for its advancement in the science of demography, and use of that science in Chinese domestic policymaking, "enhancing the scientific basis of its population work."[43] For example, after CD7, several Chinese population research institutes were established.

Over time the One-Child Policy and related birth-planning policies became increasingly irrelevant in determining fertility behavior in China as income and education levels rose and a small-family norm began to take hold even in the mid-1980s, when China remained relatively poor. A large share of rural couples were permitted to have a second child but chose not to out of concern that having a second child would interfere with income-earning activities. In some localities, 30–45 percent of couples permitted to have a second child declined to do so. At the same time, urban Chinese couples stated a preference for only one to two children.[44]

Despite low fertility rates, the CCP held the line on the One-Child Policy with only slight revision until 2013, as the following chapter will discuss. While the period following the release of CD7 had a more flexible approach to birth planning, things were to change after the 1989 Tiananmen uprising. While birth planning was supposed to elevate China by balancing its growth and dependency ratios, it had many unintended consequences as well, including chipping away at the CCP's authority.

South Korea's Grand Plan

The same underlying ideology of modernization we see in China was also present in attitudes toward population among South Korean elites. The Rhee regime (1948 to 1960) took a pronatalist view because they saw population as contributing to national power and military strength, necessary for defense against North Korea. But outside the regime, many began to worry about population growth.[45] When Rhee resigned and General Park Jung-Hee took power in 1961, economic growth was tepid. Park chaired the newly established Supreme Council for National Reconstruction (SCNR), which drafted its First Five-Year Economic Development Plan to jump-start the stagnant economy.

As with China's five-year plans, curbing population growth was a key element of this economic plan. The Social Advisory Committee and the Economic Advisory Committee of the SCNR endorsed a proposal from two Korean professors to institute a birth control policy as part of this effort, embracing the argument that South Korea's high population growth rate was aggravating poverty and restraining economic growth. Park announced the adoption of the population planning policy in October 1961, a mere two months after it had been initially proposed. The program was voluntary, but the state was heavily involved.[46] The Ministry of Health and Social Affairs was to implement the new policy; the Planned Parenthood Federation of Korea, founded just before the 1961 military takeover, was to carry out Korea's family planning program. This could not have happened without strong support from the president because of the country's authoritarian structure—political leadership was key, and family planning did indeed have strong support from the two presidents in office from 1961 to 1987, after which Korea's fertility rate started to fall below replacement level and family planning seemed far less urgent on the national agenda.[47]

As with the other countries in this region, involvement from abroad was important too. The impoverished government sought and obtained funding from foreign agencies to support family planning activities until the mid-1970s.[48] As we saw with China, the Korean belief that high population growth would mean a strong economy was tinged with eugenic ideas about population "quality." South Korea's Fifth Five Year Plan (1982–1987) revised its Maternal and Child Health Law to include permission to abort in such cases as the mother "or her spouse suffers from any eugenic or genetic mental handicap or physical disease as prescribed by the Presidential Decree."[49]

Family planning was not the only tool in South Korea's population toolbox at that time; the regime also encouraged emigration to lesson population pressures, embodied in the Overseas Emigration Law of 1962. According to the text, "The purpose of this Law is to ensure the proper population policy and the stabilization of the national economy, and to enhance the national prestige by encouraging emigration of Korean nationals."[50] There is certainly no mistaking the intent. The law was to be overseen by a newly established Overseas Emigration Bureau, which aimed to send Korean farmers under contract agreements to Latin American countries like Brazil, Argentina, Paraguay, and Bolivia. In this respect it failed, both at home and abroad: 99 percent of Koreans sent abroad to work on farms moved to cities instead.[51]

As the Park government began to play an active role in promoting Korea's industrialization and economic growth, employment and economic opportunities began to concentrate in urban industrial areas. The population of Seoul nearly tripled between 1960 and 1975. Given the capital's proximity to the North Korean border (23 km, 14 miles), this presented a clear strategic problem. In March 1977 the government announced a plan to redistribute the population by restricting in-migration to Seoul and incentivizing out-migration from the city. They also gave outlying provinces priority in construction of new factories and employment opportunities to facilitate the redistribution.[52]

Engineering an Ideal Population in Singapore

In Singapore, civil society volunteers first introduced family planning (in the form of the Family Planning Association) in 1949 out of concern over post–World War II poverty and the negative effects of frequent childbearing on mothers and children.[53] After independence, a family limitation phase was spurred early on by urban housing shortages and large-scale unemployment. The strategy of the official Singapore Family Planning and Population Board was to offer both carrots and sticks for families to stop at two children. Starting in 1969, the government put in place such incentives and disincentives to promote sterilization and discourage large families; for example, on the "sticks" side, women giving birth to their third or subsequent child were no longer eligible for paid maternity leave.[54] The government legalized abortion and sterilization in 1970 and expanded access to them in 1975. To encourage responsible reproductive behavior the government also charged progressively steeper delivery charges for higher-order births, and instituted housing and school policies that rewarded smaller families. The government also offered enhanced leave policies and financial advantages to civil servants who chose to be sterilized.[55]

By 1975, Singapore's total fertility rate had reached replacement level, 5 years ahead of its target date. As far as carrots go, this fertility decline was partly achieved through investments in human capital (primarily high-quality K-12 education) and economic policies designed to bring more women into the labor force. These investments and policies had the added benefit of contributing to Singapore's remarkable economic trajectory, one that saw it go from a desperately poor and unstable entrepôt to one of the most prosperous countries in the world.

Government ideas about the ideal family are evident during this time. Some scholars argue that the government deliberately encouraged shifts from traditional communal living arrangements to nuclear-family living arrangements and encouraged the two-child family norm in "the belief that dependence on extended family relations was antithetical to economic progress, innovation and diligence."[56] Although the desired two-child family norm was largely achieved by 1977, it was clear that there would still be a large number of women of childbearing ages (as Fig. 5.3 shows, below), and thus the government also encouraged its citizens to delay marriage and first births, and to increase the interval between their two children. Those anti-natalist messages took a turn toward eugenic ideas around 1983, as a later section will describe, before converting to pronatalist measures in the late 1980s.

Japan Charts Its Own Course to Lower Fertility

Abortion liberalization was quick in Japan, but unlike in China, contraception and family planning were slow to take hold. Indeed Japan did not

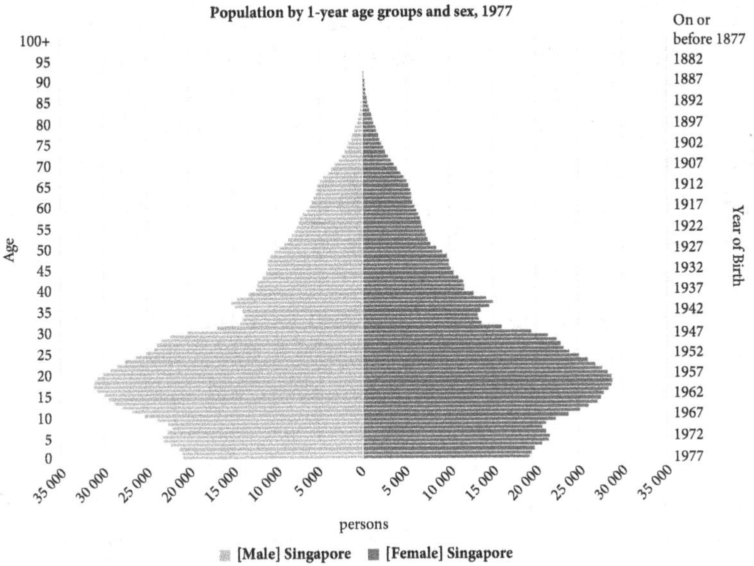

Fig. 5.3 Age structure of the population of Singapore, 1977.

Source: UN, *World Population Prospects: The 2024 Revision*, custom data acquired via website.

legalize the oral contraceptive pill until 1999, nearly four decades after the release of Enovid in Western countries. The evolution of Japanese attitudes toward abortion and contraception is a winding one, starting with the pre–World War II era when Dr. Yoshio Koya, a prominent Japanese public health researcher and student of race relations, promoted pronatalist ideas as a way to help Japanese more effectively rule over Korea. As part of its war efforts, the Japanese government took an official pronatalist stance in 1941 to reverse the downward trend in fertility rates first noted in the 1920s and encouraged women to fulfill the "national mission of motherhood" to provide soldiers and workers for the country.[57] This pronatalism took a 180 degree turn after the war, when Japanese political and intellectual elites and the Supreme Command Allied Powers (SCAP) led by General Douglas MacArthur became concerned about rapid population growth resulting from high birth rates and the forced return from former colonies of millions of Japanese military and civilian settlers.

In 1950, with a photo of a Japanese mother and child on the cover, the then-popular American periodical *Newsweek* observed that of all the pressing policy issues facing postwar Japan, including a peace treaty with Western powers, military occupation by the US, and tense relations with Russia and

"Red China," "hardly anyone discussed the great long-range problem Japan will face after a peace treaty: How to support its rapidly growing population or control it if it can't be supported."[58] With the collapse of its Asian empire Japan had lost almost half of the land that it had controlled, and with direct echoes of the Malthusian ideas resurging at the time, *Newsweek* warned that Japan only produced only enough food for a population of 65 million, but was on track to reach 100 million people by 1975, a population size actually reached by 1970.

Newsweek was wrong—plenty of people were concerned about Japan's population growth. Many American leaders believed that the expansionist colonialism of Japan's prewar governments was driven by perceived need for additional land area—Japanese *lebensraum*—to house and feed its growing population, and that this dynamic could emerge again if Japan's population continued to expand rapidly. There was real concern about the prospects for mass famine and disastrous epidemics, for which the US would be responsible as the Occupying Power. Moreover, the idea that too-rapid population growth would lead to increasing poverty and political instability, both of which might increase support for communist takeovers, would become the refrain of Cold War attitudes among the US elite about economic development in the developing world.[59]

Japan's elite, who were working toward Japan's economic recovery, were worried, too. *Newsweek* reported that the American occupation authorities placed the birth control problem "off limits," because it was so contentious, another overstatement. While they did favor a home-grown solution to high fertlity and rapid population growth, US occupying forces were not hands-off. The SCAP ordered six population counts (of varying extents) during the six years between Japan's surrender in September 1945 and October 1950.[60] Supreme Commander Douglas MacArthur appointed Dr. Yoshio Koya as the new director of the Institute of Public Health in Tokyo, which had been established by the Rockefeller Foundation in 1939. SCAP also arranged for Dr. Koya to visit the US South, primarily to assess first-hand the programs that had been established to provide family planning services to poor and ill-educated residents (mostly Black) in the still-agrarian American South.[61] As one of Japan's leading health experts, Dr. Koya was close to the center of the nation's debate over whether or not to support birth control. In the post-war period he no longer supported pronatalist policies, arguing instead that high fertility rates must be moderated if Japan was to prosper, and that using birth control to prevent pregnancies before they occurred was a superior alternative to abortion.[62]

Initially, the Japanese government did not choose to support birth control, and instead the main population policy took form as the 1948 Eugenic Protection Law (EPL) and amendments, which authorized physicians to interrupt pregnancy for economic reasons or concerns over the mother's health.[63] And Japanese women—married and unmarried—did indeed use abortion, although available data vary. Koya wrote that reported abortions numbered over 246,000 in 1949 and over 800,000 by 1952, although he estimates the actual number to be far higher.[64] Goto *et al.* chronicled 1.17 million abortions in 1955, for a rate of 50.2 per thousand (by 2005 it was 10.3).[65] Ogino wrote that abortions skyrocketed and the birth rate plummeted by half within a decade, from 34.3 per thousand in 1947 to 17.2 per thousand in 1957.[66]

Not everyone thought the EPL was a sufficient antinatalist measure. When Japan's Population Planning Council was established in 1949, it immediately recommended removal of all restrictions on voluntary methods of birth control. The Diet—Japan's law-making body—rejected this recommendation and the council was soon dissolved. But Koya persisted.

Koya thought Japan could devise a better solution, and received financial support from Dr. Clarence Gamble, a Harvard-trained physician, philanthropist, and heir to a fortune from his father who had co-founded the Proctor & Gamble Company. The younger Gamble was a prominent US eugenicist and supporter of improved maternal health services and family planning. In 1938 he had worked with Margaret Sanger to launch what was then called the "Negro Project," to reduce the birth rates of Southern, rural Blacks in the United States and thus ameliorate poverty. With Gamble's financial support and the blessing of the SCAP in Japan, Koya, who also held a post as vice president of the Japanese Association of Racial Hygiene, traveled to the United States in February through April of 1950, to visit and observe various locations of this project, including Louisiana, Mississippi, Tennessee, Kentucky, Georgia, and North Carolina. After Koya's return to Japan Gamble also provided him with financial support to conduct his own study addressed to poor rural Japanese, in what became known as his famous Three Villages Study. The insights that Koya took back from his US visit and applied in his Japanese study would today be recognized as some of the hallmarks of effective community health programs: a field-trial method that made accessing contraception free and easy (a method still used) and nurses employed as social care workers, all organized by government offices. Although its methods were voluntary, Japan's scientific approach to population legitimated intervention into private reproductive lives in order to solve what was portrayed as an "objective problem"—overpopulation. By 1951, Japan's cabinet members started to support contraception over abortion, and condom use eventually became widespread.[67]

As its name suggests, there was a eugenic element to the 1948 EPL, even if it was ostensibly aimed at lowering fertility. Like many industrialized countries including the US and much of Europe, eugenic ideas had become popular by the early 20th century among prominent Japanese intellectuals, scientists, and other elites. This movement in Japan and elsewhere was initially led by prominent scientists following the 1900 rediscovery of the genetic research of Gregor Mendel. The eugenics movement later became tainted by its association with compulsory sterilization, racism, and nativism.

The 1948 EPL in Japan was rooted in the 1940 National Eugenic Law (*Kokumin yusei-ho*), which had been modeled on the 1933 German Law for the Prevention of Hereditarily Diseased Offspring. Under Japan's EPL, more than 18,000 compulsory or strongly encouraged sterilizations were conducted between 1948 and 1996.[68] In 1952, the Japanese Society for Hygiene said that rapid population growth would lead to "a decline in the allocation of nutrition to the Japanese people, a weakening in physical strength, and an increase in the number of diseases such as tuberculosis." However, they also noted that the use of birth control could backfire and work against their goals by "trigger[ing] mistakes such as reverse selection," or "an increase in people with disabilities."[69] The Society revoked this statement only in 2017. Japan's postwar sterilization law was in place for 48 years until it was repealed in 1996. The BBC has reported that two nine-year-olds were among the 25,000 people sterilized under the eugenics law—including 16,000 forcibly sterilized—according to a report by the Japanese parliament. In 2019, the government agreed to reparations of 3.2 million yen to each survivor (US$28,600).[70] With ideologies of modernization in Japan, we see views among the public sector about both ideal qualities of a population and also an ideal population growth rate.

The private sector also played a role in helping Japan achieve an "ideal population" to support modernization and economic growth. These ideologies spurred Japan's "New Lifestyle Movement" (sometimes called "The New Life Movement"), starting in the 1940s as a loose coalition of government ministries and women's organizations, and including major corporations beginning in 1953. A quote attributed to a spokesman from the Nippon Kokan firm, the first major corporation to join, says:

> Life in the home—food, clothing, education, culture, leisure, health, child-rearing—is carried out through the initiative of the housewife. The husband, who is our employee, is nurtured within that home life. Thus, by trying to elevate the housewife, build a happy, bright family, and further construct a bright society, we will allow the husband to devote himself to production free from anxiety.[71]

This movement promoted rigid roles for husbands as "salary men," while wives were to stay home and oversee the education of two children and eliminate anxiety from her husband's life, thereby supporting Japan's chosen modernization path. By September 1956 there were 24 large public and private corporations, including Toyota Automobiles and Japan National Railways, that had adopted the birth planning program; by 1964 an estimated 115 corporations had joined, employing some 1.7 million.[72] That was to be the peak, roughly. The New Lifestyle movement faced an identity crisis by the end of the 1960s because by then the role of the full-time housewife was well established. The New Life Association dissolved in 1985, saying: "the economic environment has changed completely from the time of our movement's founding. . . . Leaders in the corporate world are hardly concerned these days with an austere New Life Movement of rationalization and self-denial."[73] Population policy had served its purpose for Japan's leaders in this phase of economic modernization, and the following period would bring unprecedented challenges that would require different approaches.

Ideologies of Identity

Ideologies around identity cast a wide shadow in the politically diverse East Asian countries under discussion here, encompassing views about femininity, womanhood, motherhood, family, and citizenship. Questions about the role of women in society—as workers, wives, mothers—are central to discussing the influence of ideologies of identity on population issues. For example, while the early Chinese Communist Party has been characterized as pioneering equal rights for women, many feminist scholars have argued that any rights granted to women were wrapped up in nationalism from the start, specifically the project to strengthen the nation. Narratives and policies that liberated women were useful for the CCP's postrevolutionary state-building project, which required putting hundreds of millions of women to work. To that end, the Marriage Law of 1950 abolished arranged marriages and granted Chinese women the right to divorce abusive husbands and to remarry, among other measures.[74]

Questions about what constitutes a family or who can be a citizen are intimately intertwined, as we see with the following example of immigration laws in South Korea. While governments across the region encouraged norms of later marriage and childbearing starting in this period, as we will see in the following chapter, citizens took deferred marriage and childbearing even further after 1990, demonstrating the limits of government control over population dynamics and the importance of what social scientists call individual and social "agency"—that decisions are made by actual people and groups and are rarely motivated by their government's goals. Still, demographic engineering is made easier by a strong and centralized state, as the following example of Singapore's carefully engineered racial balance shows. Singapore's case also demonstrates how ideologies of identity often take a eugenic tone, echoing the discussion of birth planning in postwar Japan from the preceding section.

The Construction of National Identity

The historical legend of Dangun, a mythical figure who is believed to have founded the first nation-state of Koreans around 2333 BCE, gave rise to the idea of the ethnic Korean nation. These descendants of Dangun, Korean scholars tell us, transmit and reproduce this founding tale to "create the notion of the ethnic purity and homogeneity of the Korean people."[75] For our purposes, it is irrelevant whether or not any notions of ethnic homogeneity are well founded; rather, it is the attempts to reinforce such ideas as a tool of politics that are of interest. Thus, the use of the term "myth" is not meant to imply untruth but instead to remind us that identities are created, that they do have an origin, and that they must constantly be reinforced—and reinterpreted—over time.

This idea of Korean homogeneity was codified in the post–World War II era by the 1948 Korean Nationality Act, which outlined the principles of Korean nationhood and citizenship. The United States Army Military

Government in Korea (USAMGIK) had in 1945 encouraged the interim South Korean government to devise nationality laws to deal with the large numbers of Japanese nationals who took up residence in Korea after it was colonized by the Japanese Empire in 1910. Many of these Japanese residents would later repatriate to Japan, but in 1945 still owned assets in South Korea, and the Korean Nationality Act did not come into effect until three years later.[76] The Act reflected strong gender norms of male preference, stipulating that only those with ethnically Korean fathers qualified as ethnically Korean and merited Korean full nationality. Wives could automatically gain citizenship upon marriage to a Korean national, but non-Korean husbands of Korean women could not.[77] These would prove to be important considerations for families created by relationships between Korean women and American GIs.

The lingering presence of the American military in South Korea has shaped ideologies, particularly as they set conditions for intermarriage. Military installations were often the only source of employment for local Korean residents. Because of poverty and limited opportunities, Korean women often took unattractive and low-paying jobs in "GI towns" populated by American military personnel, which offered the opportunity to meet a spouse. Intermarriage between American soldiers and Korean women has had a significant impact on the Korean American community, with one-fourth of Korean immigrants to the United States coming as relatives of interracially married women.[78]

Although the terminology is crude, in the postwar years South Korea also became known as one of the world's largest "exporters" of babies for adoption. Again, the roots of this program lie in ideologies of Korean identity, particularly prejudice against biracial children and xenophobia. In pursuit of what he called "one state for one ethnic people," South Korea's first president, Syngman Rhee, encouraged sending biracial children born to American soldiers and Korean women to "their fathers' land." Ideologies around the family were at work as well: by the end of the 1960s most of the children sent abroad were not biracial, but instead those born to unwed mothers and who were subject to a different form of prejudice.[79]

Singapore Strikes a Racial Balance

Singapore is a unique case of how states and their citizens define and debate racial and ethnic identities within the context of defining the nation.

Indeed racial and religious identity were central to Singapore's very founding as an independent nation.[80] Mui Teng Yap has argued that Singapore's geography—a small island territory with no natural resources—meant human resources were always elevated in the government's eyes and that the state paid serious attention to both ethnic composition and fertility rates early on.[81] In a speech to the first session of Singapore's first Parliament in 1965, just a year after independence, Mr. Edmund W. Barker, one of the country's founders, referred to a multiracial Singapore as a cornerstone of government policy:

> Whilst a multi-racial secular society is an ideal espoused by many, it is a dire necessity for our survival in the midst of turmoil and the pressures of big power conflict in an area where new nationalisms are seeking to assert themselves in the place of the old European empires in Asia. In such a setting a nation based on one race, one language and one religion, when its peoples are multi-racial, is one doomed for destruction.

One of the first acts of that government was to appoint a Constitutional Commission to formulate constitutional safeguards that would protect "multi-racialism and equality," particularly for minority groups.[82] The chairman, Wee Chong Jin, offered the following words on behalf of the commission:

> These immigrants brought with them their own customs and culture and as they comprised the majority of the population they and their descendants after them never had to fit themselves and to conform to a "national" way of life, even if there had been one. The result was that Singapore has emerged into nationhood with no distinct language, culture and society which it could call its own. It draws its cultural heritage from those of the many races which make up its population.[83]

Singapore's experience as a mixed-race society is illustrative for understanding how ideologies of identity create and reinforce demographic categories, which become codified in law and practice. These ideologies encourage leaders to delineate and fix boundaries that otherwise might have blurred over time, and Singapore's strong, centralized state makes such close management possible. If Singapore was a "political, economic and geographical absurdity," as founder and long-serving prime minister Lee Kuan Yew said in 1962, then to turn it from a swamp into the most prosperous state in Asia might require a strong role for its government, or so the thinking went.[84] Given his unparalleled role in creating the Singaporean state—from independence from the British, to separation from Malaysia, to creation of one of the strongest economies in the world—a deeper look at Lee's views about race demonstrates how politics becomes distorted in ideological battles over demographics.

Singapore's government, headed by Lee, took a highly active role in managing its population from the start, particularly its racial and ethnic balance. The government adopted the "four M's," multiracialism, multilingualism, multiculturalism, and multireligiosity, to organize the ethnic, religious, and linguistic diversity of Singapore into manageable categories.[85] These categories reduced the population to three main racial groups: Chinese, Malay, and Indian.[86] In common parlance, this designation is CMIO, meaning Chinese-Malay-Indian-Other, with the "Other" category a catch-all group that includes everyone from Eurasians to Filipinos to Arabs. As of mid-1963, Malays (including Indonesians) constituted 14 percent of Singapore's total population, Chinese 75 percent, Indians and Pakistanis 8 percent, and other races 3 percent, although the government noted that there was no reliable measure of Indians and Pakistanis specifically.[87]

The government has sought to retain this racial balance over time. While the categories are clear, the government was hesitant to provide too much detail; they did not recommend "any provision in the Constitution specifying, enumerating or defining the races, languages and religions which fall within the category of the racial, linguistic or religious minorities in Singapore."[88] Under the principle of multilingualism, each of the three "races" was assigned a "mother tongue" in order to reduce linguistic diversity, while English was to be used as the main language in education and official communication. Each Singaporean's birth certificate registers the "race" of the parents, and this categorization is used in schools.

In contrast to Singapore's rigid CMIO categorization, China has had a much looser approach to ethnic classification and there have been more shifts over time. While China's initial ethnic classification project named 38 ethnic groups in 1954, for reasons unknown the official number increased to 53 such categories in 1964. It rose again piecemeal until 1990, when the government officially declared 56 nationalities. With interethnic marriages, parents decide ethnicity, and children can decide at 18, but that then becomes their permanent ethnic status. Sun Yat-sen, the first provisional president of the Republic of China and first leader of the Kuomintang (Nationalist Party of China) said any Chinese person could be of China's dominant Han ethnicity if they accepted Han culture, and that Confucianism "celebrates cultural, economic, and political intermingling among ethnic and cultural groups in order to form a harmonious Han community."[89] While boundaries may be looser, there is still a clear privileging of Han identity.

In Singapore, housing was also key to population management. British imperialist Sir Thomas Raffles's 1822 Town Plan, which segregated the races, lasted until 1959, when Lee's newly elected government began to use large public housing projects to break up those segregated neighborhoods.[90] To achieve the desired ethnic mix, the Housing and Development Board (HDB) set quotas based on national ethnic proportions for public housing estates. If an owner wants to sell their flat, they must first check with the estate management authority regarding the ethnic composition of the block. Of course, in any system that uses votes to determine political office, distribution of groups in housing also means distribution of groups as voting constituents. In Singapore's case, managed distribution reinforced the hegemonic rule of Lee's People's Action Party (PAP). In the late 1980s, the PAP government enforced the Ethnic Integrated Housing Policy (EIP), which restricted any ethnic minority group from constituting more than 20 percent in a single constituency. These ethnic minorities are dispersed across 27 constituencies due to the quotas, which effectively restrict the political power of minority ethnic groups.[91]

To reinforce these racial/ethnic categories and boundaries as they built the Singaporean nation, the government prohibited dialects of Mandarin Chinese in the media, and instituted a "Speak Mandarin" campaign to homogenize Chinese groups.[92] Lee's own Chinese family was established in Singapore in the 19th century and his first language was English, notable given how the Singaporean government used language and language instruction as a tool for nation-building.

Viewed today when fear over demographic competition is high, Lee's vision of a multiracial society seems modern and even noble. However, it had its critics even at the time. One Western scholar warned in 1966 that Singapore's utopian vision was out of sync with its urban planning, which deliberately set out political, demographic, and spatial organization.[93] Among many Singaporeans, including elites, there was also a rigid view of identity, a tendency to ascribe certain characteristics to certain ethnic groups, and unequal treatment. For example, Lee's government was concerned about the Chinese becoming too westernized and took steps to counter this, but did not show the same urgency in preserving Malay or Indian values. The government encouraged the Chinese to embrace their culture by promoting Confucianism and mainstream Mandarin language, but criticized the Malays for not being "Singaporean" enough, showing a contrast in handling the two groups.[94]

Policies to manage and maintain racial proportions have at times been propelled by eugenic ideologies. We already know that Singapore had antinatalist policy early on, but by 1975 Singapore's fertility rate had reached replacement level. Yet it was not just the number of births that the government found problematic, it was differentials among Singaporean women giving birth; eugenic ideas were predominant from about 1983 to 1987.[95] Lee Kuan Yew observed what he called a "lop-sided pattern of procreation," in which better-educated women were more likely to remain single and were having smaller families than their less-educated counterparts. The result was new measures to promote larger family sizes among better-educated women. In his "Talent for the Future" speech on August 14, 1983, Lee said:

> we shouldn't get our women into jobs where they cannot, at the same time, be mothers. . . . You just can't be doing a full-time, heavy job like that of a doctor or engineer and run a home and bring up children . . . we must think deep and long on the profound changes we have unwittingly set off.[96]

Marital matchmaking was part of the proposed solution, and the Singapore government set up an agency to promote social interaction among university-educated men and women.[97] These measures generated political costs, as had China's heavy handed antinatalist policies before CD7, and Singapore's population expressed their opposition to what it saw as eugenicist policies with racial overtones. Lee's PAP lost a significant number of votes in the 1984 general election.

By 1985, Singapore's fertility rate was down to 1.5 children per woman on average. The government reversed course—now, in its eyes, fertility was too low, particularly among the highly educated Chinese majority. To try and raise fertility, in March 1987 Singapore's government launched a new population policy with the slogan, "Have Three or More Children if You Can Afford It," publicized through media campaigns and incentives. Deputy Prime Minister Goh Chok Tong was quoted in *The Straits Times* as saying that "diligence, hard work, special talents, and skills" could make up for a lack of education, countering the elitist and eugenicist tone of the preceding era and attempting to deemphasize educational qualifications for childbearing.[98] As with other government campaigns across the region aimed at raising low fertility, Singapore's did not work.

The End of the Antinatalist Era

In this period of 1945–1990, elites in these four Asian states saw interventions in the population's reproductive lives as a perfectly legitimate exercise of state power in pursuit of national goals. The desire to modernize and propel economic growth was one powerful ideology shaping state views on population. Indeed, desires for modernization drove antinatalism, particularly in the immediate post–World War II context, as women's marital and reproductive behaviors became a key concern of elites. We also see how ideologies of identity drove governments to try and engineer a desired pattern of ethnic composition. By the end of this period, population growth had slowed tremendously in each of these four countries, and contrary worries that population would in fact grow too slowly and age too quickly began to take hold. These concerns would predominate in the following period, to which we now turn.

6

Population Crisis Takes Over, 1990–2024

Overview

This chapter takes a deeper dive into population politics in East Asia since 1990 and argues that ideologies about gender—a kind of sexual politics about the place of women in the home and in the workforce and about who constitutes a family—have been the prevailing force driving discussions of demography over the last three decades. Scholars of the region have argued that during this period East Asia has been characterized by distinctively significant clashes between women's rising socioeconomic status outside the home and gender inequality within the home, and this exploration supports that assertion.[1] While ideologies of modernization drove population policies in the preceding period, which began with rapid population growth for all four Asian states, ideologies of gender particularly focused on women are the foundation on which all other demographic conflicts have been based during the period since 1990. As childbearers, women are seen as both the problem and the solution to the region's exceptionally low fertility rates.

Of course, other dynamics since 1990 set the scene for these disputes. The 1990s were the tail end of the postwar East Asian economic miracle and, generally, these states reaped the economic dividend of a young workforce well suited to fill the needs of an increasingly globalized economy at exactly the right time. Annual GDP per capita growth between 1975 and 1995 averaged 6.8 percent and brought huge gains in general wellbeing and public health across the Asian region as millions were lifted out of extreme poverty.[2]

China's GDP is by far the largest in the region, having grown dramatically from $360 billion in 1990 to $17.79 trillion (current US dollars) in 2023.[3] It was in this period that China's rise came to play such a crucial role in national security and economic politics at the global level. Investment in China began in earnest in the 1980s as American firms found China's low wages an attractive way to increase profitability and payouts to stockholders. A stronger dollar in the mid-1980s also prompted investment and

Toxic Demography. Jennifer D. Sciubba, Michael S. Teitelbaum, and Jay Winter, Oxford University Press.

DOI: 10.1093/oso/9780197745038.003.0007

increased the US trade deficit with China. The chaos of the following decade, with its numerous conflicts and crises (including economic crises in Japan and Mexico), added to China's allure as an apparently stable option for investment. By the time the new millennium arrived, China was poised to dominate much of global manufacturing. Its rise was remarkable: When the second wave of globalization began, China was poor, and while the country grew to become a node in global economy in the 1980s, during the first part of the new millennium it arguably became an important hub.

One key moment in China's rise was their accession, with support from the US Government, to the World Trade Organization in December 2001. (See discussion in Chapter 4). Hopes were high among US political and intellectual elites that China's integration into the world economy would lead to a larger and more influential Chinese middle class that would demand democratic reform. The idea that economic liberalization would beget political liberalization in China was seductive, but as the years went by and the Chinese government showed no signs of political liberalization, it became clear that such logic reflected an outmoded, post–Cold War mindset. South Korea, however, had its first free, democratic elections in 1987 after two military dictatorships that began in 1961. Globally, liberal democracratic regimes continued to strengthen alongside the free market economy as the 1990s went on, but many of those gains were lost or stalled after the turn of the 21st century.

During this time period of 1945–1989, economic changes begat changes in the national security environment as well. Korea's external security environment grew more tense, as the government of China began a rapid expansion of its military forces. In his January 29, 2002, State of the Union address President George W. Bush characterized North Korea, Iran, and Iraq as "an axis of evil, arming to threaten the peace of the world."[4] The threat from North Korea, however, was miniscule compared to the perceived threat from China felt by many of its neighbors. By the time of the opening ceremony of the 2018 Winter Olympics in Pyeongchang, South Korea, athletes from both North and South Korea united to march under one flag—white with a blue image of the unified Korean peninsula, although these warming relations later were to cool substantially.[5]

With the globalized trading regime failing to reduce geopolitical tensions, competition between the United States and China ramped up and by the early 2010s US administrations began to impose successively harsher tariffs, sanctions, and other economic measures designed to change

China's behavior. Not only had China's growing economy failed to have the democratizing domestic effects many in the West had hoped for, but following the rise to power of Xi Jinping in 2012, China's behavior grew bolder, both internationally and domestically. Meanwhile, US alliances with Japan and Korea stayed strong and provided a counterweight to growing Chinese influence in the region. While Taiwan fiercely held on to independence, the threat of forced reunification with the mainland loomed large. Japan became increasingly concerned with its low fertility as its median age rose, and began to take controversial steps toward remilitarization as a form of self-protection in the increasingly tense region.

The rising economies of the region gradually created income-earning opportunities for women outside the home and incentivized young women to pursue higher levels of education. They also drove up housing costs, which, all combined, drove fertility declines even further below replacement levels, a surprising development for a region whose rapid population had greatly worried both foreign and domestic leaders mere decades before. But as feminist scholars have maintained, there is a sexual order to the political economy and this is apparent in the ways population has been seen in the political arena in these Asian states since 1990.

Ideologies of identity have also marked discussions of demography in East Asia since 1990 as some elites have done whatever they could to preserve homogeneity in the face of labor shortages and rising immigration that threatened to change ethnic or racial composition. After an overview of mortality, fertility, and migration trends in the region, the chapter looks deeper into ideology, population, and policy since 1990.

Population Trends

As the new century approached, Japan became the first country in the world to reach a median age of 40 years. It became clear that low fertility would be the norm across developed countries, and by the end of the period fertility declines were underway even in countries that had not reached high-income status. These fertility declines shifted the states' age profiles toward smaller proportions of children and larger proportions of older adults. Worries about overpopulation gave way to fears of depopulation. Low fertility was increasingly portrayed as an existential threat by governments of these four Asian states, who scrambled to raise fertility while holding on to the status quo national identity. Prime Minister Fumio Kishida has warned that Japan's population trends are so dire that the country is "on the verge of being unable to maintain its social functions."[6]

By today, the region of East Asia has the lowest fertility rate in the world at 1.0 child per woman, uniquely low coupled with unique gender and ethnic dynamics that elevate demographic issues on the political agendas of China, Japan, Singapore, and South Korea.[7] Mortality continued to improve across the region, and in 1986 Japanese females rose to the top of the league in life expectancy, a crown they wear still today. Immigration remains limited or highly regulated—particularly in Singapore's case—across these four states. As the populations of these countries began to shrink—Japan starting in 2011, South Korea in 2020, and China in 2022—it altered the framework within which decisions are made. The exception, of course, is Singapore, which manages its population size through immigration.

Mortality

This region is known as one of exceptional longevity, and rapid economic growth in the region continued to improve life expectancy, particularly at the start of this period. Three aspects of mortality trends since 1990 stand out. The first is continued rapid gains in life expectancy in South Korea that brought them on par with Japan and Singapore, as Fig. 6.1 shows. The second is the relatively lower life expectancy at birth in China. Keeping in mind that the Chinese population is so large that individual provinces are the size of populous countries, life expectancy across China is highly dependent on both geography (province and rural-urban ratios) and sex. Women in Beijing have the highest life expectancy in China, and among men, those in Shanghai hold the record.[8] Western Chinese provinces such as Xinjiang, Qinghai, and Tibet are heavily populated by ethnic minorities, and have higher levels of poverty and higher infant mortality. Future gains in life expectancy in these poorer regions are expected to come mainly from improved life expectancy at younger ages instead of from gains in longevity, as is the case in most Chinese provinces.[9] Still, China has seen remarkable progress: their infant mortality rate had been 42 per thousand births in the period 1985–1990 but by 2000–2005 had declined to 27.[10]

The third notable aspect is, of course, COVID-19. In December 2019, the first COVID-19 case was discovered in Wuhan, Hubei province, and after

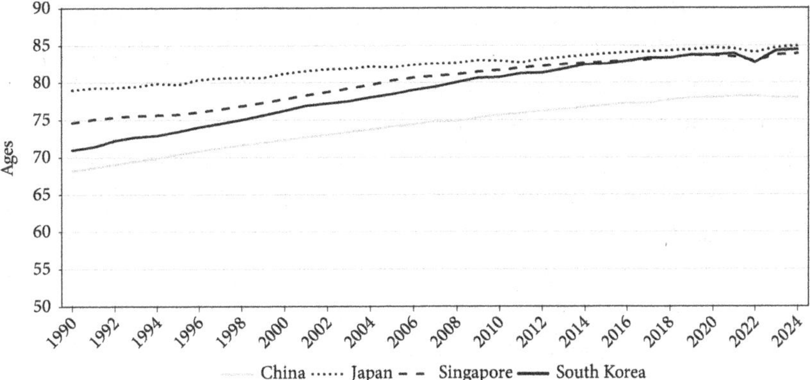

Fig. 6.1 Life expectancy at birth in China, Japan, Singapore, and Republic of Korea, 1990–2024.

Source: Population Division, UN Department of Economic and Social Affairs, *World Population Prospects, the 2024 Revision* (UN DESA, 2024). https://population.un.org/wpp/.

hundreds of cases were discovered over the next few weeks China began a series of lockdowns. Other countries took similar measures as the pandemic spread globally. As cases broke out in different areas of the country, China took more extreme measures. The government decreed in 2021 that any community or building with a COVID-positive individual would be classified as high-risk and people in the high-risk area would be forbidden to go out. The policy became known as Zero COVID and lasted until November 2022, when it was finally relaxed after immense civil society pressure. The sudden loosening of restrictions led to a large spike in infections,[11] although estimates differ. Du *et al.* estimated over 1 million deaths in China from COVID in the first month after the Zero COVID policy was lifted, the vast majority of which were to those aged 80 and over.[12] Xiao and Wang estimated 1.87 million excess deaths occurred among individuals 30 years and older during the first 2 months after Zero COVID was lifted.[13]

Japan experienced a lower cumulative incidence of COVID-19 cases and lower excess mortality due to COVID. These outcomes were primarily reflections of robust health at higher ages, high vaccine coverage, as well as particular healthcare initiatives and high compliance to them.[14] Initially COVID-19 did not hit South Korea as hard as it hit China, but still South Korea recorded over 370,000 COVID-related deaths in 2022. Given that life expectancy estimates reflect mortality conditions, South Korea's statistics agency anticipates that babies born in 2022 will have a life expectancy of

82.7 years, down nearly one year from those born in 2021. Japan's life expectancy fell for two consecutive years as of 2023, reducing life expectancy by 0.62 years for women and 0.51 for men.[15] Singapore self-reported one of the world's lowest COVID death rates and as of end-June 2022 reported only 1,403 COVID-related deaths. Again, the government attributes its relative success to high vaccination rates. As of mid-March 2022 only 5 percent of the population was not vaccinated.[16]

Fertility

It was well known in Japan that births had been declining sharply since the mid-1970s, but those declines took on new significance in June 1990 when major Japanese newspapers reported that in 1989 the total fertility rate had fallen to 1.57, even lower than the previous record low of 1966, which was an inauspicious year according to the Chinese zodiac. The furor over the news coined a new Japanese phrase: the "1.57 shock." But there were more shocks to follow. The collapse of Japan's economic bubble in the mid-1990s made it harder for men and women to find jobs, pushing the marriage age upward even more and intensifying fertility declines. Childlessness rapidly increased in Japan, from about 11 percent for the cohorts born in the early 1950s to 28 percent for those born in the 1970s.[17] By 2024, the total fertility rate was 1.2. In response to political pressure, the government created a new ministry in 2005 to identify the drivers of Japanese fertility decline and to suggest appropriate responses.[18]

Similar "ultra-low" fertility appeared in China as well. Not long into the 1990s, China's fertility rate fell below replacement level. Demographers at the UN, as shown in Fig. 6.2, estimated China's total fertility rate as above 1.5 for the first two decades of the century, but other demographers have estimated that it fell further and faster. A total fertility rate of 1.1 was most commonly cited in 2024.[19] In 2013, China finally officially abandoned its One-Child policy decades after it was no longer demographically useful. The new Only Child policy allowed parents to have two children if one or both of them were only children. In 2016, China's leadership loosened the policy further to a Two-Child Policy, and then to a Three-Child Policy in 2021. Actively encouraging couples to have three children is a policy sea change for China but has been to no avail, demonstrating that even though state policy played a large role in initial fertility declines in China, norms around

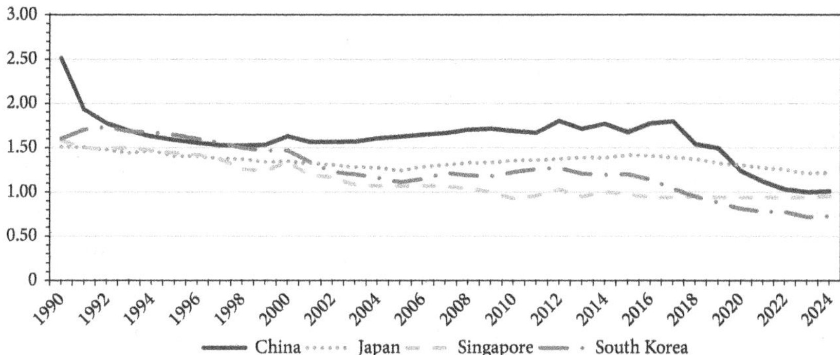

Fig. 6.2 Total fertility rate, China, Japan, Republic of Korea, and Singapore, 1990–2024.

Source: Population Division, UN Department of Economic and Social Affairs, *World Population Prospects, the 2024 Revision* (UN DESA, 2024), https://population.un.org/wpp/.

smaller families have firmly taken hold and continue despite government pronatalist efforts.

Similarly, fertility has also been "ultralow" in Singapore despite government efforts to increase it. In 2001, for example, Singapore's government announced a Baby Bonus of SGD 9,000 (approximately $7,000 USD) for a second child and SGD 18,000 (approximately $14,000 USD) for a third, distributed over six years, to cover the cost of childrearing. Nonetheless, between 2010 and 2020, the proportion of ever-married females who had only 1 child increased from 19 percent to 24 percent and those having none from 9.3 percent in 2010 to 13.5 percent in 2020.[20] Singapore's total fertility rate is now below 1 child per woman.

High housing costs and often high unemployment among Singaporean youth have made family formation even more difficult; for these and other reasons marriage rates are declining and the average age at first marriage has been rising. For example, between the 2010 and 2020 census, the proportion of singles in Singapore rose across age groups. The increase was most prominent for those 25–34 years, meaning that Singaporeans continue to get married later and later. That coincides with later childbearing and fewer children overall. Childbearing outside of wedlock remains rare in all these states, reflecting a strong cultural taboo not present in low-fertility European societies. In 2020, the average number of children born to women aged 30–39 was 1.40, but to women aged 40–49 was 1.76; 10 years earlier the numbers were 1.49 and 2.02, respectively.[21] Ethnic Chinese in Singapore have the highest proportion of singles, showing that the cultural drivers of change in marriage and childbearing transcend national boundaries.

The mean age at first marriage stayed low in China through the 1990s but then rose from 23.4 in 2000 to 24.9 in 2010 and 27.95 in 2020—large upward shifts in this marriage indicator.[22] In response, China's Communist Youth League announced in May 2017 that it would "help unmarried young people find significant others" through activities such as mass blind dates, and "educate young people to establish proper values for love and marriage."[23] In May 2023 China's Family Planning Association launched pilot projects in 20 cities to increase births by reducing the costs of marriage and childbearing. The projects aim to build a new marriage and childbearing culture that will make the social environment more conducive to having children. Bride price, money or goods given to a bride's family by a groom's, and other "outdated" customs will be curbed, and parents will be encouraged to have children at "appropriate" ages and to share childrearing. This project follows a 2022 pilot for a new culture of marriage and childbirth in 20 Chinese cities. Earlier in 2023, the government launched a campaign against extravagant and costly wedding ceremonies.[24]

The government's approach is shaped by rigid ideologies about who constitutes a family. Even though China's leaders are worried about low fertility, they do not want to encourage childbearing outside of marriage. In fact, single women could be penalized for having children and denied a birth certificate for their child if they did not have a valid "reproduction permit."[25] These inflexible ideologies likely pressure fertility rates even lower because they only sanction childbearing within a two-parent, heterosexual relationship characterized by traditional gender roles around childrearing and work.

As low as these fertility rates are, they do not compare to the years of record-setting low fertility in South Korea, reaching 0.72 in 2023 nationwide and as low as 0.55 in Seoul.[26] The influence of ideologies on South Korea's fertility trajectory is detailed in later sections.

In the preceding time period starting after World War II, governments had gotten what they wished for when fertility rates plummeted, although government action was not solely responsible for the shift. When fertility decines blew past targeted lows and it became clear that national populations would shrink (unless supported by immigration, as in Singapore), any illusion of control was shattered and governments would pivot to trying to engineer the population in the other direction—including sponsoring matchmaking.

Migration

In the post-1990 period, immigration to these states remained limited, as Fig. 6.3 shows, and highly regulated despite generally shrinking workforces.

Immigrants constitute only a small proportion of these populations, excepting Singapore, but Japan and South Korea have liberalized somewhat to bring in foreign workers for certain fields with labor shortages. In 2019, Japan created its Specified Skilled Workers (SSW) Program, a status of residence to allow foreign workers in 14 industry fields (amended in 2021 to a reorganized list of 12 fields.). As of May 2022, Japan had signed memoranda of cooperation as part of the SSW program with 14 Asian countries: the Philippines, Cambodia, Nepal, Myanmar, Mongolia, Sri Lanka, Indonesia, Vietnam, Bangladesh, Uzbekistan, Pakistan, Thailand, India, and Malaysia.[27] South Korea began accepting temporary foreign workers in the 1990s to fill manufacturing and agriculture jobs, jobs with long hours and low pay. The government reported 1,124,057 total immigrants in 2022 of which they counted 657,519 as foreigners and 466,538 as Korean nationals.[28] As it did globally, COVID disrupted immigration to these countries, and as of this writing numbers have not completely rebounded.

The outlier among this group with regard to immigration is Singapore. Its total fertility rate is around 1 child per woman, and as the annual rate of natural population increase has declined in this period, immigration has become more important for the government's goal of population growth. The immigrant population in Singapore grew from approximately 727,000

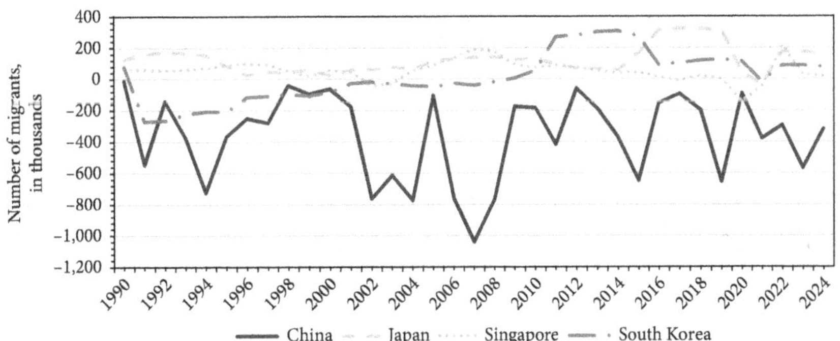

Fig. 6.3 Total net migration, China, Japan, Republic of Korea, and Singapore, 1990–2024.

in 1990 to 1.35 million in 2000 and 2.23 million in 2013, the vast majority of whom were from Malaysia (1.04 million in 2013). As the preceding chapter showed, preserving racial balance is a government priority, and immigration is highly regulated. According to the government, Singapore's "pace of immigration continues to be measured and stable." New Singaporean citizens are naturalized from its permanent resident pool. The government's view on who qualifies to become a citizen reflects that emphasis on stability: "New citizenships are granted to individuals who can integrate and contribute to Singapore, and are committed to making Singapore their home. New citizens either share family ties with Singaporeans (for example, through marriage), or have studied, worked or lived in Singapore for some time."[29]

China has experienced a net outflow of migrants throughout the post-1990 period and has a vast diaspora. The United States is the top destination for Chinese immigrants worldwide and hosts 28 percent of the 8.6 million Chinese living outside China, Hong Kong, or Macau. South Korea (which is home to 803,000 of those Chinese migrants), Japan (776,000), and Singapore (514,000) join Canada and Australia as other top destinations.[30] Although offset by emigration, China does have some immigration and saw an increase in foreign residents during the 2010s. That flow was largely reversed by the hardline policies of Xi Jinping, including the Zero COVID restrictions. Border crossings of foreigners (including short-term visitors) declined sharply in 2022, to only 4.47 million foreigners (excluding residents of Hong Kong, Macau, and Chinese Taipei) from 97.68 million in 2019. Multinational firms have had difficulty attracting foreigners to work in China.[31]

Women on Strike—National Goals versus Individual Agency

One of the most notable developments in global reproductive politics was the 1994 UN population conference in Cairo. Preceding population conferences (including Mexico City in 1984 and Bucharest in 1974) had been in part a battle between enthusiasts for focused policies designed to lower very high fertility rates and policy proponents of more comprehensive development and reproductive health services that included family planning, and the former view generally prevailed. The 1994 population conference in Cairo represented a break with that history, as feminist and broad-based development groups successfully reframed population issues as both rights-based and determined by development (this was the first population conference on both population *and* development). Despite resistance from some groups, including US environmentalists and the Vatican, Cairo was a watershed moment. The more comprehensive approach focused on reproductive health programs instead of more focused "family planning," and led many states to end population "targets" that opponents criticized as incentivizing excessively zealous policies (including forced sterilization in India), and gave more emphasis to increasing girls' education as a long-term fertility-reduction strategy.

It is difficult to measure the impact of Cairo on population rhetoric and politics across Asia, because by the mid-1990s all four of these states had fertility rates well below replacement-level and the impetus to curb births had waned. On the one hand, the Fourth World Conference on Women in Beijing in 1995 echoed Cairo's emphasis on rights and reproductive health, and in 1996 South Korea replaced its fertility regulation policy with the goal of "improving the quality of the population."[32] On the other hand, rhetorical and policy shifts in line with the messages of Cairo and the types of policies we would expect to follow have been unevenly reflected across the region. As demographer Yen-hsin Alice Cheng argues, there is a:

> persistence of cultural norms that place a high value on female chastity, see marriage as *the* ideal context for childbearing and strongly disapprove of non-marital births. This is a vivid example of a region where the modernisation narrative—i.e. that family diversity and unconventional family practices tend to follow economic development—does not hold. In the case of East Asia, it appears that conventional family practices are rather deeply ingrained.[33]

It has become more obvious in the post-1990 world that population politics in Asia is interwoven with gender politics. Women are at the center of these states' population strategies: their governments want them to have more children, work more, and take care of the rapidly increasing older population. In 2007, Hakuo Yanagisawa, Minister of Health, Labor, and Welfare, famously referred to women as "childbearing machines" and entreated them to bear more children, a goal that is often at odds with efforts of labor ministries to increase female labor force participation.[34] It appears, however, that Japanese women do not buy into this plan to birth more *and* work more. Neither do Korean women. When asked in a 2023 survey whether women have a societal obligation to bear more children, only 8 percent of Koreans and 7 percent of Japanese aged 18–34 answered in the affirmative, although over half of South Korean adults ages 55 and over answered this question in the affirmative. Meanwhile, those ideologies appear to be weaker generally in Japan—only 18 percent of those 55-and-over answered in the affirmative. There is a gender gap as well: 34 percent of South Korean men of all ages said women have a duty to bear children, while only 23 percent of Korean women do.[35] Many women in these countries actively resist the imposition of gender ideologies around marriage and childbearing.

We see this rejection in two expressions in Korean society. One is the "Sampo Generation," which refers to young people who have given up three longstanding rites of passage: dating, marriage, and having children. Some expand this to the "N-Po Generation," where the "N-" represents the multitude of things younger people feel that they have given up, or given up on, including jobs and homeownership. Alongside this is the "4 Nos," or the "4B Movement," a reflection of what some see as a gender war in which Korean women have rejected social norms by saying no to dating, marriage, childbirth, and sex with men.[36]

Many scholars argue marriage and childbirth trends are evidence that women are no longer willing to accept deeply unequal marriages that they perceive as reproducing patriarchal structures and do not serve women's best interests. With women's economic independence increasing over time, marriage is no longer necessary to provide financial security and instead may actually make women more vulnerable to insecurity, at least in China's case. In China in 2011, the Supreme People's Court reinterpreted the country's Marriage Law of 1950 as allocating ownership of marital property to the person who owns the home and whose name is on the deed—generally the husband—rather than being divided between spouses. Statistics relevant to this matter vary greatly: the government reports that 39.9 percent of women jointly owned property with their husbands as of 2020, but survey-based studies report much lower figures in a range of 8–24 percent. Joint bank accounts are also exceedingly rare in China and indeed were prohibited by major state banks until 2013.[37] The 2011 reinterpretation of the 1950 Marriage Law represents a sharp departure from past interpretations, as recently as 2001, that provided women some financial protection by more equal division of property, suggesting increasing influence of gender ideologies in more recent years. Compounding the issue, it is still common for family members to pool assets to help male but not female family members purchase a home, unsurprising since assets given to female members would be at risk given the law's interpretation.[38] Marriage is also legally necessary for some privileges in China. Starting in mid-2012 Shanghai declared that single residents without a *hukou* (official household registration permit) were not allowed to purchase a home, while married residents without a *hukou* were permitted to do so.[39]

Marriage is important financially for women, but even more so culturally. The Chinese government has been working to promote marriage by stigmatizing urban, professional women who remain single and in 2007 launched a propaganda campaign to that effect. Starting in that year, China's Women's Federation began using the term "leftover women" to refer to single women older than 27. The term has been used in the state-run Xinhua News Agency and has been added to the official lexicon of China's Ministry of Education.[40]

Gender and Modernization—Ideologies at Work

Gender ideologies affect how these various states approach the issue of women in the workforce in their campaign toward modernization. Japan and China fall at the extremes among this set of four national cases. In 1999, investment strategists at Goldman Sachs Japan led by Kathy Matsui recommended making gender equality the centerpiece of Japan's economic revitalization strategy, a strategy they called "Womenomics." Prime Minister Shinzo Abe started his second term in 2012 by declaring that "Abenomics is Womenomics," and released his Womenomics agenda in January 2014. Provisions included raising female labor force participation, increasing the percentage of women returning to work after the birth of their first child, expanding childcare capacity and eliminating daycare waitlists, and increasing the percentage of new fathers taking paternity leave.[41] Progress has been mixed. Female labor force participation (ages 15–64) did increase to 74.4 percent in 2022 from 63.4 percent in 2012 (and up from 57.4 percent in 1990) but the proportion of fathers taking paternity leave stayed flat at only about 3 percent.[42]

Still, the Japanese government's approach to work, gender, and fertility recognizes that larger cultural issues are at play, including an incredibly demanding work culture (also an issue in Korea). Thus they recommend shorter working hours for both men and women, and that men contribute more unpaid labor at home. In its 2010 revision to the Child Care and Family Care Leave Law, Japan's government noted that "Although about

30 percent of men want to take child care leave, their actual leave-taking rate is 1.56 percent. The hours spent by Japanese men on child care and housework are shorter than men in any other developed country."[43] Turning recommendations into outcomes has proven challenging. According to the most recently available data from the OECD, Japanese men spend an average of 40.8 minutes in unpaid work per day at home, while Japanese women spend 224.5 (the OECD average for men is 136.5 minutes versus 263.4 minutes for women).[44]

While women have been the centerpiece of the Japanese government's strategy, in China gender ideologies structure the workplace in a far different way. Pushing women out of the workplace and into the home has been a long-standing strategy for Chinese leaders to address unemployment. In 1978, for example, China's State Council mandated that women in both labor-intensive and white-collar fields must retire 10 years earlier than men. Around that same time, when state-owned enterprises started firing millions of employees, women were the first to go. As unemployment increased in the late 1980s and 1990s, the "Women Return to the Home" (*nuren hui jia*) movement, which called on women to give up their jobs for men, gained popularity.[45]

Chinese women have indeed been returning to the home, or at least exiting the workforce. Over time, rising discrimination against women in hiring (and youth more generally) has reduced the relatively high female-labor force participation of China's early Communist days. Women's labor force participation rate (over age 15) has fallen from nearly 73 percent in 1991 to 60.5 percent in 2023.[46] Encouraging women to leave the workplace for the home has become a strategy to raise fertility as well. In October 2023, at the 13th National Women's Congress, Xi said, "We should actively foster a new type of marriage and childbearing culture," and party officials should influence young people's views on "love and marriage, fertility and family." Xi, however, made no mention of women at work.[47] Rather than birth more and work more, Xi appears to prefer that women birth more and leave the work to the men.

Economic constraints caused by trade wars with the United States, reduced domestic consumption (some of which may be driven by an aging population), and the impact of COVID on the economy, such as rising business closures and job losses, has arguably fallen hardest on Chinese women and youth. Research by Yun Zhou has found that young, urban Chinese women saw the One-Child Policy as actually offering protection against labor market discrimination since it reduced the risk that employers would see potential motherhood as an excuse not to hire women of child-bearing age. These women also felt that as children they had faced less competition within the family because of the general absence of male siblings.[48] Chinese youth have also been especially vulnerable. While urban unemployment for those aged 25–59 has been steady at under 6 percent for the past few years, unemployment among those aged 16–24 years has risen from 13.3 percent in 2018 to 16.8 percent in summer 2020, and to 19.9 percent in summer 2022.[49] The Chinese government caps eligibility for most civil servant positions at age 35, and other employers follow suit.[50] This type of discrimination essentially negates arguments about the importance of population aging and the shrinking of the prime-age workforce and demonstrates how much ideology distorts discussions of demography. The inability of many young Chinese—men and women—to attain stable employment and careers in China likely results in further postponement of marriage and childbearing.

At least rhetorically, South Korea has been trending more toward the Japanese model, but as in Japan gender ideologies in Korea have proven difficult to overcome. Starting in the 2000s the government tried to increase births through measures like childcare support but with only limited efforts to support gender equality or enforce a rights-based framework around reproduction, which some Korean youth have seen as inadequate and a reflection of traditional norms.[51] Korean feminists have noted that in contrast to Japan's plan to tackle unequal gender roles at work and at home, South Korea has taken a different tack by focusing its policies on reducing the financial burden of children. Such financial support to parents began in June 2009, and the Yoon administration added a universal financial voucher for childrearing of 2,000 Korean Won (one-time payment) (approximately $1,500 USD). They also increased the universal cash support from 300 Won (about $230 USD) to 700 Won (about $530 USD) in 2022.

There have been multiple revisions in the language of the "Plan for Aging Society and Population" since its announcement in 2006. According to the third revision 2019–2020, one main goal is "Establishing a gender-equal society," which is echoed in the fourth revision.[52] As in Japan, however, rhetoric and government action have yet to bring about a large-scale cultural shift. Korean men spend an average of 49 minutes a day on unpaid labor at home versus 215 minutes for women, and their uptake of available paternity leave is low.[53] When the Korean government issued a "birth map" in 2016, they were forced to pull the publication in the face of accusations that the government was blaming women for the low birth rate. As one blogger saw it, "They counted fertile women like they counted the number of livestock."[54]

Patriarchal norms are even embedded in data collection practices in South Korea, as "data in Korean censuses on children ever born are collected only for the women who have ever married," leaving researchers studying Korean fertility trends no choice but to code all the women who have never married as childless.[55]

In South Korea, government family policies, like spending on families and social protection, have expanded since the late 1990s. However, the 1997 Asian financial crisis also reduced labor market opportunities for young people. Young women, in particular, felt that crunch at the same time that married women began to place higher value on their own employment. A high share of the female labor force is self-employed, on temporary or nonstandard work contracts, or in the informal sector. This is particularly the case for Korean women, especially married women, in their 40s and 50s returning to the labor market after taking time for family and childrearing responsibilities.[56]

The evolution of traditional Korean preference for sons over daughters also is relevant. Remarkably, South Korea was able to combat this strong cultural norm through legal changes, including property inheritance rights. South Korea's low fertility is indisputably driven by rigid gender norms and institutions that often discriminate against women (see Case Study: Missing Women—The Ultimate Demographic Distortion), yet much of the Korean government's response to low fertility has been to reinforce those norms, rather than try to improve the situation of women. A survey by the Korean Population, Health and Welfare Association showed that a quarter of female respondents said they were hesitant to marry because of "the culture of patriarchy and gender inequality." Men's and women's answers to the survey questions about having children showed stark differences. Men tended to point to strong finances and a stable job as prerequisites, while a high percentage of young women cited their partners' participation in household duties, including childcare, and parental leave as prerequisites.[57]

The patriarchal structures reinforced by leadership are not unique to South Korea, and arguably extend to all four Asian cases in Chapters 5 and 6. But the population policies promoted by the regimes of these four states across the decades are best understood within the context of those structures. For example, the failure of pronatalist policies to revise the social structures that depress fertility in the first place are a large reason why those pronatalist policies have failed. Too often—and not just in Asia, as other chapters show—governments address population issues by setting specific population targets: for growth rates, overall size, specific fertility levels. The population outcome is the goal, with little or no consideration of what the standards of living or quality of life of that population are, particularly for women or immigrants (or women immigrants). This approach sets policy makers up for failure because it does not address underlying drivers of fertility trends. South Korea's government set a numerical target for total fertility rate in its third plan for aging society at 1.5 children per woman by 2020.[58] Its population policy missed the mark.

Case Study: Missing Women—The Ultimate Demographic Distortion

The ultimate demographic distortion in this region may be the millions of "missing females" in China and South Korea due to historical son preference coupled with the availability of sex-selective abortion. The influence of patrilineality, the organization of society along male familial lines, on Chinese policy and demography is well documented among feminist scholars. Susan Greenhalgh has argued that the loosened birth planning policies after 1983 are evidence of the state's strong desire to preserve the patrilineal family because they allow a second child if the first is a girl, if the husband and wife live near the wife's family, "if only one son in a family is able to reproduce, or if a family has produced only one son for three generations in a row."[59]

Quite remarkably, the year 1990 was a clear inflection point for reversing South Korea's skewed sex ratio at birth, as Fig. 6.4 shows. By the early 1970s the new Korean government headed by Chun Doo-Hwan worried about a second baby boom from the post–Korean War baby boom generation entering reproductive ages around 1980, so Korea's Fifth Five-Year Plan (1982–87) included a comprehensive approach to control population growth that revitalized family planning. One part of the approach was to get all government ministries involved in family planning; another tried to change social norms away from traditional Korean preferences for both larger families and sons. Concretely, this meant abolishing many gender-discriminatory items in the family law and in medical-insurance regulations in order to weaken the basis for son preference.[60] Gender ideologies were at play as well. The government launched propaganda to boost the value of girls and counter son preference on the assumption

continued

continued

that fertility declines would be impeded as couples might keep bearing children until they had a son.[61]

Boosting the value of girls was no small feat. In Korean culture, the first-born son traditiaonlly had all of the institutional responsibility, including the expectation that he would care for his parents in their old age, and second-born and higher-order sons were not as important except as backups. In essence, both second sons and all daughters represented additional mouths to feed once survival rates improved after the early 1960s.[62] When the South Korean government started promoting a two-child norm in the 1970s, they attempted to overcome the cultural preference for sons with their slogan, "Daughter or son, stop at two, and raise well." But government policy has its limits, as we have seen time and again. A 1971 survey showed that a son was seen as so vital that 50 percent of women (and 68 percent of rural women) said failure to have a son was a sufficient reason for a husband to have a child with another woman.[63]

Den Boer and Hudson argue that there are many settings with strong cultural preference for sons that do not have abnormal sex ratios at birth, so it is "government-led fertility policies and the resulting incentive structures" that catalyze acting on those preferences.[64] In particular, whether son preference translates to action depends on the strength and rigidity of patrilineal practices, according to den Boer and Hudson. Laws, policies, and practices are powerful; they not only can support patrilineality, but can also undo it. South Korea is a prime example, where a vastly abnormal sex ratio corrected to normal in less than a generation. Family law in South Korea codified the patrilineal system. Starting in 1977, women gained some inheritance rights, but only 25 percent of the inheritance their brothers received. Upon divorce, fathers had complete child custody rights and generally received the lion's share of marital assets. Undergirded by the 1987 UN Committee on the Elimination of All Forms of Discrimination Against Women (CEDAW), Korean women's rights groups effectively lobbied for changes. A new law effective in 1991 ensured that inheritances would be shared equally between sons and daughters, that a married couple's domicile would be decided jointly, and that the wife's name would be entered into her husband's family register, or he into her family's register if he so chose. The new law also removed the automatic paternal right to child custody.[65]

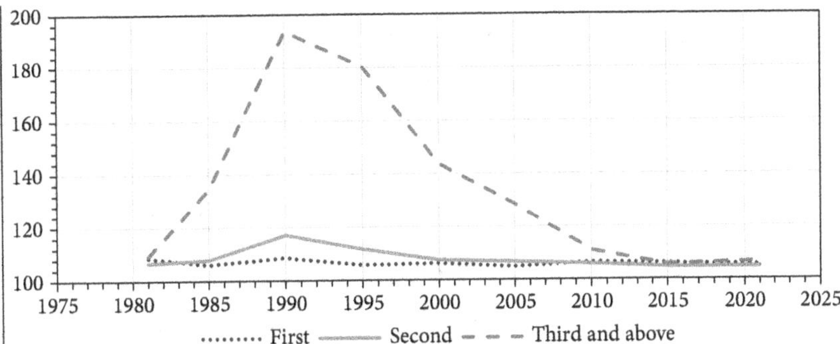

Fig. 6.4 Sex ratio at birth by birth order, South Korea, 1981–2014.

Sources: Through 1985, Quanbao Jiang et al., "Changes in Sex Ratio at Birth in China: A Decomposition by Birth Order," *Journal of Biosocial Science* 49, no. 6 (2017), https://www.ncbi.nlm.nih.gov/entrez/eutils/elink.fcgi?dbfrom=pubmed&retmode=ref&cmd=prlinks&id=27834160; data for 1990 onward, "Sex Ratio at Birth by Birth Order for Provinces," Statistics Korea, https://kosis.kr/statHtml/statHtml.do?orgId=101&tblId=DT_1B81A19&vw_cd=MT_ETITLE&list_id=A21&scrId=&seqNo=&language=en&obj_var_id=&itm_id=&conn_path=A6&path=%252Feng%252Fsearch%252FsearchList.do (updated August 24, 2022, accessed June 29, 2023). https://kosis.kr/statHtml/statHtml.do?orgId=101&tblId=DT_1B81A19&conn_path=I2&language=en.

The overall legal environment was influential. However, for the sex ratio to become as skewed as it did parents must not only have a strong preference for sons over daughters, but be willing to act on that preference through sex-selective abortion. And for parents to act on their son preferences, they need access to both prenatal sex screening and abortion, both regulated by government policies.[66] Although the Korean government made little attempt to enforce antiabortion laws, it did try to enforce the ban on fetal sex identification, first legislated in 1987 and then strengthened in 1994.[67] It helped, as Fig. 6.4 shows. The abortion story is more complicated, but instructive for thinking about how reproductive policies might change in the new era of global low fertility that stretches across cultures, income levels, and government regime types.

South Korea criminalized abortion in 1953, but the Maternal and Child Health Law of 1973 included numerous exemptions and enforcement of abortion laws was lax.[68] In response to low births, the Korean government adopted the "Comprehensive Plan for the Prevention of Illegal Abortion" in February 2010. According to a 2011 Korean women's NGO report, in response, most obstetricians stopped conducting abortion operations.[69] By then, however, the ratio of females

continued

continued

to males at birth had basically normalized for first and second births, as seen in the preceding graph, and had dropped to almost 111 males per 100 females for third births.

Ideologies of Identity—Who Belongs?

Ideologies of identity distort discussions of population against a background of low fertility rates since 1990. The degree to which immigration—in what form and at what levels—should be employed to offset population decline and shifts toward older age compositions is hotly debated in Japan, Singapore, and South Korea (less so in China, which remains a net emigration country). In Japan, even the term "immigration" itself is highly contested, as reflected in a November 5, 2018, exchange between then prime minister Shinzo Abe and Saito Renho of the Constitutional Democratic Party of Japan (a leading left-center party) in a budget meeting of the Diet. Renho questioned the prime minister as to why he avoided using the term "immigration."[70] In response, Abe said, "The definition of immigration is ambiguous and there is no specific definition, but what we are saying is that we are currently experiencing a serious labor shortage. In order to respond to this, the current system for accepting foreign human resources in specialized and technical fields will be expanded."[71] The influence of strong norms about ethnohomogeneity on policymaking around immigration and the labor force is clear in their exchange.

While immigration has not shaped party politics in Japan or Korea to the degree it has in the United States or especially Europe, that may be changing. Japan's right-wing Sanseito political party, founded in 2020, is pursuing an anti-immigration platform, protectionist policies, and was partly founded as a response to COVID, calling for the freedom to opt out of masks and vaccines. In the 2022 House of Councillors (Upper House) election, Sanseito ran candidates in all 45 electoral districts and 5 in the proportional representation segment in the Upper House election. It lost in all but one, a seat in a proportional representation segment, but the party gained about 1.76 million votes, 500,000 more than the number gained by the long-standing Social Democratic Party.[72] Unlike in the United States or Europe, in Korea, left-wing politics is often more nationalist, as those on the left are more likely to support unification with the North. In a 2024 poll in Korea, 64 percent of supporters of the then-ruling and conservative People Power Party said they supported admission of more immigrants, while support was lower among the more liberal Democratic Party of Korea supporters (55 percent in favor) and the more progressive Justice Party supporters (58 percent). Also, immigration is a relatively new political issue so it is likely to be politically dynamic.[73]

In South Korea, ideological conflicts over who is Korean have a strong demographic component in terms of both ethnicity and gender. As in Japan, the national narrative is rooted in the idea of ethnic homogeneity, an ideology that makes it difficult to increase immigration in response to shrinking labor forces from low fertility. A strong sense of ethnic nationalism becomes reinforced by rules about immigration and citizenship. Immigration to South Korea has increased steadily since 1990 with a spike between 2010 and 2015, as Fig. 6.3 shows, but indeed it has a strong ethnic component. In 1999, the National Assembly passed the Overseas Korean Act, which gave eligible immigrants with Korean background a form of dual citizenship rights with the creation of the "Overseas Korean" visa category.[74] But, of course, defining that diaspora is where the politics of population comes in. The category targeted more than five million people of Korean descent residing largely in China, the United States, Japan, and the former Soviet Union. However these ethnic Koreans are still not treated equally, with those from the United States and Japan favored over those from China and the former Soviet Union. Ethnically Korean immigrants from the US and Japan are seen as more desirable "cosmopolitan professionals from wealthy countries" while ethnically Korean immigrants from China and the fomer Soviet Union are seen as less desirable immigrants because they come from poor, nondemocratic, and "backwards" settings.[75]

Indeed, until 2003, ethnic Koreans from China and the former Soviet Union had been excluded from obtaining Overseas Korean status because the provision limited eligibility to those who left the Korean peninsula after the founding of the Republic in 1948, effectively excluding more than half of all Korean diasporic populations. Most of the post-1948 emigrants were in the United States and Japan, and although over 70 percent of Korean residents in Japan are also descendants of pre-1948 emigrants, they qualified for immigration under an exception to the Overseas Korean Act. The way immigration laws, the various visas, and labor schemes, are constructed with two categories of coethnic immigrants reflects "anxieties among bureaucratic elites about the mass influx of Korean Chinese in search of higher paying jobs and opportunities."[76] Still, Korean Chinese formed the largest foreign community in Korea by far after the normalization of diplomatic relations between South Korea and mainland China in 1992, increasing from 32,443 in 2000 to almost 680,000 in 2017.[77]

As Korean policymakers have pushed for more open immigration policies to supplement the aging labor force, the narrative that Korea is ethnically homogeneous has become harder to sustain. Civil society groups have also pressured to redefine Korean identity in a more expansive and less exclusive way. Scholar Yoonkyung Lee argues that there are opposing forces around ethnocentrism and ethnonationalism today, between "Koreans' attachment to the nationalist identity that undergirded their political survival and economic success during the nation's turbulent modern decades and the present realities of a multi-ethnicizing population that demands pluralist and fluid understandings of social membership and collective identity."[78] Lee sees other roots for change in "Korea's economic globalization, which has increased movements of people across borders, and to democratic development, which has allowed critical voices to be raised within."[79]

Koreans have been slow to embrace those of non-Korean backgrounds, however, as ideologies of identity and of gender shape policymaking. Two types of visa categories in particular—coethnic immigration and marriage migrant visas—have allowed Korea to meet labor demands while maintaining restrictive policies, but have in effect created second-class Koreans.[80] Korea's former President Yook Suk Yeol said in 2023 that "Despite such growth in the number of immigrants, our social perceptions have still not changed properly. . . . I also think that because of the many restrictions they face in their role as members of society, which is needed to induce changes in social perceptions, immigrants themselves have made efforts that are far lacking or have not had the opportunity to properly do so."[81]

Even in multiethnic Singapore, it is clear that leaders prefer natural population growth from increasing births rather than immigration. Prime Minister Lee Hsien Loong noted in 2019 that the ratio of births to additional permanent residents in Singapore's population increase was nearly one to one. While immigration remained important and "adds a vibrancy to the place," he also said, "To secure our future, we must make our own babies, enough of them. Because if all of the next generation are not our own, then where do they come from and what is the point of this?"[82] For Lee, managing Singapore's overall population size *and* its national character are both important: "If we could open our doors, we could double our population overnight, and that would not be a wise idea." In his words, Singapore's immigration scheme allows "flexibility depending on the needs of the economy and the business cycle," while ensuring that immigrants "are able to fit in and not cause too much of a social dislocation."[83]

Maintaining the balance in the CMIO (Chinese/Malay/Indian/Others) racialization of identity that was established at Singapore's modern founding (see preceding chapter) is paramount for Singapore's leaders, even amid low fertility. More specifically, immigration and citizenship laws codify the vision of Singapore as a "Chinese majority enclave within a Malay-Muslim region."[84] New migrants from other Asian countries who become citizens or permanent residents are also included in the CMIO system, with those from Bangladesh, Pakistan, Sri Lanka, North India, and South India grouped under the "Indian" label.[85] Even Singapore's rigid housing system, administered through their Housing and Development Board (HDB), is a tool for enforcing Singapore's particular take on multicultural ideology, a core of Singapore's national identity. The HDB uses ethnic quotas to distribute residents among the public housing blocks. Public schools are another tool. Students are assigned a "mother tongue" based on their ethnicity, as denoted on their identity cards. For example, though all Singapore students study English, a Malay student must also study Malay and an Indian student must study Tamil.[86]

One way Singapore's leaders enforce their demographic ideal is through the concept of the "Singaporean core," which was first articulated in Parliament in 2011 by Dr. Amy Khor, minister of state for health and chairman of REACH, the lead government agency that facilitates feedback between Singaporeans and their government. On the heels of a difficult electoral victory for the long-dominant People's Action Party and citizens' dissatisfaction with Singapore's foreign labor policy, her aim was to impose a quota on foreign workers and protect locals' employment prospects. Some Singaporeans have since interpreted the idea of the "Singaporean core" as more of a euphemism for domestic (i.e., Singaporean) labor as a central fixture, but only alongside a permanent periphery of foreign labor at a ratio of two

Singaporeans to every one foreign worker.[87] In a 2015 interview that more fully articulates the concept of the Singaporean core, Manpower Minister Lim Swee Say said, "It's important that we ensure that two thirds of our workforce will form a strong Singaporean core in our economy." Under this strategy, Singapore would continue to bring in foreign workers, but ensure there was an emphasis on high-quality, high-skilled workers who would complement, not compete with, Singaporeans. "We don't want Singapore to be their learning ground," he said.[88] There are notable differences in total fertility rates among the three major ethnic groups. The average number of children born to resident ever-married females aged 40–49 was 1.65 for Chinese, 2.43 for Malay, and 1.86 for Indians in 2020.[89] Singapore's immigration scheme allows a way to preserve racial balance, which would eventually be upset by fertility differences.

Case Study: Korea and the International Marriage Market

We have seen how interwoven the ideologies of colonialism, modernization, ethnicity, and gender in South Korea's approaches toward international marriage have become since 1990. Historically, most international marriages of Koreans were associated with the invasion of Korea by other countries. During China's Chung Dynasty, Korean women were captured as spoils of war and when returned home were shamed and forced to live in a segregated area. Korean women who engaged in sexual labor or were married to American soldiers during the Korean War were referred to in a derogatory way by terms such as "GI Brides."[90] International marriages in general, and especially those involving Korean women, were condemned as betrayals of Korean nationalism. Still, before 1990, Korean women were mostly the ones who had international marriages. Korean men's rate of international marriage started to increase in 1992, when Korea reestablished official relations with China. After 1995, the number of men with international marriages surpassed that of women.

Marriage migration to Korea was led by the *Joseonjok* (ethnic Koreans residing in China) since the government-controlled immigration influx by: (1) an open-door policy for *Joseonjok* women as "cross-border" brides and (2) a closed-door policy for unskilled migrant workers in general and *Joseonjok* in particular. In the 1990s, the government limited the entrance of *Joseonjok* since many were visiting and working illegally; therefore the easiest way to migrate to South Korea became through marriage. Marriage migration also provided a route for others to return to Korea, because *Joseonjok* wives are allowed to send two invitation letters to their parents to come to Korea.[91]

Korea's international marriage policies offer citizenship status only for certain women. For example, migrant hostesses brought in for US military "camptown" clubs on entertainer visas since 1996, mostly women from the Philippines and the former Soviet Union, were excluded from making claims as either migrant workers or migrant women. Starting in the 1990s, civil society activists advocated for reforms to migration laws and their protests have brought significant policy changes. In 2004 feminist organizations succeeded in efforts to have these women reclassified as victims eligible for state protection under the new law, rather than as criminals in the sexual commerce business.[92]

One clear example of the stickiness of gender ideologies is the Korean government's campaign to recruit female migrants as marriage partners for unmarried men in rural districts experiencing population decline and demographic aging. This is not new; the 1992 treaty to establish diplomatic and trade relations between South Korea and mainland China allowed local government officials and agricultural associations in rural areas to arrange marriage meetings between Korean men and ethnic Korean women from China, and deregulation in 1999 led to the establishment of international marriage agencies and widened the pool to include Southeast Asia and Russia. The majority of foreign brides are Vietnamese and Chinese, which Korean men prefer, according to a Korean Sociological Association survey, because "they look similar to Koreans" (36.8 percent of the responses), "they are likely to be obedient" (36.3 percent), and "the children will look like Koreans."[93]

Before the Nationality Law was revised in 1998 it had incorporated traditional patrilineal and gender biases, expressed in the common view that "A married daughter is no longer a daughter." For example, the nationalities of children reflected those of their fathers only, meaning that children with a Korean mother and a foreign father could not acquire Korean nationality by birth. Female foreigners who married Korean men were permitted to obtain Korean citizenship immediately following their marriages, while male foreigners who married Korean women had to wait

continued

continued

two years, and meet certain eligibility requirements in order to apply for Korean nationality.[94]

As low fertility became the norm and it became clear that sex-selective abortion meant millions of "missing" Korean females of marriageable ages, as discussed in a preceding section, the idea of international marriage took on new significance. The creation of the marriage migrant visa "solidified the idea that foreign female spouses of native Korean men had three principal duties: bear (Korean) children, care for their aging (Korean) in-laws, and become (Korean) citizens," according to scholar Erin Chung, and the marriage migrant visa was entirely derivative of the spousal status.[95] The Nationality Act again was amended in 2004 to allow some spouses of Korean nationals to acquire Korean nationality even if they did not meet naturalization requirements.

In 2011, South Korea introduced the "marriage migrant" (F-6) visa, which provided a higher status—in fact, the highest status visa, top of the hierarchy of noncitizens—for the female migrants who were predominantly the spouses of nationals and removed the requirement for female migrants to remain married to Korean spouses. The marriage migrant visa provided access to health insurance, pensions, property rights, investment rights, unlimited employment rights, and social welfare benefits, just as the Overseas Korean Visa did. Additionally, marriage migrant visa holders were eligible for simplified naturalization and dual citizenship rights, along with access to 200 multicultural family centers to facilitate their integration. These centers ran social integration programs that educated migrants on how to operate within a traditional Korean structure and serve as wives, daughters-in-law, and mothers. Immigrant wives were instructed on how to cook for traditional holidays, maintain shrines, and speak with honorifics to address their husbands' families.[96] Proactive efforts by state and nonstate actors to recruit female migrants to marry Korean citizens have made them one of the fastest-growing immigrant groups, and marriage to a native citizen has become one of the most recognized paths to acquiring citizenship. However, marriage migrants are incorporated as dependents, leading to a highly vulnerable position vis-à-vis their principal sponsors (Korean husbands and in-laws), which has led to domestic violence, growing divorce rates, and growing numbers of undocumented female migrants.

Ideologies of identity and ideologies of modernization seem likely to come into increasing conflict as these societies and their leaders navigate a path for keeping their economies healthy amid shrinking labor forces. Immigration also seems likely to rise in importance on the political agendas if low fertility persists and the population declines substantially in size.

Conclusion—Ramping Up Population Politics

If we view the trajectory of fertility, mortality, and migration trends in these states alongside their reproductive politics, we see how governments are always chasing an elusive "sweet spot" when it comes to population. Japan's government shifted from thinking there were "too many" births to "too few", just as leaders of China, South Korea, Singapore, and indeed many other states did. In the pre-1990 period, ideologies of modernization drove population distortions as these states sought to reduce fertility rates to propel economic growth. In the post-1990 period, with fertility rates plummeting, ideologies of gender rose to the fore. In both periods, ideologies of identity remained a powerful force for distortion.

Yet, in this period we also see movements in the other direction, correcting distortions of the past. For example, Japan has been reckoning with the legacy of its Eugenic Protection Law, described in the preceding chapter. At the landmark 1994 International Conference on Family Planning in Cairo, a Japanese woman with disabilities spoke out against Japan's Eugenic Protection Law, garnering international attention that, along with domestic social movement activism, forced changes in the law just two years later. In 1996, the Eugenic Protection Law was renamed the "Maternal Protection Law" and its eugenic provisions repealed to allow only voluntary sterilization and abortion. In June 2023, Japan's Diet published a report that revealed that around 16,000 people had been sterilized without consent under the law over the 48 years of its existence, including two nine-year-old children.[97] South Korea also has focused on shifting rhetoric around low fertility to be more in line with women's empowerment as elsewhere in the world.

While this chapter privileges ideologies of gender, ideologies of modernization are still visible in domestic attitudes toward immigration, namely as leaders in Japan, Singapore, and South Korea consider a greater role for immigrants in supplementing a contracting workforce due to low domestic fertility. As Justice Minister Han Dong-hoon said in July 2023, "Without immigration, South Korea has no future."[98]

We also see from this region that political systems matter for channeling ideological distortions into actual policy and demographic outcomes. With rapidly shrinking populations, Chinese, Japanese, and South Korean elites worry that their countries are in an existential crisis, but it is policymakers in Singapore and China, with their more autocratic regimes, that have freer rein when it comes to population policy. Singapore has demonstrated a remarkable ability to control immigration and manage ethnic composition, even though the state has been limited in the degree to which it can effectively incentivize marriage and childbearing thus far. These political systems will continue to matter in the future. All four of these Asian countries see population instrumentally, and desire more births for the sake of the nation (whether the ethnic/political nation or the economy), but it is in China where reproductive autonomy is at greatest risk because of both norms and political institutions. As China's population continues to shrink and age, coercive pronatal policies could come to replace the former One-Child Policy. Such moves might backfire, however, and incite popular opposition to the government. This happened with China's Zero COVID policies when Chinese protestors used blank sheets of paper as symbols of censorship and repression, giving their movement the nickname "white-paper movement" at the end of 2022.

The population shifts happening in Asia are unprecedented and will test the limits of even democratic institutions. With the lowest fertility in the world, claims of labor shortages, a caregiving crisis, and straining national budgets, population dynamics have created an atmosphere ripe for future demographic distortion.

Conclusion

Population Politics

Yesterday, Today, and Tomorrow

This book has shown what population politics looks like in three regions of the world grappling with low birth rates alongside generally—although not universally—improving health and increased longevity, and facing wildly different levels of migration. These trends, and attitudes about them, vary among and within the regions, but the braiding together of discussions of population issues and political values is universal.

Demographic data describe empirical processes that—when collected and analyzed by careful and objective researchers—can provide important insights into the past, present, and even future. What we have shown is that such data never exist purely on their own; they are always embedded in political and social context and their interpretation is conditioned by those contexts. Demographers cannot pretend that if their studies are value-neutral their findings will remain outside the political and social fray. In the hands of ideologues or political and economic interest groups, these same data can be manipulated and even weaponized to serve their own purposes.

Those interested in understanding the powerful demographic trends underway should exercise care in assessing the credibility of demographic claims put forward by interested parties. We cannot stop distortion, but we can try to separate the production of knowledge from its distortion by those who convert demographic phenomena into political narratives, an aim we work towards by cataloging how population politics has been and still is at play in these regions.

There has never been a one-to-one correspondence between demographic change and political or social dynamics. Different political regimes share similar demographic profiles, and countries with similar demographic trends sometimes share little in the way they organize their political lives. The sheer complexity and subtlety of the causes of demographic change mean that politics is only one variable in the story.

Toxic Demography. Jennifer D. Sciubba, Michael S. Teitelbaum, and Jay Winter, Oxford University Press.

DOI: 10.1093/oso/9780197745038.003.0008

The most significant of these changes is the move to low fertility for two-thirds of the globe—and unprecedentedly low levels of fertility in many nations. This demographic shift touches all continents, and remarkably, the response of political elites has been similar despite geographic and cultural differences. Political leaders who think they can reverse low fertility rates via costly tax incentives, cash bonuses, and parental leave policies need to think again and consider the evidence that such policies generally are failing to raise fertility to replacement levels, although they may lighten the costs of parenting and serve a purpose in improving well-being. Overall, and too often, uninformed advocates and political leaders all over the world assume they understand what causes population dynamics to change and what remedies will work to produce a better future for the nation. They hide their ignorance under a fig leaf of overly confident language.

This is not to say that politics has no effects on population phenomena; we can cite multiple instances of successful promotion of fertility decline, deadly genocides, ethnic cleansing, and effective border enforcement to prove the contrary. Migration, in particular, is always subject to political intervention under the global system of sovereign states, although the commitment of determined people to evade border controls sometimes is greater than that of national leaders to enforce them in the context of opposition by domestic interest groups. Our conclusion is that while states and their leaders frequently try to affect population phenomena, much of the time they have only limited success in doing so.

In large part, that is because states are not the main actors in the unfolding of patterns of fertility or mortality decline. Social and economic factors, coupled with the work of associations outside the apparatus of the state and decisions made by millions of individuals and couples play at least as great and at times a greater role in changing strategies of family formation and the life chances of different age groups. We expect that population dynamics will remain an area of concern for political elites because they are integral to economic and other political dynamics, but also that those elites will grow increasingly frustrated at their inability actually to control those dynamics. Population issues—particularly immigration, ethnic change, and low fertility rates—will be only more contentious in the coming decades.

How can we do better in understanding these now-common and powerful phenomena? The first step is to admit that we do not have an adequate "theory of demographic transition" that can provide a satisfactory explanation of current historically low levels of fertility being reported in many parts of the world today. There is evidence that so many factors drive these low rates, from a shift in values and fear of the future, to costs of children, to gender dynamics, that no elegant theory could possibly emerge to account for them all. The second step is to counter alarmism by stripping from the term "population decline" the menace that demagogues routinely attach to it. Yes, national totals of populations in certain states have gone down in recent years. No, Italy or Japan are not about to disappear. There will be a new, smaller normal, but countries with smaller populations have opportunities to reduce their environmental footprints in ways those with relatively rapid rates of population growth find very challenging. Given the handwringing over negative or even slowing population growth, however, it seems unlikely that depopulating nations will seize this opportunity, and instead will seek to expand consumption to boost economic growth.

In addition to unprecedentedly low fertility, we are in the midst of a dramatic shift in global ethnic composition. European states dominated Africa, Asia, and Latin America for centuries, but no longer, and future population growth will be concentrated in the non-European world, and in particular in sub-Saharan Africa, the region of the world with the highest fertility rates. Although it too now has below-replacement fertility, India's population will continue to grow for several decades, riding a wave of demographic momentum from earlier high fertility. The populations of countries such as Pakistan, Nigeria, Indonesia, and parts of the Middle East also seem quite certain to continue to expand. Japan, Russia, China, and Germany, however, have already peaked in size, and over the next 30 years a large number of countries in Latin American and the Caribbean will also peak.[1]

It is at this point that responsible and informed demographic agencies and publications matter. They are essential in limiting the damage fearmongering can do. Population research institutions such as the Population Association of America, the International Union for the Scientific Study of Population, the *Institut national d'études démographiques* (INED), and others offer appropriate forums for thoughtful discussion and debate about the ethical implications of population science. Noble intentions do not suffice—a data point is never just a data point.

As we identified in our Introduction, one source of demographic distortion is simple misunderstanding. Such debates and discussions should be part of data science curricula and graduate programs in demography and international affairs. Demographers need training in other social sciences, like political science and economics; likewise, other social scientists need to better understand the science behind demography, including appropriate attention to both the power and the limitations of demographic analysis. Professional associations and universities have a role to play in facilitating exchanges between demographers and other social scientists, and in educating the public and policymakers about the potential insights as well as the unavoidable limitations of analyses focused on the implications of demographic data and projections.

The three regions we have examined have vastly different histories, politics, economies, and cultures, and yet it is remarkable how similar the dynamics of demographic distortion are in all three. The convergence of the three regional cases we examine here is striking for many reasons. It is evident that the braiding of ideological conflicts into debates over population issues is inherent in all political systems and structures. There are numerous structural parallels in the overlap between population and politics in our three regions. In all of them population becomes a prominent, and sometimes predominant, political matter at certain times and under certain conditions. There is a common set of factors that determines the contours of population politics in particular cases. We discuss them in turn.

The Powers of the State

Population politics reflect long-term ideological divisions over where the boundary *should be* between the state and the domain of private life. Some people see the need for constant vigilance over the creeping expansion of state power; others see the state as the necessary agent of social reform, whose commitment to protect the rights of the nation as a whole take precedence over local or private rights.

There is also the vexed question of whether the family is a domain so much at the heart of personal freedom that it must be walled off against intrusions by state actors into its autonomous space. Should governments encourage higher fertility? Play matchmaker to promote marriage? How do governments perceive the role of women, their bodies in particular, in pursuing state goals, whether population, economic, or other? Does the state, or its highest courts, have the right to block a woman's choice to limit her fertility through abortion, contraception, or sterilization? Is the fetus a "person" protected by national laws, constitutions, or international human rights principles, and if so, does such protection begin at conception or at a particular gestation age? It is evident that the balance of powers in different states among legislative, executive, and judicial authorities will determine how and in what forms debates over population questions are posed, evaluated, and resolved.

These political institutions—the means by which policies get made and implemented—matter. For example, while authoritarian China has a history of highly coercive policies, Japan's liberal democratic government still actively tries to intervene in raising fertility, but has not been coercive. We might go further in thinking about the role of democracy: A recent study by the United Nations showed that countries with *no* professed fertility policy have scores on the Democracy Index nearly twice as high as the average score of countries with policies to *raise* fertility.[2] While measures to raise population totals have rarely been effective, both democratic and authoritarian regimes have tried to implement them.

Ethnic, Racial and Religious Composition of the Population

Changing ethnic, racial, or religious composition of the population has ignited political firestorms that almost always have led to the distortion of demographic analysis and data, especially under conditions that combine high or rising migration with low or declining fertility. A study from the United Nations found that "Exposure to rhetoric, messaging or media about global or domestic population size correlated to viewing immigration rates as too high."[3] These shifts in composition, particularly when minorities are seen as threatening the "domination" of a state by its majority ethnic group, provide impetus for political campaigns to return to a past in which the majority felt less under siege.

To go back to "once upon a time" always distorts the past and clouds responsible discussion about the future, and yet demographers cannot ignore the facts of political life that frame their work. There can be real benefits of immigration for both the immigrants and their receiving societies (and in many cases their sending societies). And yet it is also true that that high rates of immigration to countries with low levels of fertility can lead to relatively rapid rates of change in demographic composition, which often contribute to worsening ethnic tensions and anti-immigrant political rhetoric, sentiment, and behavior. In part, that grim generalization is due to insufficient attention to managing some of the predictable stresses that may accompany proportionally large immigration. In one of its lead articles in 2024, the editors of *The Economist* argued that Canada offers a case study of such insufficient attention by the decade-old government then led by Justin Trudeau. The leader states that the Trudeau government adopted policies designed to substantially expand immigration admissions, but neglected to ensure comparable expansion of schooling, housing, and healthcare services. There ensued severe housing shortages and rising housing costs, inadequate education and health services, and popular anger against both Prime Minister Trudeau and his Liberal Party, and more generally against Canadian immigration policy.[4]

Demographers do public service by providing useful data on and analysis of fertility or ethnicity, and in many cases, data are used to apportion resources (financial, educational, infrastructural), and to allocate political representation. But demographers do not get to decide how people use their data once brought into public debate. A journal article on changing racial composition can be used just as easily to promote national solidarity as to fuel fears of "replacement."

One development of European origin warrants brief attention here: a right-wing conspiracy theory called the "Great Replacement theory," initiated by the French writer Jean Raspail around 1973 and then reconfigured in 2010 by the French writer and *agent provocateur* Renaud Camus. These fear-filled diatribes have been embraced later by some activists in many other European countries and subsequently in the United States and Canada. They rest on anxiety about the intentional replacement of Europeans and White North Americans by those of non-European descent and their supporters.[5] This view may be termed "White extinction anxiety," since what matters more than the replacement of one ethnic group by another is the profound sense of loss of control of the future by the "replaced" group. Such anxiety over demographic replacement is in no way limited to these geographies, but instead stretches worldwide and includes the effects of internal migration in multiethnic low-income societies such as India.[6] This is one reason why eugenics has failed to disappear from conversations about population. Indeed, improvements in reproductive technology continue to raise the possibility of designing babies not just with fewer intellectual or physical disabilities, but with selected physical and mental traits. The furor over "Great Replacement" arguments is both regrettable and likely to continue well into the foreseeable future.

The Threat of Globalization and Nostalgia for the World We Have Lost

States may lose territory, shift borders, or establish outposts an ocean away, but the core of a state is really its people. Because population is at the heart of what makes a state, changes to that population can be elevated to the level of an existential threat. Millions of citizens of one country choose to live in another; other groups see themselves as forced to escape the violence or poverty of their own place of birth to find better conditions of life elsewhere. A nation's people includes its diaspora, who in many ways share the experiences of their kinsmen in the home country. And yet while expatriate populations have grown, national populations in many parts of the world have ceased to grow. As hard as China's leaders have worked to position the country as a global powerhouse and regional hegemon, it is no surprise that news of China's slow loss of population, which some estimate may have begun in 2022, would yield official concern. In the unlikely event that fertility rates in China were to remain constant at current (2024) low levels to the end of the 21st century, the Chinese population would be almost 900 million smaller than it is today.[7]

Anxiety over current or prospective population decline seems to elide easily with fears of a loss of standing and influence in global affairs. Declining national population totals, even if small in size, touch many such fears. Among them is fear of the eclipse of the sovereignty of European nations by the European Union, or of national economies by multinational companies and trading blocs.

The profile of global institutions such as the United Nations Security Council or the World Economic Forum are likely to reflect the demographic past more so than the demographic future. Yet the prospect of reform is a perfect example of the blending of demographic and political anxieties.

Consider the following scenario: What would be the reaction to proposing that India replace France on the UN Security Council in 2045, one hundred years after the founding of the United Nations? Should the most populous nation—estimates for India in 2045 cluster around 1.6 billion—deserve a place on the Security Council? India's population is likely to be nearly 25 times larger than that of France. If France's replacement by India on the Security Council were seriously proposed, should we expect some European political leaders to play on racial fears of the same kind as Jean

Raspail conjured up in his 1973 nightmare novel *The Camp of the Saints*? His dystopia told the story of the uninvited mass arrival of the wretched and the poor from India to France. His novel of physical displacement carried an emotional charge that surely would be transferred to a debate over the political displacement of France by India on the UN Security Council. Even if the Security Council's number of permanent members were to grow to accommodate India, it would be hard to avoid the sight of politicians capitalizing on the image of a decline in European power on the world stage.

Think about similar anxieties over the ethnic composition of the United States. In 2018 the Brookings Institution published a report stating that in 2045 the United States will become a minority White nation. They said, in that year "whites will comprise 49.7 percent of the population in contrast to 24.6 percent for Hispanics, 13.1 percent for blacks, 7.9 percent for Asians, and 3.8 percent for multiracial populations."[8] Even though official US terminology is confusing ("Hispanic" means those who respond yes to the question, "Are you of Hispanic origin?," but some who identify as "Hispanic" also self-report their "race" as "White"), it is foolish to imagine that nativist parties in the United States would not use incendiary language to decry the decline of the White race in the United States. The United States is not alone; in Lebanon, India, Nigeria, and many other countries around the world, an accurate count of different ethnic, religious, and racial groups has explosive implications.

Rage over declining numbers or declining fertility always entails distortion. There is nothing intrinsically malevolent about population decline, however defined. Some ecologists welcome it as an important prerequisite for future environmental stability. What matters is not the demographic reality, but how that reality is inserted into the engines of political anxiety.

Immigration is neither intrinsically positive nor negative with respect to the development of any society, though large-scale immigration does often test social cohesion in many ways. The presence of large numbers of new immigrants exposes the native-born to worry about the loss of the world they knew in their youth. That world has gone, they cry, and no one can bring it back.

Let us put this kind of nostalgic anxiety in a relatively trivial context. If we have a look at a photograph of the last English football team that won the World Cup in 1966, we can see what "replacement theory" is all about. That 1966 team was all White. In 2021, three Black players on England's national football team missed penalty kicks in the European championship game against Italy, sending England crashing out of the competition. The online racial abuse they suffered hinted at the underlying problem.[9] A totally White Britain—something that never existed anyway—represents for many people the powerful Britain of the past. Turning away from the European Union in 2016 was an attempt to resurrect that vision of the United Kingdom as a world power independent of her European neighbors. Immigration fears were not only about racial, linguistic, or ethnic differences, but also about the loss of Britain's standing as a great power. Many people living in nations with a brilliant past behind them see immigration as another nail hammered into the coffin of their former greatness.

It is true that joining the European Union did mean sacrificing a degree of national sovereignty for a modicum of collective economic and strategic security. Other countries have similar tensions over how to preserve national identities within the European Union. Those worried about declining national population totals tend to see them as self-evident signs of national decline, and interpret immigration as an additional threat to the (indigenous) nation's future.

Whatever splits emerge within European countries, the demographic future looks clear. The forces pushing down European fertility, like those pushing up extra-European migration to Europe, may be too strong to counter without the adoption of policies presenting conflicts with commitments to individual and human rights. Depending on unpredictable political developments, it is possible that both smaller families and repeated waves of migratory flows may be Europe's future. Smaller families are the East Asian future too, though forceful actions to control migration may be more acceptable in political and cultural terms there than in either Europe or North America.

Family Forms and Gender Roles

There are some ironies in the reality that culturally conservative notions of what is women's "natural" place in society may be one driver of the low fertility rates that vex many people who hold conservative views, especially in East Asia. Citizens take it upon themselves to make different decisions about marriage and childbearing (and therefore work to redefine "the family" in a way that runs counter to state preferences). The state scrambles to recover the old ways through policies to encourage marriage and childbearing, but to date with only limited effect. Women's shifting preferences for labor market participation, education, and childbearing have been at the heart of this development across all of our regions from 1945 on. What remains clear is that the more family forms change, particularly as marriage and childbearing rates decline, and the more gender equality rules are enforced, the more likely it is that there will be a conservative backlash against threats to "the family." Yet, attempts to double down on patriarchal norms in the name of raising fertility rates will only result in more extreme antagonism, particularly among women, the targets of such attempts. We see this backlash in the "4B movement" in South Korea. Elites in China, where patriarchal policies are already in place, and in the United States, where proponents of traditionalist rhetoric are becoming more vocal, would be wise to see South Korea's experience as a warning.

Adapting to Demographic Decline

Perhaps the best way to conclude this book is to say that those who think they can hold back the demographic tide of low fertility need to think again. Even costly measures intended to increase very low fertility rates have so far not proven to be as effective as desired by many governments. Financial approaches to low fertility do not account for the powerful shift in values that has driven the move to smaller families in many societies. These values certainly could shift again in the future, and a larger-family norm begin to take hold. But because of the long-lasting momentum of demographic change, countries in which such countershifts might occur after their populations were already declining would continue to register negative growth for several decades. Thus, even with the potential for higher births in the future, the norm for the next several decades in much of the world seems likely to be low fertility, which in the absence of very large immigration inflows would imply slowly growing or declining population sizes, and shifts toward older age compositions. Those that do seek or allow high levels of immigration in this context would likely see unusually rapid changes in ethnic/religious/racial/linguistic composition, with attendant cultural and perhaps political effects.

Although they are limited in their ability to control fertility rates, particularly when they respect the human rights regimes that currently prevail in most developed countries, governments could decide to implement far more effective measures to restrain irregular and disorderly transnational migration than those of the past decades. The sticking point is that in liberal democracies such measures are likely to be opposed, and possibly blocked, by a variety of activist and interest groups. Indeed, the feared future of low fertility combined with high migration is already with us in many countries, even if the future is less terrifying than fearmongers want us to believe. Yet decades of elite support for expansive immigration and globalization policies have failed to win over substantial sections of these countries' populations, and over the last decades substantial numbers have begun to vote in support of political movements that oppose liberal immigration and free trade policies.

Humility is in order here. No one can accurately forecast the course of cultural and political shifts. We can, though, let the past be our guide and use what we have learned about the ways cultural, political, *and* demographic shifts work in tandem to anticipate how they might play out in the future. Chronicling these developments is a first step in helping the public understand their consequences and to adapt to them with as much compassion and good sense as we can muster. Considering how population data and research will be used as we undertake them is also essential.

This does not mean that scientific work should be changed or watered down; it means that there is a role for those who provide well-informed and accurate translations of such research for policymakers and advocates to use. Good data continue to be important, and so does interpretation of data. Yet, the plethora of data already available and improvements underway in data collection, quality, and analysis, including AI, have not reduced the likelihood of garbled interpretations and weaponization of evidence based on population research. Perception will always matter and mistrust is rampant. Informed and balanced demographic information is required for rational public debate, and can offer political leaders and broader publics alike a valuable forum to consider what may be needed to address the unprecedented demographic changes that are already underway and seem likely to continue for the foreseeable future.

Given what we know about population history even well before the period we chronicle here, we expect population politics of the future to be just as volatile as it is today, because it is always tied to core identities and values. The other driver of distortion is intentional manipulation, and that is much harder to combat than misunderstanding or ignorance.

The declines in population size that would likely result from long-term low fertility are not necessarily a problem to be solved today (although systems such as entitlements that were built around an assumption of high fertility are a problem), but we recognize that governments see them as such, and some are aiming to raise fertility rates, adjust public pension systems, or increase immigration. Continuing to bring a political lens to bear on these issues is crucial because they are in no sense apolitical.

National-level policymakers can play an important role in establishing antialarmist norms, and policymakers, civil society leaders, and local citizens can work to foster strong, inclusive communities of conversation. Local leaders can, in theory, be more reactive to the pain points caused by real or perceived demographic change and put in place supports to rectify omissions and launch remedies. These include creating local forums for community members to come together, providing adequate human resources in schools so that students of all backgrounds can learn, and making sure that housing, health, and other local infrastructure are not overtaxed in a way that creates volatile resentments of one group against another.

Friction over demographic change seems inevitable, given the effects low fertility and age structure changes have on the economy and society, the political incentives for sounding alarms, and even the human tendencies toward dividing the world in two between in-groups and out-groups. Still, we hope that our book raises awareness of the inevitability of invective and distortions so that naming them moderates their dangerous consequences. A more rational conversation about demographic change is in everyone's interest. Helping to make population politics a useful tool rather than merely a cudgel to beat one's opponents over their heads has been our purpose in this book. To have taken a step in the direction of greater sanity in a field that is marred throughout the world by exaggeration and invective is not a choice; it is a necessity.

Notes

Introduction

1. Population Division UN Department of Economic and Social Affairs, *World Population Prospects 2022: Summary of Results*, United Nations (New York, July 2022), https://www.un.org/development/desa/pd/sites/www.un.org.development.desa.pd/files/wpp2022_summary_of_results.pdf. The 2019 edition had reported the proportion as "close to half," so this was a remarkable shift.
2. Carl Minzner, "China's Population Decline Is Not Yet a Crisis. Beijing's Response Could Make It One," *CFR Blog* (January 26, 2023), https://www.cfr.org/blog/chinas-population-decline-not-yet-crisis-beijings-response-could-make-it-one.
3. Sara Hertog, Patrick Gerland, and John Wilmoth, *India Overtakes China as the World's Most Populous Country*, United Nations, Department of Economic and Social Affairs (New York, April 2023), https://www.un.org/development/desa/dpad/wp-content/uploads/sites/45/PB153.pdf.
4. Elon Musk tweeted on January 17, 2023, "Population collapse is an existential problem for humanity, not overpopulation!" https://twitter.com/elonmusk/status/1615275639564816386.
5. UN, *World Population Prospects, 2024 Revision*, ed. United Nations Department of Economic and Social Affairs (New York, 2024).
6. Vegard Skirbekk, *Decline and Prosper* (London: Palgrave Macmillan, 2022).
7. Eric Hobsbawm, *Nations and Nationalism since 1780: Programme, Myth, Reality* (Cambridge: Cambridge University Press, 1992), 6.
8. Amy Gutmann, *Identity in Democracy* (Princeton, NJ: Princeton University Press, 2003); and Susan J. Henders, ed., *Democratization and Identity* (Boulder, CO: Lexington Books, 2004).
9. Susan J. Henders, "Political Regimes and Ethnic Identities in East and Southeast Asia: Beyond the 'Asian Values' Debate," in Henders, *Democratization and Identity*, 1–24.
10. Gutmann, *Identity in Democracy*.
11. Anthony D. Smith, *National Identity* (London: Penguin, 1991).
12. Jessie Yeung and Junko Ogura, "It's 'Now or Never' to Reverse Japan's Population Crisis, Prime Minister Says," *CNN.com* (January 24, 2023), https://www.cnn.com/2023/01/23/asia/japan-kishida-birth-rate-population-intl-hnk/index.html.
13. Vladimir Putin, *Annual Address to the Federal Assembly* (Moscow, May 10, 2006), http://archive.kremlin.ru/eng/speeches/2006/05/10/1823_type70029type82912_105566.shtml.
14. Thilo Sarrazin, *Deutschland schafft sich ab: Wie wir unser Land aufs Spiel setzen* (München: Deutsche Verlags-Anstalt, 2010).
15. See Philippa Levine, *Eugenics: A Very Short Introduction* (New York: Oxford University Press, 2017).
16. Sarah Mellors Rodriguez, *Reproductive Realities in Modern China: Birth Control and Abortion, 1911–2021*, ed. Jacob Eyferth, Daniel Leese, and Michael Schoenhals, Cambridge Studies in the History of the People's Republic of China (Cambridge: Cambridge University Press, 2023), 18.
17. Gunnar Thorvaldsen, *Censuses and Census Takers: A Global History* (Abingdon, UK: Routledge, 2018).
18. Nicole Acevedo, "Large Share of Latinos Don't Identify with Current Race Categories, Census Bureau Numbers Show" (March 31, 2023), https://www.nbcnews.com/news/latino/latinos-census-dont-identify-racial-categories-rcna77592.
19. See: https://www.foreignaffairs.com/articles/world/2022-01-19/privacy-power.

Chapter 1

1. Agnès Pizzini and Julien Johan, *Children of* (2022), a documentary film available on Terranoa. This film was a joint French, Belgian, and Polish production. https://www.film-documentaire.fr/4DACTION/w_fiche_film/67269_0.
2. Tara Tzara, *The Lost Children: Reconstructing Europe's Families after World War II* (Cambridge, MA: Harvard University Press, 2015), 3.
3. *Dokumentation der Vertreibung der Deutschen aus Ost-Mitteleuropa*, Theodor Schieder (compiler) in collaboration with A. Diestelkamp [et al.] (Bonn: Bundesministerium für Vertriebene, 1953), 78, 155, 160.
4. Volker R. Berghahn, "The United States and the Shaping of West Germany's Social Compact, 1945–1966," *International Labor and Working-Class History* 50 (Fall 1996): 125–32.
5. Benn Steil, *The Battle of Bretton Woods: John Maynard Keynes, Harry Dexter White, and the Making of a New World Order* (Princeton, NJ: Princeton University Press, 2013).
6. Andreas Heinrich, "The Emergence of the Socialist Healthcare Model after the First World War," in *International Impacts on Social Policy: Short Histories in Global Perspective*, ed. Frank Nullmeier, Delia González de Reufels, and Herbert Obinger (London: Palgrave Macmillan, 2022), 5–46.
7. Conférence de presse de M. Pierre Pfimlin, April 5, 1946, 80/AJ/75, Archives nationales, Paris (AN).
8. Louis Chevalier, *Le problème démographique Nord-Africain* (Paris: Presses Universitaires de France, 1947), 209, as cited in Tara Zahra, *The Lost Children: Reconstructing Europe's Families after World War II* (Cambridge, MA: Harvard University Press, 2011), 166.
9. Charles Webster, "Eugenic Sterilization: Europe's Shame," *Health Matters* 31 (Winter 1997), http://groups.csail.mit.edu/mac/users/rauch/nvp/misc/eugenic.html.
10. Philippa Levine, *Eugenics: A Very Short Introduction* (Oxford: Oxford University Press, 2017), ch. 5.
11. R. D. Buchanan, *Playing with Fire: The Controversial Career of Hans J. Eysenck* (Oxford: Oxford University Press, 2010).
12. John Hajnal, "The Marriage Boom," *Population Index* 19, no. 2 (1953): 80–101.
13. John Hajnal, "European Marriage Patterns in Perspective," in *Population in History: Essays in Historical Demography*, ed. David Glass and D. E. C. Eversley (London: Edward Arnold, 1970), 101–43.
14. Ceri Peach, "Postwar Migration to Europe: Reflux, Influx, Refuge," *Social Science Quarterly* 78, no. 2 (June 1997): 269–83.
15. Peach, "Postwar Migration," 270.
16. Caroline Elkins, *Imperial Reckoning: The Untold Story of Britain's Gulag in Kenya* (New York: Henry Holt, 2005).
17. Jim House and Neil MacMaster. *Paris 1961: Algerians, State Terror, and Memory* (Oxford: Oxford University Press, 2006).
18. David Dufresnes, "Procès Einaudi," *Libération*, March 27, 1999.
19. House and MacMaster, *Paris 1961*.
20. Simon Heffer, *Like the Roman: The Life of Enoch Powell* (London: Orion, 1998).
21. Jerzy Berent, "Causes of Fertility Decline in Eastern Europe and the Soviet Union: Part I. The Influence of Demographic Factors," *Population Studies* 24, no. 1 (1970): 35–58; Jerzy Berent, "Causes of Fertility Decline in Eastern Europe and the Soviet Union II: Economic and Social Factors," *Population Studies* 24, no. 2 (1970): 247–92.
22. Berent, "Causes of Fertility Decline I," 39.
23. Michael S. Teitelbaum, "Fertility Effects of the Abolition of Legal Abortion in Romania," *Population Studies* 26, no. 3 (1972): 405–17.
24. Berent, "Causes of Fertility Decline I," 54.
25. Berent, "Causes of Fertility Decline II," 251.
26. Berent, "Causes of Fertility Decline II," 261–62.
27. Berent, "Causes of Fertility Decline II," 281.
28. Michael Kitson and Jonathan Michie, "The Deindustrial Revolution: The Rise and Fall of UK Manufacturing, 1870–1910," University of Cambridge, Center for Business Research, working paper 459 (June 2014), Table 3, p. 16.
29. Kitson and Michie, "The Deindustrial Revolution," 13.

30. J.-P. Fitoussi and E. S. Phelps, "Causes of the 1980s Slump in Europe," https://core.ac.uk/download/pdf/6252244.pdf.
31. Susan George, "A Short History of Neo-Liberalism," *TNI*, March 24, 1999. https://www.tni.org/en/article/a-short-history-of-neoliberalism
32. Philip Martin, "Germany's Guestworkers," *Challenge* 24, no. 3 (1981): 34–42.
33. "Kohl Defends Plan to Halve Turkish Population," *Spiegel online*, August 2, 2013, https://www.spiegel.de/international/germany/helmut-kohl-admits-to-old-plan-to-halve-turkish-population-a-914572.html.
34. Philip L. Martin, "Germany's Guestworkers," *Challenge* (July–August 1981): 35.
35. Philip Ogden, "France: Recession, Politics, and Migration Policy," *Geography* 70, no. 2 (1985), Table 1.
36. Wendy Williams, *Windrush Lessons Learned Review* (London: HMSO, 2020).
37. Paul Ehrlich, *The Population Bomb* (New York: Ballantine Books, 1968), prologue.
38. Suzanne White Junod and Lara Marks, "Women's Trials: The Approval of the First Oral Contraceptive Pill in the United States and Great Britain," *Journal of the History of Medicine and Allied Sciences* 57, no. 2 (April 2002): 117–160, esp. 158.
39. Michael Murphy, "The Contraceptive Pill and Women's Employment as Factors in Fertility Change in Britain 1963–1980: A Challenge to the Conventional View," *Population Studies* 47, no. 2 (1993): 221–43.
40. Peter Kim Streatfield, "The Role of Abortion in Fertility Control," *Journal of Health, Population and Nutrition*, 19, no. 4 (2001): 265–67.
41. Barbara Crane, "The Transnational Politics of Abortion," *Population and Development Review* 20 (1994): Supplement, 241–62.
42. Judith Blake and Prithwis Das Gupta, "Reproductive Motivation versus Contraceptive Technology: Is Recent American Experience an Exception?," *Population and Development Review* 1, no. 2 (December 1975): 229–49.
43. Michael S. Teitelbaum, and Jay Winter, *The Global Spread of Fertility Decline* (New Haven, CT: Yale University Press, 2013).
44. Dirk J. van de Kaa, "Europe's Second Demographic Transition," *Population Bulletin* 44, no. 1 (March 1987): 1–55
45. Peter McDonald, "Gender Equity in Theories of Fertility Transition," *Population and Development Review* 26, no. 3 (2000): 427–39, and Nancy Folbre, "Of Patriarchy Born: The Political Economy of Fertility Decisions," *Feminist Studies* 9, no. 2 (1983): 261–84.
46. Berent, "Causes of Fertility Decline II."
47. France Meslé, Jacques Vallin, and Zoe Andreyev, "Mortality in Europe: The Divergence between East and West," *Population*, 57, no. 1 (2002): 160, English edition.
48. Meslé, Vallin and Andreyev, "Mortality in Europe," 160.
49. Meslé, Vallin and Andreyev, "Mortality in Europe," 160.
50. Jean Raspail, *The Camp of the Saints*, trans. Norman Shapiro (New York: Scribners, 1975), 2.
51. Raspail, *The Camp of the Saints*, 13.
52. Raspail, *The Camp of the Saints*, 10.
53. "The Untranslated Writings of Jean Raspail," *Instauration* (January 1980): 6–10. The author's name is not listed, but is probably American White supremacist Sumner Humphrey. The text may be found at https://www.jstor.org/stable/pdf/community.28144968.pdf?refreqid=fastly-default%3Aedbc032212f25cb21be7fd496dac4783&ab_segments=0%2Fbasic_search_gsv2%2Fcontrol&origin=&initiator=search-results&acceptTC=1.
54. Marc Weitzmann, "A Visit with Jean Raspail, Creator of the 'Great Replacement Theory,'" *Tablet*, March 27, 2017, https://www.tabletmag.com/sections/news/articles/steve-bannon-jean-raspail
55. James McAuley, "How Gay Icon Renaud Camus Became the Ideologue of White Supremacy," *The Nation*, June 17, 2019.
56. Marc Weitzmann, "The Global Language of Hatred Is French: And Anti-Semites and Islamophobes Both Speak It," *Foreign Affairs* 98, no. 1 (April 1, 2019).
57. "Gérald Darmanin annonce engager la dissolution de l'organisation catholique intégriste Civitas après des propos antisémites," *Le Monde*, August 7, 2023.
58. "Un appel de 343 femmes," *Nouvel Observateur*, no. 334, April 5, 1971.

59. "Qui a engrossé les 343 salopes du manifeste sur l'avortement?,"' *Charlie Hebdo*, April 12, 1971. Cabu was murdered in January 2015 in an Islamist terrorist attack on the offices of *Charlie Hebdo* in Paris.
60. Lucie Bras, "Décès de Simone Veil: Retour sur trois jours de débats à l'Assemblée qui ont marqué l'histoire," *20 Minutes*, June 30, 2017, https://www.20minutes.fr/societe/2096983-20170630-deces-simone-veil-retour-trois-jours-debats-assemblee-marque-histoire.
61. Bras, "Décès de Simone Veil."
62. Chloé Leprince, "Violence en politique: Les débats sur l'avortement pour la loi Veil, summum historique," *Radio France*, February 2, 2023; Ronan Tésoriere, "VIDEO. La loi sur l'IVG, le discours historique de Simone Veil," *La Parisienne*, June 30, 2017. https://www.leparisien.fr/laparisienne/actualites/la-loi-sur-l-ivg-le-jour-de-gloire-de-simone-veil-30-06-2017-7100400.php.
63. Dorothy M. Stetson, "Abortion Law Reform in France," *Journal of Comparative Family Studies* 17, no. 3 (1986): 277–90.

Chapter 2

1. Charles S. Maier, "The Collapse of Communism: Approaches for a Future History," *History Workshop* 31 (Spring 1991): 34–59.
2. REF:JART Allen Lynch, "Deng's and Gorbachev's Reform Strategies Compared", *Russia in Global Affairs*, no. 2. (April–June 2012), https://eng.globalaffairs.ru/articles/dengs-and-gorbachevs-reform-strategies-compared/. Accessed June 24, 2025.
3. Sheila Fitzpatrick, *The Shortest History of the Soviet Union* (New York: Columbia University Press, 2022).
4. Christine Danton, "Human Rights in Russia and the Former Soviet Republics: The Health Crisis in Russia," *Human Rights and Human Welfare* 7, no. 1 (2007): Article 41, https://digitalcommons.du.edu/hrhw/vol7/iss1/41.
5. Rifat A. Atun, "The Health Crisis in Russia: Countries in the EU and G8 Must Help Russia Tackle Its Health Crisis," *BMJ: British Medical Journal* 331, no. 7530 (December 17, 2005): 1418–19.
6. Ibid.
7. Rifat A. Atun et al., "Analysis of How Health System Context Influences HIV Control: Case Studies from the Russian Federation," *Bulletin of the World Health Organization*, no. 83 (2005): 730–38.
8. Pavel Grigoriev, France Meslé, Vladimir M. Shkolnikov, Evgeny Andreev, Agnieszka Fihel, Marketa Pechholdova, and Jacques Vallin, "The Recent Mortality Decline in Russia: Beginning of the Cardiovascular Revolution?," *Population and Development Review* 40, no. 1 (March 2014): 107–29.
9. Simon Matskeplishvili and Anna Kontsevaya, "Cardiovascular Health, Disease, and Care in Russia," *Circulation* 144, no. 8 (August 24, 2021): 586–88.
10. Nick Townsend, Lauren Wilson, Prachi Bhatnagar, Kremlin Wickramasinghe, Mike Rayner, and Melanie Nichols, "Cardiovascular Disease in Europe: Epidemiological Update 2016," *European Heart Journal* 37 (2016): 3232–45.
11. Tomas Frejka and Tomáš Sobotka, "Overview Chapter 1: Fertility in Europe: Diverse, Delayed and below Replacement," *Demographic Research*, no. 19 (July–December 2008): 15–46, at 17–20 and Fig. 3.
12. Michèle Picard and Asta Zinbo, "The Long Road to Admission: The Report of the Government of the Republika Srpska," in *Investigating Srebrenica: Institutions, Facts, Responsibilities*, ed. Isabelle Delpla, XavierBougarel, and Jean-Louis Fournel (New York: Berghahn Books, 2012), 141.
13. Timothy J. Hatton, Wolfram F. Richter, and Riccardo Faini, "Seeking Asylum in Europe," *Economic Policy* 19, no. 38 (2004): 5–62. Hatton was the author of the paper, on which Richter and Faini commented.
14. Timothy J. Hatton, "Seeking Asylum in Europe," *Economic Policy* 19, no. 38 (2004): 9.
15. Gert Krell, Hans Nicklas, and Anne Ostermann, "Immigration, Asylum, and Anti-Foreigner Violence in Germany," *Journal of Peace Research* 33, no. 2 (May 1996): 153–70.
16. Paul Kubicek, "Turkish Accession to the European Union: Challenges and Opportunities," *World Affairs* 168, no. 2 (Fall 2005): 67.

17. Brent E. Sasley, "Turkish Leaders and Foreign Policy Decision-Making: Lobbying for European Union Membership," *Middle Eastern Studies* 48, no. 4 (July 2012): 553–66.
18. Martin Malek, "Russia's Asymmetric Wars in Chechnya since 1994," *Connections* 8, no. 4 (Fall 2009): 81–98.
19. Luis Martinez, *The Algerian Civil War 1990–1998*, trans. Jonathan Derrick (London: Hurst & Co., 1998); Dalia Ghanem, "The Birth of Political Islam in Algeria," in *The Shifting Foundations of Political Islam in Algeria*, Carnegie Endowment for International Peace (2019), 1–4, http://www.jstor.com/stable/resrep20971.4.
20. Its director was Xavier Beauvois.
21. https://www.statista.com/statistics/747053/age-algerian-immigrants-in-france/; Alec G. Hargreaves, "Third-Generation Algerians in France: Between Genealogy and History," *French Review* 83, no. 6 (May 2010): 1290–99, and "7 millions de Franco-Algériences," *L'Expression*, February 4, 2015, http://www.lexpressiondz.com/actualite/210070-7-millions-de-franco-algeriens.html.
22. William B. Cohen, "Legacy of Empire: The Algerian Connection," *Journal of Contemporary History* 15, no. 1 (January 1980): 97–123.
23. David Coleman, "The Demographic Effects of International Migration in Europe," *Oxford Review of Economic Policy* 24, no. 3 (2008): 452–76.
24. Shulamit Volkov, "Antisemitism as a Cultural Code: Reflections on the History and Historiography of Antisemitism in Imperial Germany," *The Leo Baeck Institute Year Book*, no. 23 (1978), 25–46, https://doi.org/10.1093/leobaeck/23.1.25.
25. https://www.worldometers.info/coronavirus/#countries.
26. Thomas Piketty, *Capital in the 21st Century* (Cambridge, MA: Harvard University Press, 2013), and Heather Boushey, J. Bradford DeLong, and Marshall Steinbaum, eds., *After Piketty: The Agenda for Economics and Inequality* (Cambridge, MA: Harvard University Press, 2017).
27. Charles Maier, *The Project-State and Its Rivals: A New History of the Twentieth and Twenty-First Centuries* (Cambridge, MA: Harvard University Press, 2023), 373.
28. McKinsey Global Institute, *The Rise and Rise of the Global Balance Sheet* (November 2021), www.mckinsey.com/mgi.
29. "Share of Vote for Major Center-Right and Left Parties in Legislative Elections in France from 1962 to 2024," *Statista Research Department*, September 2, 2024, https://www.statista.com/statistics/1038009/share-of-vote-for-center-right-and-left-parties-in-france/
30. R. Daniel Kelemen, "The European Union's Main Democratic Deficits in Comparative Perspective," in *Dilemmas of European Democracy: New Perspectives on Democratic Politics in the European Union*, edited by Niklas Bremberg and Ludvig Norman (Edinburgh: Edinburgh University Press, 2023), 181–97.
31. https://www.consilium.europa.eu/en/policies/schengen-area/.
32. Robert Tombs, "The English Revolt: Brexit, Euroscepticism and the Future of the United Kingdom," *New Statesman*, July 24, 2016.
33. John Harris, "Britain Is in the Midst of a Working-Class Revolt," *Guardian*, June 17, 2016.
34. D. Clark, "The Brexit Referendum—Statistics & Facts," *Statista*, July 3, 2024, https://www.statista.com/topics/2971/eu-referendum/#editorsPicks.
35. David Coleman, "A Demographic Rationale for Brexit," *Population and Development Review* 44, no. 4 (December 2016): 682.
36. Coleman, "A Demographic Rationale," 683.
37. Coleman, "A Demographic Rationale," 685.
38. Coleman, "A Demographic Rationale," 685.
39. Vote Leave (2016).
40. Alan Bradshaw and Paul Haynes, "The Assemblage of British Politics' Breaking Point," *Journal of Consumer Culture* 23, no. 4 (2023): 971–89.
41. J. Welby, Archbishop of Canterbury, interview in *The House* magazine (2016), https://www.archbishopofcanterbury.org/speaking-and-writing/articles/archbishop-canterbury-interview-house-magazine.
42. Paul Kirby and Jessica Parker, "Germany's Far Right Hails 'Historic' Election Victory in East," BBC, September 2, 2024, https://www.bbc.com/news/articles/cn02w01xr2jo. For earlier developments, see Alec MacGillis, "The Complicated Rise of the Right in Germany's Left-Behind Places," *New Yorker*, September 11, 2024.
43. https://www.einsteinforum.de/veranstaltungen/meaney/.

44. Thomas Meaney, "Teutonic Tremors," *National Interest*, no. 150 (July/August 2017): 52–61.
45. Thilo Sarrazin, *Deutschland schafft sich ab: Wie wir unser Land aufs Spiel setzen* (München: Deutsche Verlags-Anstalt, 2010).
46. Thomas Meaney, "A Celebrity Philosopher Explains the Populist Insurgency," *New Yorker*, February 19, 2018.
47. The European Commission case was *Horváth and Kiss v. Hungary*. In Hungary, it is known by the name of the village in which the Romani families who brought the case lived: the Gyöngyöspata case. See Bernard Rorke, "Antigypsyism in Hungary: The Gyöngyöspata Case versus 'the People's Sense of Justice,'" in *Romani Communities and Transformative Change: A New Social Europe*, ed. Andrew Ryder, Marius Taba, and Nidhi Trehan (Bristol: Bristol University Press, 2021), 83.
48. Peter Krasztev and Jon Van Til, eds., *The Hungarian Patient: Social Opposition to an Illiberal Democracy* (Budapest: Central European University, 2015).
49. "Viktor Orbán Has Not Arrived on the Far Right Just Now by His 'Mixed Race' Comment," Heinrich Böll Stiftung, Prague, August 10, 2022. https://cz.boell.org/en/2022/08/10/viktor-orban-has-not-arrived-far-right-just-now-his-mixed-race-comment
50. "Viktor Orbán Has Not Arrived on the Far Right Just Now."
51. "Budapest Declaration on the Demographic Renewal of Europe," *Population and Development Review* 44, no. 4 (December 2021): 1230–32.
52. "Viktor Orbán Has Not Arrived on the Far Right Just Now."
53. "The Council and the European Parliament Reach Breakthrough in Reform of EU Asylum and Migration System," Council of the EU, Press release, December 20, 2023, https://www.consilium.europa.eu/en/press/press-releases/2023/12/20/the-council-and-the-european-parliament-reach-breakthrough-in-reform-of-eu-asylum-and-migration-system/
54. Barbara Janta (RAND Europe), Lynn M. Davies (Requat Advisory Ltd.), Victoria Jordan (RAND Europe), and Katherine Stewart (RAND Europe), *Recent Trends in Child and Family Policy in the EU European Platform for Investing in Children: Annual Thematic Report* (Brussels: EU, 2019).
55. Myriam Khlat, Walid Ghosn (main coauthors), Michel Guillot, Stéphanie Vandentorren, and the DcCOVMIG Research Team, "Impact of the COVID-19 Crisis on the Mortality Profiles of the Foreign-Born in France during the First Pandemic Wave," *Social Science and Medicine* 313 (2022): 115160, https://www.ined.fr/en/everything_about_population/demographic-facts-sheets/focus-on/high-excess-mortality-for-immigrant-populations-during-the-first-wave-of-the-COVID-19-pandemic-in-france/.
56. "Situational Brief: Migration and COVID-19 in Scandinavian Countries," *Lancet Policy Briefs* (2020): 1–10; "What Has Been the Impact of the COVID-19 Pandemic on Immigrants? An Update on Recent Evidence," in *Tackling Coronavirus (COVID-19): Contributing to a Global Effort* (Paris: OECD, August 2022), http://www.oecd.org/coronavirus/en/?_ga=2.253115657.1094217564.1646294989-529802111.1635931837; and WHO Bureau for Europe, *Report on the Health of Refugees and Migrants in the WHO European Region: No Public Health without Refugee and Migrant Health* (Geneva: WHO, 2018), https://iris.who.int/bitstream/handle/10665/311348/9789289053785-eng.pdf.
57. Clare Bambra, Julia Lynch, and Katherine E. Smith, *The Unequal Pandemic: COVID-19 and Health Inequalities* (Bristol: Bristol University Press, 2021).
58. Elisa J. Sobo and Elżbieta Drążkiewicz, "Rights, Responsibilities and Revelations: COVID-19 Conspiracy Theories and the State," in *Viral Loads: Anthropologies of Urgency in the Time of COVID-19*, ed. Lenore Manderson, Nancy J. Burke, and Ayo Wahlberg (London: UCL Press, 2021), 21–44.
59. Barbara Adam, Ulrich Beck, and Joost van Loon, *The Risk Society and Beyond* (London: Sage, 2000), 6–8.
60. Two of the authors of this book made this argument in *The Global Spread of Low Fertility* (New Haven, CT: Yale University Press, 2013).
61. David Pierson, "China Dismisses Latest Claim That Lab Leak Likely Caused COVID," *New York Times*, February 27, 2023.
62. O. J. Watson, G. Barnsley, J. Toor, A. B. Hogan, P. Winskill, and A. C. Ghani, "Global Impact of the First Year of COVID-19 Vaccination: A Mathematical Modelling Study," *The Lancet Infectious Diseases* 22, no. 9 (June 2022): 1293–302, https://doi.org/10.1016/s1473-3099(22)00320-6.

63. Binoy Kampmark, "The Pandemic Surveillance State: An Enduring Legacy of COVID-19," *Journal of Global Faultlines* 7, no. 1 (2020): 59–70.
64. Jack Goodman and Flora Carmichael, "The Coronavirus Pandemic 'Great Reset' Theory and a False Vaccine Claim Debunked," BBC News (November 22, 2020), https://www.bbc.com/news/55017002.
65. Liram Koblentz-Stenzler and Alexander Pack, "Infected by Hate: Far-Right Attempts to Leverage Anti-Vaccine Sentiment," *International Institute for Counter-Terrorism (ICT)* (2021), https://www.jstor.org/stable/resrep30926.
66. https://www.statista.com/statistics/1102288/coronavirus-deaths-development-europe/.
67. For the data on totals infected and totals who died from COVID, see these statistical sources: https://www.who.int/data/stories/the-true-death-toll-of-COVID-19-estimating-global-excess-mortality; https://www.statista.com/statistics/1102288/coronavirus-deaths-development-europe/; https://www.worldometers.info/coronavirus/.
68. Romain Imbach, "Why Did Donald Trump Accuse NATO Members of Not Paying?," *Le Monde*, November 3, 2024.
69. Olha Pyshchulina and Vasyl Yurchyshyn, *Migration Patterns and Impacts: Lessons from Ukraine Annual Report 2023* (Kiev: Razumkov Centre, 2023), and Stanislav Secrieru, "How Big Is the Storm? Assessing the Impact of the Russian–Ukrainian War on the Eastern Neighbourhood," *European Union Institute for Security Studies (EUISS)* (2022).
70. Marcia Shore, *The Ukrainian Night: An Intimate History of Revolution* (New Haven, CT: Yale University Press, 2018).

Chapter 3

1. UN *World Population Prospects, 2024 Revision.*
2. Development of other forms of modern contraception, especially IUDs, lagged, slowed by concerns about particular devices that proved to have higher risks than their developers had appreciated, in one case leading to the bankruptcy of a major device producer. As such problematic designs were withdrawn and new ones developed, IUDs continued to attract a substantial number of users.
3. Jeff Diamant, Besheer Mohamed, and Rebecca Leppert, "What the Data Says about Abortion in the U.S.," Pew Research Center, March 25, 2024, https://pewrsr.ch/3TRbxDV (accessed June 6, 2025).
4. At a very micro-level, one of the authors (MST) was asked to review plans by his local school board to permanently close one of its four elementary schools, based on earlier projections of continuing enrollment declines. His new projections based on up-to-date data suggested that enrollment increases over the coming decade were more likely than the declines anticipated from the older projections, leading the board to conclude that its planned school closure would be unwise. In the event enrollments did increase (actually close to the upper variant of the new projections), meaning that the board decision had avoided the substantial costs of building new school facilities within the next decade.
5. The beginning of the first wave of feminism is commonly dated to the mid-19th century, continuing into the early 20th century as a major force demanding women's suffrage and legalization of contraception.
6. A second "Red Scare," entwined with the Cold War that followed World War II, was led by Senator Joseph McCarthy (Republican, Wisconsin).
7. The 1918 Sedition Act is more accurately described as a set of amendments to the 1917 Espionage Act.
8. Bombing targets included plutocrats J. P. Morgan and John D. Rockefeller, Supreme Court Justice Oliver Wendell Holmes, and Attorney General A. Mitchell Palmer. In the bombing of Palmer's house, the bomber died and was identified as an Italian American radical from Philadelphia, thereby exacerbating concerns about radicalism imported from southern Europe.
9. One of the most prominent such groups was based in New England and known as the *Galleanisti*, as followers of the Italian anarchist Luigi Galleani, who advocated for violent "direct action" via bombs and assassinations and wrote a "how-to" book on bomb-making. Galleani himself was deported to Italy following the coordinated bombings in eight US cities in June 1919. For a fuller discussion see for example, Leah

Weinryb Grohsgal, "The Anarchist's Chronicle," National Endowment for the Humanities, January 13, 2016, https://www.neh.gov/divisions/preservation/featured-project/the-anarchist%E2%80%99s-chronicle (accessed June 17, 2025).

10. Office of the Historian, United States Department of State, *Milestones: 1921–1936: The Immigration Act of 1924 (The Johnson-Reed Act)*, (accessed July 18, 2020), https://history.state.gov/milestones/1921-1936/immigration-act.
11. Also known as the Hart-Celler Act after its lead sponsors in the US Senate and House of Representatives.
12. US Senate, Subcommittee on Immigration and Naturalization of the Committee on the Judiciary, Washington, DC, February 10, 1965, pp. 71, 119.
13. United States, Congress, House, Subcommittee No. 1 of the Committee on the Judiciary, *Immigration*, Hearings, 88th Congress, 1st sess., 1065, p. 14. Cited in David M. Reimers, "An Unintended Reform: The 1965 Immigration Act and Third World Immigration to the United States," *Journal of American Ethnic History* 3, no. 1 (Fall, 1983): 9–28, https://www.jstor.org/stable/27500293.
14. Cited in Reimers, "An Unintended Reform," 16.
15. Bill Ong Hing, *Defining America: Through Immigration Policy* (Philadelphia: Temple University Press, 2012), 95.
16. US Congress, Senate, Congressional Record, September 20, 1965, 111: 24503.
17. See, for example, Reimers, "An Unintended Reform."
18. Especially Bulgaria, Romania, Hungary, Albania, Poland, and Czechoslovakia.
19. For a more detailed discussion, see Michael S. Teitelbaum, *Falling Behind? Boom, Bust, and the Global Race for Scientific Talent* (Princeton, NJ: Princeton University Press, 2014), 25–69 and 217–18.
20. John T. Correll, "Airpower and the Cuban Missile Crisis," *Air Force Magazine* 88, no. 8 (August 2005), https://www.airandspaceforces.com/article/0805u2/. Archived from the original on June 13, 2013 (accessed June 10, 2025).
21. There is a large literature on the Cuban missile crisis. Well-received book-length volumes include: Max Frankel, *High Noon in the Cold War* (New York: Presidio Press, 2004); and Sheldon M. Stern, *The Cuban Missile Crisis in American Memory: Myths versus Reality* (Stanford, CA: Stanford University Press, 2012).
22. Arthur M. Schlesinger Jr., "New Foreword to 1999 Edition" of Robert F. Kennedy, *Thirteen Days: A Memoir of the Cuban Missile Crisis* (New York: W.W. Norton, 1999), 7.
23. Public Law 89–732, November 2, 1966, To adjust the status of Cuban refugees to that of lawful permanent residents, https://uscode.house.gov/statutes/pl/89/732.pdf (accessed June 17, 2025)
24. M. S. Hamm, "Abandoned Ones: The Imprisonment and Uprising of the Mariel Boat People," NJCRS virtual library, 1995, https://www.ojp.gov/ncjrs/virtual-library/abstracts/abandoned-ones-imprisonment-and-uprising-mariel-boat-people (accessed June 14, 2024).
25. JFK Library, "Military Advisors in Vietnam: 1963," https://www.jfklibrary.org/learn/education/teachers/curricular-resources/military-advisors-in-vietnam-1963.
26. Spencer C. Tucker, *The Encyclopedia of the Vietnam War: A Political, Social, and Military History*, 2nd ed., 4 vols. (Santa Barbara, CA: ABC-CLIO, 2011).
27. Historians often identify this as the Second US Red Scare, in reference to the multiyear First Red Scare that followed the end of World War I, the Bolshevik Revolution of 1917, and a series of domestic bomb attacks by anarchist political groups that continued for several years.
28. Similarly, Democratic Congressional majorities in 1953–1960 and 1969–1976 were also constrained by divided government and the veto powers of Republican presidents Eisenhower, Nixon, and Ford.
29. As used in US English since the 1930s, the word "liberal" carries connotations of progressive or center-left politics rather than the laissez-faire and conservative connotations of the same English word as used in the United States and in Europe during the 19th century—and indeed to the present day in most countries. This is a source of considerable confusion in cross-national political discussion, and accordingly we use the terms "liberal" and "center-left" interchangeably.
30. Cass R. Sunstein, "Did Brown Matter?," *New Yorker*, April 25, 2004, https://www.newyorker.com/magazine/2004/05/03/did-brown-matter here (accessed June 17, 2025).

31. Led by luminaries such as Martin Luther King Jr., Dorothy Height, John Lewis, Bayard Rustin, James Farmer, Roy Wilkins, A. Philip Randolph, and Whitney M. Young Jr.
32. Sara Diamond, *Roads to Dominion: Right-Wing Movements and Political Power in the United States* (New York: Guilford Press, 199).
33. "About Us," The Federalist Society, https://fedsoc.org/about-us (accessed June 16, 2025).
34. Bork, a longtime faculty member at Yale Law School who initially had specialized in antitrust law, had played an important role in the 1973 "Saturday Night Massacre" related to the Watergate investigation. Subsequently Bork was appointed by President Nixon as the US solicitor general, in which position he served from 1973 to1978, and later was nominated and confirmed as a member of one of the most influential second-tier Federal courts, the Court of Appeals for the District of Columbia Circuit.
35. In its 1965 ruling *Griswold v. Connecticut*, the Supreme Court declared unconstitutional a Connecticut law prohibiting the use of contraceptives. The majority decision, written by Justice William O. Douglas, found there to be a "zone of privacy" within a "penumbra" of fundamental constitutional guarantees embodied in the First, Fourth, and Fifth Amendments. This precedent was central to the Court's subsequent and far more controversial decision declaring unconstitutional State laws prohibiting abortion before the 24th week of pregnancy (*Roe v. Wade*, 1973). Nearly 50 years later the Supreme Court overruled its *Roe v. Wade* precedent and returned power to regulate abortion to the States. *Dobbs v. Jackson Women's Health Organization*, No. 19–1392, 597 U.S. (2022).
36. *The Economist*, Lexington, "A Hell of a Senator: Ted Kennedy's Death Leaves a Messy Hole in American Public Life," United States section of the print edition, August 27, 2009, https://www.economist.com/united-states/2009/08/27/a-hell-of-a-senator (accessed June 14, 2025).
37. Cited in Nina Totenberg, "Robert Bork's Supreme Court Nomination 'Changed Everything, Maybe Forever,'" National Public Radio, *It's All Politics*, December 19, 2012, 4:33 p.m., https://www.npr.org/sections/itsallpolitics/2012/12/19/167645600/robert-borks-supreme-court-nomination-changed-everything-maybe-forever (accessed June 4, 2023).
38. Ron Elving, "How the Supreme Court's Conservative Majority Came to Be," National Public Radio, July 1, 2023, 10:00 a.m. ET, https://www.npr.org/2023/07/13/1185496055/supreme-court-conservative-majority-th omas-trump-bush.
39. Allegedly these supporters included David Rockefeller, former secretary of state Henry Kissinger, elder statesman John J. McCloy, and Carter's national security adviser Zbigniew Brzezinski, a group that Brzezinski described as "influential friends of the shah." There is controversy about the roles played by these political heavyweights, as well as about what and when they knew about the shah's health. Rockefeller and Kissinger denied playing the major roles alleged by some commentators. For the perspective of one insider, a US diplomat who was one of those taken hostage, see William J. Daugherty, "Jimmy Carter and the 1979 Decision to Admit the Shah into the United States," AmericanDiplomacy.org (2003), http://www.unc.edu/depts/diplomat/archives_roll/2003_01-03/dauherty_shah/dauherty_shah.html (accessed May 26, 2023).
40. The quality of the medical treatment provided for the Shah's lymphoma, which some authors describe as a "political cancer," is itself a topic of controversy. See for example Ardavan Khoshnood and Arvin Khoshnood, "The Death of an Emperor—Mohammad Reza Shah Pahlavi and His Political Cancer," *Alexandria Journal of Medicine* 52, no. 3 (2016): 201–208, https://doi.org/10.1016/j.ajme.2015.11.002.

Chapter 4

1. Brady E. Hamilton, Joyce A. Martin, and Michelle J. K. Osterman, "Births: Provisional Data for 2024," *Vital Statistics Rapid Release*, National Center for Health Statistics, Report No. 38, April 2025, https://www.cdc.gov/nchs/data/vsrr/vsrr038.pdf (accessed June 19, 2025).
2. Lawrence L. Wu and Nicholas D. E. Mark, "Is US Fertility Below Replacement? Evidence from Period vs. Cohort Trends," *Population Research and Policy Review* 42 (2023): 76, https://doi.org/10.1007/s11113-023-09821-y (accessed March 10, 2024).
3. Wu and Mark, "Is US Fertility Below Replacement?," 17–18.
4. KFF, "Recent Widening of Racial Disparities in U.S. Life Expectancy Was Largely Driven by COVID-19 Mortality," 2, https://www.kff.org/racial-equity-and-health-policy/press-release/recent-widening-of-racial-disparities-in-u-s-life-expectancy-was-largely-driven-by-covid-19-mortality/

5. Steven A. Camarota and Karen Zeigler, "Estimating the Impact of Immigration on U.S. Population Growth," *Center for Immigration Studies*, March 2023, Table 1, https://cis.org/sites/default/files/2023-03/camarota-population-growth_1.pdf (accessed August 7, 2023).
6. Camarota and Zeigler, "Estimating the Impact of Immigration on U.S. Population Growth," 4 and Table 2.
7. US Congress, 99th Congress (1985–1986), "S.1200—Immigration Reform and Control Act of 1986," https://www.congress.gov/bill/99th-congress/senate-bill/1200. For a retrospective view of the Act two decades later by its principal cosponsors, see Romano L. Mazzoli and Alan K. Simpson, "Enacting Immigration Reform, Again," *Washington Post*, September 15, 2006.
8. Jeffrey S. Passel and Jens Manuel Krogstad, "What We Know about Unauthorized Immigrants Living in the U.S," Pew Research Center, July 22, 2024, https://www.pewresearch.org/short-reads/2024/0722/what-we-know-about-unauthorized-immigrants-living-in-the-us/
9. Passel and Krogstad, "What Has Happened with Unauthorized Migration since July 2022?"
10. Mark Gross, Jacqueline Lamas, Yeris H. Mayol-Garcia, and Eric Jensen, "Census Bureau Improves Methodology to Better Estimate Increase in Net International Migration," Washington, DC: US Census Bureau, December 19, 2024, https://www.census.gov/newsroom/blogs/random-samplings/2024/12/international-migration-population-estimates.html(accessed April 2, 2025).
11. Steven A. Camarota and Karen Zeigler, "Foreign-Born Number and Share of U.S. Population at All-Time Highs in January 2025," Washington: Center for Immigration Studies, March 12, 2025, https://cis.org/Report/ForeignBorn-number-and-share-US-Population-AllTime-Highs-January-2025 (accessed April 3, 2025).
12. The main categories are: temporary workers and families; students and families; exchange visitors and families; and diplomats, other representatives, and families. The first category accounts for about one-half of the total. *Estimates of the Resident Nonimmigrant Population in the United States: 2008* (dhs.gov).
13. Data accessed online at: *Estimates of the Resident Nonimmigrant Population in the United States: 2008*, dhs.gov; *Population Estimate Nonimmigrants Residing in the United States: Fiscal Years 2017–2019* (May 2021), dhs.gov.
14. Mahamad Moslimani, "How Temporary Protected Status Has Expanded under the Biden Administration," Pew Research Center, April 21, 2023, https://www.pewresearch.org/short-reads/2024/03/29/how-temporary-protected-status-has-expanded-under-the-biden-administration (accessed August 8, 2023).
15. A useful summary of this CHNV program was published by Refugees International, an organization advocating for its development and continuation. See Yael Schacher, "Setting the Record Straight on CHNV," Refugees International, March 28, 2025, https://www.refugeesinternational.org/perspectives-and-commentaries/setting-the-record-straight-on-chnv/
16. The US Government distinguishes between "affirmative" and "defensive" asylum claims. "Affirmative" asylum claims are typically submitted by persons already inside the United States who are not currently subject to removal proceedings. "Defensive" asylum claims mostly are submitted as a defense against being removed from the country by persons who have been apprehended and placed in removal proceedings. For an informative discussion of this complex system, see Kathleen Bush-Joseph, *Outmatched: The U.S. Asylum System Faces Record Demands; In Search of Control*, United States of America Country Report, Washington: Migration Policy Institute, February 2024, pp. 20–27.
17. Francis Fukuyama, "The End of History?," *The National Interest*, no. 16 (Summer 1989).
18. Until passage of the Homeland Security Act of 2002 that created the Department of Homeland Security in response to the 2001 attacks on the World Trade Center and the Pentagon, responsibility for US immigration policy was vested in the Department of Justice and hence directed by the attorney general.
19. Demetrios G. Papademetriou, "New Directions for Managing U.S.-Mexican Migration," in *Migration, Free Trade and Regional Integration in North America* (Paris: OECD, 1998), 279–87. See also Demetrios G. Papademetriou, "Shifting Expectations of Free Trade and Migration," in *NAFTA's Promise and Reality*, ed. John J. Audley, Demetrios G. Papademetriou, Sandra Polaski, and Scott Vaughan (Washington, DC: Carnegie Endowment for International Peach, 2004), 42, https://carnegieendowment.org/research/2003/11/naftas-

promise-and-reality-lessons-from-mexico-for-the-hemishphere?lan=en(accessed online June 20, 2025).

20. Alison Mitchell, "The China Trade Wrangle: The Bush Speech; Bush, Invoking 3 Presidents, Casts 'Vote' for China Trade," *New York Times*, May 18, 2000, https://www.nytimes.com/2000/05/18/world/china-trade-wrangle-bush-speech-bush-invoking-3-presidents-casts-vote-for-china.html
21. According to a 2018 article in the center-left American magazine *The Atlantic*, "permanent normal trade relations" (PNTR) was a euphemism designed to replace the traditional international trade terminology "most favored nation" (MFN) status, which meant that Chinese imports would be treated as favorably as those arriving from the "most favored nation." Granting China "most favored nation" status had become politically awkward after 1989, when the Chinese government violently suppressed student protests in Tiananmen Square. *The Atlantic* article concluded that adoption of the euphemism "permanent normal trade relations" was effective in gaining US political support for liberalizing trade policies with China. Reihan Salam, "Normalizing Trade Relations with China Was a Mistake," *The Atlantic*, June 8, 2018, https://www.theatlantic.com/ideas/archive/2018/06/normalizing-trade-relations-with-china-was-a mistake/562403/ (accessed June 20, 2025).
22. For an interesting perspective on this shift in bipartisan perspective, see Farah Stockman, "The Queen Bee of Bidenomics," *New York Times*, June 17, 2024, https://www.nytimes.com/2024/06/17/opinion/jennifer-harris-bidenomics.html (accessed June 20, 2025).
23. See, for example, *The Economist*, "The World Is in the Grip of a Manufacturing Delusion," July 13, 2023. https://www.economist.com/finance-and-economics/2023/07/13/the-world-is-in-the-grip-of-a-manufacturing-delusion (accessed June 20, 2025).
24. *The Economist*, "Frenemies: On the Left and Right Economic Philosophy Is Not Just Changing—It Is Converging," July 15, 2023, pp. 17–18.
25. According to Open Secrets, the SEIU union and its affiliates allocated $185 million in political contributions 1990–2022; $26 million for lobbying 1998–2022; and $82 million in "outside spending" 2000–2022. See Open Secrets, "Organization Profiles," 1990–2022.
26. See John B. Judis and Ruy Teixeira, *The Emerging Democratic Majority* (New York: Scribner, 2002). The title of this 2002 book, was a play on a much earlier book by a prominent Republican strategist Kevin Phillips (Kevin P. Phillips, *The Emerging Republican Majority* (New York: Arlington House, 1969)). Phillips had predicted the rise of Republican voting majorities during the subsequent decades, and had helped develop the party's "southern strategy" designed to achieve political realignment of white but conservative Southern voters from reliable Democratic voters to Republican supporters. Decades later Phillips became disenchanted with the Republican Party and became a political Independent. A retrospective article in the progressive magazine *The Atlantic* declared that Phillips's 1969 book "has loomed large in the minds of political operatives and observers ever since, as an essential guide to the Republican 'southern strategy' that gave modern conservatism the depth and durability of New Deal liberalism." Dov Grohsgal and Kevin M. Kruse, "How the Republican Majority Emerged," *The Atlantic*, August 6, 2019, https://www.theatlantic.com/ideas/archive/2019/08/emerging-republican-majority/595504 (accessed June 20, 2025).
27. Phillips, *The Emerging Republican Majority*, 69–71.
28. Ruy Teixeira and John B. Judis, *Where Have All the Democrats Gone? The Soul of the Party in the Age of Extremes* (New York: Henry Holt, 2023).
29. Lori Robertson, "Breaking Down the Immigration Figures," FactCheck.org, Annenberg Public Policy Center, February 27, 2024, https://www.factcheck.org/2024/02/breaking-down-the-immigration-figures/ (accessed June 20, 2025).
30. Juan A. Lozano, "Program That Allows 30,000 Migrants from 4 Countries into the US Each Month Upheld by Judge," Associated Press, March 8, 2024, https://apnews.com/article/immigration-biden-haiti-cuba-nicaragua-venezuela-trial- fac9dc853231ba04ff0ea4e7442057ef (accessed online June 20, 2025).
31. *Actions—H.Res.863–118th Congress (2023–2024): Impeaching Alejandro Nicholas Mayorkas, Secretary of Homeland Security, for high crimes and misdemeanors*, https://www.congress.gov/bill/118th-congress/house-resolution/863/all-actions (accessed June 20, 2025).
32. *Text—H.Res.863–118th Congress (2023–2024): Impeaching Alejandro Nicholas Mayorkas, Secretary of Homeland Security, for high crimes and misdemeanors*, https://www.congress.gov/bill/118th-congress/house-resolution/863/text (accessed June 20, 2025).

33. The first was the unanimous impeachment of Secretary of War William W. Belknap in 1876, who was accused of involvement in a financial scandal. Belknap resigned the same day and hence was never convicted by the Senate.
34. See, for example, Rachel Dobkin, "Economy, Immigration among Key Reasons Voters Backed Trump: Survey," *Newsweek*, November 6, 2024, https://www.newsweek.com/economy-immigration-donald-trump-wins-election-ap-votecast-1981414. See also: *Wall Street Journal*, "How Donald Trump Defeated Kamala Harris and Won Back the White House," *Wall Street Journal*, November 6, 2024, https://www.wsj.com/video/how-donald-trump-defeated-kamala-harris-and-won-back-the-white-house/013A070A-422A-4AB1-89EA-D4822A22B511?page=1
35. Pew Research Center, "How Americans View the Situation at the U.S.-Mexico Border, Its Causes and Consequences," February 2024, https://www.pewresearch.org/politics/2024/02/15/how-americans-view-the-situation-at-the-u-s-mexico-border-its-causes-and-consequences/ (accessed June 16, 2024).
36. According to the BBC, in March 2021 Biden "put Vice-President Kamala Harris in charge of controlling migration at the southern border following a big influx of new arrivals." The BBC described this role as Biden's "immigration czar" and other media used "border czar," though the term "czar" was not a formal designation of her charge. BBC News, "Biden Tasks Harris with Tackling Migrant Influx on US-Mexico Border," March 24, 2021, https://www.bbc.com/news/world-us-canada-56516332.
37. See, for example, Dobkin, "Economy, Immigration among Key Reasons Voters Backed Trump."
38. Title X of the Public Health Services Act, adopted in 1970 by large and bipartisan majorities, increasingly became a partisan issue. Pro-life groups and conservative Republicans began to criticize Title X funding for Planned Parenthood, noting that the organization was the leading provider of abortion services and an active advocate against the restrictions promoted by pro-life groups. Supporters responded by noting that none of Planned Parenthood's Title X funds financed only family planning services and none supported any abortion services or advocacy. While critics acknowledged this to be true, they maintained that this federal funding was fungible and had enabled Planned Parenthood to allocate much of its nongovernmental funding to its abortion services and advocacy.
39. See for example Alexandra Desanctis, "Yes, Some Contraceptives Are Abortifacients," *National Review*, November 4, 2016, https://www.nationalreview.com/2016/11/contraception-birth-control-abortion-abortifacients-ella-plan-b-iud-embryo-life/. For a recent analysis of views among physicians, see Laura E. T. Swan et al., "Physician Beliefs about Contraceptive Methods as Abortifacients," *American Journal of Obstetrics and Gynecology* 228, no. 2 (February 2023): 237–39. https://www.ajog.org/article/S0002-9378(22)00772-4/abstract (accessed June 5, 2025).
40. See preceding chapter.
41. US Department of the Treasury, "FACT SHEET: The American Rescue Plan Will Deliver Immediate Economic Relief to Families," March 28, 2021, https:// home.treasury.gov/news/featured-stories/fact-sheet-the-american-rescue-plan-will-deliver-immediate-economic-relief-to-families (accessed June 5, 2025).
42. In addition, this Act provided "Economic Impact Payments" of up to $1,400 per year for eligible individuals or $2,800 for married couples filing jointly, plus $1,400 for each qualifying dependent including adult dependents. US Treasury, "Economic Impact Payments, 2021," https://home.treasury.gov/policy-issues/coronavirus/assistance-for-american-families-and-workers/economic-impact-payments
43. BBC News, "Why the US Is Launching a $300 Monthly Child Benefit," July 15, 2021, https://www.bbc.com/news/business-55986366 (accessed July 18, 2023).
44. Sarah Al-Arshani, "Decreased Immigration Is Contributing to Rising Prices and Heightened Inflation as Businesses Struggle to Find Necessary Staff amid Labor Crunch," *Business Insider*, May 7, 2022, https://www.businessinsider.com/decreased-immigration-contributing-to-rising-prices-inflation-labor-crunch-2022-5 (accessed June 5, 2024).
45. Teixeira and Judis, *Where Have All the Democrats Gone?*. See also: E. J. Dionne, "Is There Such a Thing as Progressive Nationalism?" *The American Prospect*, April 1, 2019, https://www.americanproject.org/thing-progressive-nationalism/ (accessed June 12, 2025).

46. In a decision that focused heavily on alleged negative impacts on Asian American applicants, the US Supreme Court ruled in a 6-3 decision dated June 29, 2023, that the race-conscious admission policies of Harvard College and the University of North Carolina violated the Constitution, bringing an end to legally sanctioned affirmative action admissions in higher education. US Supreme Court, *Fair Admissions, Inc. v. President and Fellows of Harvard College*, and *Students for Fair Admissions, Inc. v. University of North Carolina*. Ruling available online at: "Read Full Text of the Supreme Court Affirmative Action Decision and Ruling in High-Stakes Case," *CBS News*, https://www.cbsnews.com/news/read-supreme-court-affirmative-action-decision-case-full-text-opinion-ruling/ (accessed June 20, 2025).
47. Gladys Gerbaud, Chase Harrison, and Khalea Robertson, "How Latinos Voted in the 2024 U.S. Presidential Election," *Americas Society and Council of the Americas*, November 6, 2024, https://www.as-coa.org/articles/how-latinos-voted-2024-us-presidential-election
48. Dante Alighieri, *Inferno*, part 1 of *The Divine Comedy*, Canto XX: Circle Eight (Bolgia 4).
49. Kenneth Prewitt, *What Is Your Race? The Census and Our Flawed Efforts to Classify Americans* (Princeton, NJ: Princeton University Press, 2013), 40–41.
50. Cited in Prewitt, *What Is Your Race?*, 41.
51. The actual categories reported in the 1790 census were:

    free white males of 16 years and upwards including heads of families,
    free white males under 16 years,
    free white females including heads of families,
    all other free persons,
    slaves,
    and total inhabitants.
52. Willcox was eminent enough to have been elected to the presidencies of both the American Statistical Association and the American Economic Association. His scientific prominence however may not have precluded him from making assertions that now seem scientifically unfounded, even bizarre. In 1911 he was quoted in the press as declaring to the annual conference of the American Statistical Association in St. Louis that US fertility declines meant that there would be "no children in the United States under five years of age" by 2020, and that the only option for avoiding "race suicide" would be to import babies from France. Of course, it is possible that Willcox was misquoted in this press report. *Fort Scott Daily Tribune* and *Fort Scott Daily Monitor*, "Baby Crop Will Exhaust," January 2, 2011, p. 2
53. Walter Willcox, "Census Statistics of the Negro," *Yale Review* 13 (1904): 204. Cited in Prewitt, *What Is Your Race?*, 60.
54. Prewitt, *What Is Your Race?*, 70.
55. Prewitt, *What Is Your Race?*, 71–72.
56. Prewitt, *What Is Your Race?*, 72.
57. Prewitt, *What Is Your Race?*, 174–82.
58. Office of Management and Budget, "Revisions to OMB's Statistical Policy Directive No. 15: Standards for Maintaining, Collecting, and Presenting Federal Data on Race and Ethnicity," March 29, 2024, https://www.federalregister.gov/documents/2024/03/29/2024-06469/revisions-to-ombs-statistical-policy-directive-no-15-standards-for-maintaining-collecting-and

Chapter 5

1. The gap between Eastern Asia and Europe in 1960 was actually 32 years, because the impact of the Great Famine in China brought down life expectancy for the region in aggregate. Population Division UN Department of Economic and Social Affairs, *World Population Prospects, the 2022 Revision* (UN DESA, 2022), https://population.un.org/wpp/.
2. Deborah Oakley, "American–Japanese Interaction in the Development of Population Policy in Japan, 1945–52," *Population and Development Review* 4, no. 4 (1978).
3. Zhongwei Zhao and Yohannes Kinfu, "Mortality Transition in East Asia," *Asian Population Studies* 1, no. 1 (2005): 6.
4. Adeline Seow and Lee Hin-Peng, "From Colony to City State: Changes in Health Needs in Singapore from 1950 to 1990," *Journal of Public Health Medicine* 16, no. 2 (1994): 149–158, https://www.jstor.org/stable/45160472?read-now=1#page_scan_tab_contents.
5. Ik Ki Kim, "Demographic Changes in Korea during the Period of 1960–2000," in *Generational Change and Social Policy Challenges Australia and South Korea*, ed. Ruth Phillips (Sydney: Sydney University Press, 2007), 60.

6. Eui Hang Shin, "Effects of the Korean War on Social Structures of the Republic of Korea," *International Journal of Korean Studies* 5, no. 1 (2001): 134.
7. Son-Ung Kim, "Population Policies in Korea," in *Economic Development, Population Policy, and Demographic Transition in the Republic of Korea*, ed. Robert Repetto et al., Series in the Modernization of The Republic of Korea: 1945–1975 (Cambridge, MA: Harvard University Press, 1981), 198.
8. Kim, "Demographic Changes in Korea during the Period of 1960–2000."
9. Zhao and Kinfu, "Mortality Transition in East Asia," 5.
10. Vaclav Smil, "China's Great Famine: 40 Years Later," *BMJ (Clinical Research Ed.)* 319, no. 7225 (1999), https://doi.org/doi:10.1136/bmj.319.7225.1619.
11. Kimberly Singer Babiarz et al., "An Exploration of China's Mortality Decline under Mao: A Provincial Analysis, 1950–80," *Population Studies* 69, no. 1 (2015), https://doi.org/doi:10.1080/00324728.2014.972432, https://www.ncbi.nlm.nih.gov/pmc/articles/PMC4331212/.
12. Tyrene White, "China's Population Policy in Historical Context," in *Reproductive States: Global Perspectives on the Invention and Implementation of Population Policy*, ed. Rickie Solinger and Mie Nakachi (New York: Oxford University Press, 2016), 336.
13. Shin, "Effects of the Korean War on Social Structures of the Republic of Korea," 136.
14. Tai-Hwan Kwon, "The National Family Planning Program and Fertility Transition in South Korea," in *Population Policies and Programs in East Asia*, ed. Andrew Mason, East-West Center Occasional Papers: Population and Health Series (Honolulu: East-West Center, 2001).
15. Kwon, "The National Family Planning Program and Fertility Transition in South Korea," 42–43, 44, 51.
16. Kim, "Demographic Changes in Korea during the Period of 1960–2000," 66.
17. Kyung Ae Cho, "Korea's Low Birth Rate Issue and Policy Directions," *Issues and Perspectives* 27, no. 1 (2021): 6, https://www.ncbi.nlm.nih.gov/pmc/articles/PMC9334168/pdf/kjwhn-2021-02-16.pdf.
18. Oakley, "American–Japanese Interaction in the Development of Population Policy in Japan, 1945–52," 619.
19. "History," 2024, https://www.taiwan.gov.tw/content_3.php (accessed February 27, 2024).
20. Laavanya Kathiravelu and Junjia Ye, "Jurong West, Singapore," in *Diversities Old and New: Migration and Socio-Spatial Patterns in New York, Singapore and Johannesburg*, ed. Steven Vertovec (Basingstoke Palgrave Macmillan, 2015), 46.
21. Mui Teng Yap, "Population Policies and Programs in Singapore," in Mason, *Population Policies and Programs in East Asia*, 90.
22. Kwon, "The National Family Planning Program and Fertility Transition in South Korea," 51–52. Demographers are divided as to the role of population pressure from high fertility in leading to rapid urbanization between 1945 and 1970.
23. Tai Hwan Kwon, *Demography of Korea: Population Change and Its Components, 1925–1966* (Seoul: Seoul National University Press, 1977), 203–205; Shin, "Effects of the Korean War on Social Structures of the Republic of Korea," 134–35.
24. Shin, "Effects of the Korean War on Social Structures of the Republic of Korea," 136.
25. Shin, "Effects of the Korean War on Social Structures of the Republic of Korea," 136.
26. Kim, "Demographic Changes in Korea during the Period of 1960–2000," 55–56.
27. Yap, "Population Policies and Programs in Singapore," 91.
28. See Sarah Mellors Rodriguez, *Reproductive Realities in Modern China: Birth Control and Abortion, 1911–2021*, Cambridge Studies in the History of the People's Republic of China (Cambridge: Cambridge University Press, 2023), 24.
29. Rodriguez, *Reproductive Realities in Modern China*, 4.
30. Frank Dikötter, *The Discourse of Race in Modern China* (Hong Kong: Hong Kong University Press, 1992), https://www.frankdikotter.com/publications/discourse-of-race.pdf.
31. Fifth National People's Congress, "China's New Marriage Law," *Population and Development Review* 7, no. 2 (1981): 370, https://www.jstor.org/stable/1972649.
32. Rodriguez, *Reproductive Realities in Modern China*, 3.
33. White, "China's Population Policy in Historical Context," 333.
34. Ma Jisen, "The Politics of China's Population Growth," *Asian Perspective* 22, no. 1 (1998): 45–46, http://www.jstor.org/stable/42704155.

35. Yi Chen and Yi Zhao, "The Timing of First Marriage and Subsequent Life Outcomes: Evidence from a Natural Experiment," *Journal of Comparative Economics* 50, no. 3 (2022): 713–731, https://www.sciencedirect.com/science/article/abs/pii/S0147596722000245.
36. Tyrene White, *China's Longest Campaign: Birth Planning in the People's Republic, 1949–2005* (Ithaca, NY: Cornell University Press, 2006), 135.
37. White, "China's Population Policy in Historical Context," 336.
38. In Susan Greenhalgh, *Just One Child: Science and Policy in Deng's China* (Berkeley: University of California Press, 2008), 88.
39. White, *China's Longest Campaign*, 137.
40. Susan Greenhalgh, "Shifts in China's Population Policy, 1984–1986: Views from the Central, Provincial, and Local Levels," *Population and Development Review* 12, no. 3 (1986): 492–94.
41. Greenhalgh, "Shifts in China's Population Policy, 1984–1986," 492–93.
42. Greenhalgh (1986) cites Huang, 1985, on p. 493. Huang, Huiliang. 1985. "Difficulties of controlling Shaanxi's population analyzed." *Shaanxi Ribao*, August 5, 1985, in *JPRS, Political, Sociological and Military—China Report*, October 10, 1985: 101–102.
43. Greenhalgh, "Shifts in China's Population Policy, 1984–1986," 498.
44. Greenhalgh, "Shifts in China's Population Policy, 1984–1986," 506, 509.
45. Kim, "Population Policies in Korea," 201.
46. Scholars debate the relative size of public-private roles in this policy. See Kwon, "The National Family Planning Program and Fertility Transition in South Korea," 42.
47. Kwon, "The National Family Planning Program and Fertility Transition in South Korea," 40.
48. Kwon, "The National Family Planning Program and Fertility Transition in South Korea," 49.
49. "Mother-Child Health Act of 10 May 1986," Republic of Korea (1990), https://www.ilo.org/dyn/travail/docs/1755/mother%20and%20child%20care%20Act.pdf.
50. "The Emigration Law," in *Law No. 1030, March 9, 1962, last amended by Law No. 1439, November 5, 1963*, Republic of Korea (1962).
51. Kim, "Population Policies in Korea"; "The Emigration Law."
52. Kim, "Population Policies in Korea," 205–207.
53. Yap, "Population Policies and Programs in Singapore," 91–92.
54. Theresa Wong and Brenda S. A. Yeoh, *Fertility and the Family: An Overview of Pro-Natalist Population Policies in Singapore*, Asian MetaCentre for Population and Sustainable Development Analysis (Singapore, 2003), 7.
55. Yap, "Population Policies and Programs in Singapore," 94–97.
56. In Wong and Yeoh, *Fertility and the Family*, 8.
57. Miho Ogino, "From Abortion to ART: A History of Conflict between the State and the Women's Reproductive Rights Movement in Japan after World War II," in *Reproductive States: Global Perspectives on the Invention and Implementation of Population Policy*, ed. Rickie Solinger and Mie Nakachi (New York: Oxford University Press, 2016), 99.
58. "Too Many Babies? Japan Tries All-Out Birth Control," *Newsweek*, May 8, 1950, 42.
59. Charles F. Westoff, "The Commission on Population Growth and the American Future: Its Origins, Operations, and Aftermath," *Population Index* 39, no. 4 (1973).
60. Oakley, "American-Japanese Interaction in the Development of Population Policy in Japan, 1945–52," 622.
61. Aiko Takeuchi-Demirci, "The Color of Democracy: A Japanese Public Health Official's Reconnaissance Trip to the US South," *Southern Spaces* (March 18, 2011), https://southernspaces.org/2011/color-democracy-japanese-public-health-officials-reconnaissance-trip-us-south/.
62. Takeuchi-Demirci, "The Color of Democracy: A Japanese Public Health Official's Reconnaissance Trip to the US South." Homei, Aya. "The Science of Population and Birth Control in Post-War Japan," in *Science, Technology and Medicine in the Modern Japanese Empire*, ed. David G. Wittner and Philip C. Brown (New York: Routledge, 2016), 227–243, Chap. 14.
63. The EPL legalized abortion without a lengthy fight between civil society and the central government, unlike in many Western contexts. Koya, Yoshio. "A Study of Induced Abortion in Japan and Its Significance," *The Milbank Memorial Fund Quarterly* 32, no. 3 (1954): 282–293.
64. Koya, "A Study of Induced Abortion in Japan and Its Significance," 282.
65. Aya Goto et al., "Abortion Trends in Japan, 1975–95," *Studies in Family Planning* 31, no. 4 (2000): 301–308, https://www.jstor.org/stable/172238.
66. Ogino, "From Abortion to ART" 100.

67. Ogino, "From Abortion to ART."
68. Ogino, "From Abortion to ART," 107.
69. "Academic Society to Retract Push for Eugenic Protection Law 66 Yrs after Its Proposal," *The Mainichi* (December 19, 2018), https://mainichi.jp/english/articles/20181219/p2a/00m/0dm/006000c.
70. Derek Cai, "Japan Sterilisation Law Victims Included Nine-Year-Olds," BBC News (June 20, 2023).
71. Kawasaki was a part of this larger firm. Some sources attribute the beginning of the movement to Kawasaki and some to Nippon Kokan, but they are connected. Andrew Gordon, "Managing the Japanese Household: The New Life Movement in Postwar Japan," *Social Politics*, 4, no. 2 (Summer1997): 247.
72. Hisao Aoki, "Family Planning Programs in Industrial Companies," in *Basic Readings on Population and Family Planning in Japan*, ed. Minoru Muramatsu and Tameyoshi Katagiri (Tokyo: JOICFP, 1985), 83.
73. Gordon, "Managing the Japanese Household," 275.
74. Leta Hong Fincher, *Betraying Big Brother: The Feminist Awakening in China* (London: Verso, 2018).
75. Yoonkyung Lee, "Migration, Migrants, and Contested Ethno-Nationalism in Korea," *Critical Asian Studies* 41, no. 3 (2009): 365.
76. Chulwoo Lee, *Report on Citizenship Law: The Republic of Korea*, Robert Schuman Centre for Advanced Studies: European University Institute (Italy, 2019).
77. Lee, *Report on Citizenship Law*, 367. Citing Hyun-sun Kim, "The Construction of Korean Nationality: Full-, Half-, and Non-Koreans," *Sahwe yeongu* (*Social Research*) 12, no. 2 (2006): 77–106 [in Korean].
78. Shin, "Effects of the Korean War on Social Structures of the Republic of Korea," 144–47.
79. Choe Sang-Hun, "World's Largest 'Baby Exporter' Confronts Its Painful Past," *New York Times* (September 17, 2023), https://www.nytimes.com/2023/09/17/world/asia/south-korea-adoption.html.
80. Singapore's leaders frequently use the term "racial" rather than "ethnic."
81. Yap, "Population Policies and Programs in Singapore," 90.
82. *Papers Presented to Parliament, Command Paper. Cmd. 29 of 1966*, Parliament of Singapore (PARL) (Singapore, December 21, 1966), 1–2, https://www.nas.gov.sg/archivesonline/government_records/record-details/7f9c0085-e437-11e7-be76-001a4a5ba61b.
83. *Papers Presented to Parliament, Command Paper. Cmd. 29 of 1966*, 2–3.
84. *Transcript of the Broadcast on August 13 at 10:30pm over Radio Singapore*, National Archives of Singapore: National Library Board (1962), https://www.nas.gov.sg/archivesonline/data/pdfdoc/lky19620726c.pdf.
85. Andreas Ackermann, "'They Give Us the Categories and We Fill Ourselves In': Ethnic Thinking in Singapore," *International Journal on Minority and Group Rights* 4 (1997), 451–467.
86. Singapore's government grouped Indians and Pakistanis together "as a racial group on purely practical considerations." See *Papers Presented to Parliament, Command Paper. Cmd. 29 of 1966*,
87. *Papers Presented to Parliament, Command Paper. Cmd. 29 of 1966.*
88. *Papers Presented to Parliament, Command Paper. Cmd. 29 of 1966*, 4.
89. Xiaowei Zang, "Chapter 1: Introduction: Who Are Ethnic Minorities and How Well Do They Do in China?," in *Handbook on Ethnic Minorities in China*, ed. Xiaowei Zang (Cheltenham, UK: Elgar, 2016), 2–4.
90. Subramaniam Aiyer, "From Colonial Segregation to Postcolonial 'Integration'—Constructing Ethnic Difference through Singapore's Little India and the Singapore 'Indian'" (Doctor of Philosophy University of Canterbury, 2006), 19, https://ir.canterbury.ac.nz/server/api/core/bitstreams/e5349cc0-eb1a-4b18-a95c-bbbdcb50c435/content.
91. Netina Tan, "Constitutional Engineering and Regulating Ethnic Politics in Singapore" (Constitutional Design and Ethnic Conflict Conference, New York University, November 17, 2012).
92. Kathiravelu and Ye, "Jurong West, Singapore," 47.
93. Warwick Neville, "Singapore: Ethnic Diversity and Its Implications," *Annals of the Association of American Geographers* 56, no. 2 (1966), https://www.tandfonline.com/doi/abs/10.1111/j.1467-8306.1966.tb00556.x.

94. Ackermann, "'They Give Us the Categories and We Fill Ourselves In.'"
95. Wong and Yeoh, *Fertility and the Family* 6.
96. Quoted in Wong and Yeoh, *Fertility and the Family*, 8.
97. Yap, "Population Policies and Programs in Singapore," 97–98.
98. Jagdish N. Bhagwati, Klaus-Werner Schatz, and Kar-yiu Wong, "The West German Gastarbeiter System of Immigration," *European Economic Review* 26 (1984).

Chapter 6

1. Yen-hsin Alice Cheng, "Ultra-Low Fertility in East Asia: Confucianism and Its Discontents," *Vienna Yearbook of Population Research* 18 (2020), 83–120.; Erin Hye-Won Kim, "Division of Domestic Labour and Lowest-Low Fertility in South Korea," *Demographic Research* 37, no. 24 (2017), 743–68.
2. David E. Bloom, David Canning, and Jaypee Sevilla, *The Demographic Dividend: A New Perspective on the Economic Consequences of Population Change*, Population Matters (Santa Monica, CA: RAND, 2003). And see https://www.adb.org/publications/growth-and-poverty-lessons-east-asian-miracle-revisited.
3. "World Development Indicators," The World Bank (Washington, DC, 2024, https://databank.worldbank.org/source/world-development-indicators.
4. George W. Bush, "The President's State of the Union Address," news release, January 29, 2002, https://georgewbush-whitehouse.archives.gov/news/releases/2002/01/20020129-11.html.
5. Motoko Rich, "Olympics Open with Koreas Marching Together, Offering Hope for Peace," *New York Times*, February 9, 2018, https://www.nytimes.com/2018/02/09/world/asia/olympics-opening-ceremony-north-korea.html.
6. Andrea Rizzi, "A Look at Japan's Demographic Collapse, Through the Eyes of Its Youth," *El País (USA)* (June 6, 2023), https://english.elpais.com/international/2023-06-06/a-look-at-japans-demographic-collapse-through-the-eyes-of-its-youth.html.
7. *2024 World Population Data Sheet*, Population Reference Bureau (Washington, DC, 2024).
8. Ruhai Bai et al., "Projections of Future Life Expectancy in China up to 2035: A Modelling Study," *Lancet* 8, no. 12 (2023), E915–22, https://www.thelancet.com/journals/lanpub/article/PIIS2468-2667(22)00338-3/fulltext.
9. Bai et al., "Projections of Future Life Expectancy in China up to 2035."
10. Population Division, UN Department of Economic and Social Affairs, *World Population Prospects, the 2022 Revision*, (UN DESA, 2022), https://population.un.org/wpp/.
11. Haizheng Li and Xiangyuan Li, "The COVID-19 Pandemic's Impact on the Chinese Economy," *China Currents* 22, no. 1 (2023), https://www.chinacenter.net/2023/china-currents/22-1/the-COVID-19-pandemics-impact-on-the-chinese-economy/.
12. Zhanwei Du et al., "Estimate of COVID-19 Deaths, China," *Emerging Infectious Diseases* 29, no. 10 (2023), 2121–24, https://wwwnc.cdc.gov/eid/article/29/10/23-0585_article.
13. Hong Xiao and Zhicheng Wang, "Excess All-Cause Mortality in China after Ending the Zero COVID Policy," *Infectious Diseases* 6, no. 8 (2023), e2330877, https://doi.org/doi:10.1001/jamanetworkopen.2023.30877, https://jamanetwork.com/journals/jamanetworkopen/fullarticle/2808734.
14. Shinya Tsuzuki and Philippe Beutels, "The Estimated Disease Burden of COVID-19 in Japan from 2020 to 2021," *Journal of Infection and Public Health* 16, no. 8 (2023), 1236–43, https://www.ncbi.nlm.nih.gov/pmc/articles/PMC10210821/.
15. Hyonhee Shin, "COVID-19 Shrinks Life Expectancy in S. Korea for First Time since 1970," *Reuters* (December 1, 2023), https://www.reuters.com/business/healthcare-pharmaceuticals/COVID-19-shrinks-life-expectancy-skorea-first-time-since-1970-2023-12-01/.
16. *Report on Excess Mortality during the COVID-19 Pandemic up to June 2022*, Ministry of Health Singapore (Singapore, September 2022), https://www.moh.gov.sg/docs/librariesprovider5/resources-statistics/reports/report-on-excess-mortality-during-the-COVID-pandemic-18sep2022.pdf.
17. Cheng, "Ultra-Low Fertility in East Asia: Confucianism and Its Discontents."
18. Florian Coulmas, *Population Decline and Ageing in Japan—The Social Consequences*, Routledge Contemporary Japan Series (London: Routledge, 2007), 49.
19. *2023 World Population Data Sheet*, Population Reference Bureau (Washington, DC, 2024).

20. Singapore Department of Statistics, *Key Findings: Census of Population 2020 Statistical Release 1* (2020), 14, https://www.singstat.gov.sg/-/media/files/publications/cop2020/sr1/findings.pdf.
21. Singapore Department of Statistics, *Key Findings: Census of Population 2020 Statistical Release 1.*
22. Cheng, "Ultra-Low Fertility in East Asia," 92.
23. Dai Wangyun, "Unlucky in Love? The Party Is Here to Help," *Sixth Tone* (August 16, 2018), http://www.sixthtone.com/news/1002782/unlucky-in-love-the-party-is-here-to-help.
24. "Pilot Projects Launched in 20 More Cities to Build New-Era Marriage Culture," *Global Times* (May 14, 2023), https://www.globaltimes.cn/page/202305/1290693.shtml.
25. Leta Hong Fincher, *Betraying Big Brother: The Feminist Awakening in China* (London: Verso, 2018), 175, 79.
26. Sam Kim, "South Korea's World's-Lowest Fertility Rate Drops to New Record, Again," *Time* (February 28, 2024), https://time.com/6835865/south-korea-fertility-rate-2023-record-low/. Statistics Korea uses actual population statistics, while the UN uses projections, so figures differ.
27. *International Migration Outlook 2022*, OECD (2022), https://www.oecd-ilibrary.org/sites/cf203c31-en/index.html?itemId=/content/component/cf203c31-en.
28. "International Migration by Age and Sex (National and Foreign)," KOSIS: Korean Statistical Information Service (2023), https://kosis.kr/statHtml/statHtml.do?orgId=101&tblId=DT_1B28025&conn_path=I2&language=en.
29. *Population in Brief 2023*, National Population and Talent Division, Strategy Group, Prime Minister's Office (September 2023).
30. Raquel Rosenbloom and Jeanne Batalova, "Chinese Immigrants in the United States," *Migration Information Source* (January 12, 2023), https://www.migrationpolicy.org/article/chinese-immigrants-united-states.
31. OECD, *International Migration Outlook 2023*, OECD (2023).
32. Kyung Ae Cho, "Korea's Low Birth Rate Issue and Policy Directions," *Issues and Perspectives* 27, no. 1 (2021): 8, https://www.ncbi.nlm.nih.gov/pmc/articles/PMC9334168/pdf/kjwhn-2021-02-16.pdf.
33. Cheng, "Ultra-Low Fertility in East Asia," 97.
34. "Yanagisawa Calls Women Child-Bearing Machines," *Japan Times* (January 28, 2007), https://www.japantimes.co.jp/news/2007/01/28/national/yanagisawa-calls-women-child-bearing-machines/.
35. Kirsten Lesage, *Few East Asian Adults Believe Women Have an Obligation to Society to Have Children*, Pew Research Center (Washington, DC, 2024), https://www.pewresearch.org/short-reads/2024/04/03/few-east-asian-adults-believe-women-have-an-obligation-to-society-to-have-children/.
36. Min Joo Lee, "South Korea's 'N-Po Generation' of Millennials Have 'Given Up' and Its Feminist 4B Movement Is Refusing to Date, Marry or Have Kids," *Fortune* (May 15, 2023), https://fortune.com/2023/05/15/south-korea-millennial-npo-generation-given-up-4b-movement-women/; Anna Louie Sussman, "A World without Men" (March 8, 2023), https://www.thecut.com/2023/03/4b-movement-feminism-south-korea.html.
37. Leta Hong Fincher, *Leftover Women: The Resurgence of Gender Inequality in China*, Asian Arguments (London: Bloomsbury Academic, 2023), 98, 100.
38. Fincher, *Leftover Women*, 80.
39. Fincher, *Leftover Women.*
40. Fincher, *Leftover Women*, 22.
41. Kathy Matsui, "Is Womenomics Working?," *Project Syndicate* (June 7, 2019), https://www.project-syndicate.org/onpoint/is-womenomics-working-by-kathy-matsui-2019-06.
42. "OECD Data Explorer," OECD (2024), https://data-explorer.oecd.org/.
43. *Introduction to the Revised Child Care and Family Care Leave Law*, Japan Ministry of Health, Labour and Welfare (2010), https://www.mhlw.go.jp/english/policy/affairs/dl/05.pdf.
44. "Time Spent in Paid and Unpaid Work, by Sex," OECD.stat (2024), https://stats.oecd.org/index.aspx?queryid=54757#.
45. Fincher, *Betraying Big Brother*, 125–26.
46. "World Bank Gender Data Portal," World Bank (2024), https://genderdata.worldbank.org/countries/china/.

47. Alexandra Stevenson, "China's Male Leaders Signal to Women That Their Place Is in the Home," *New York Times*, November 2, 2023, https://www.nytimes.com/2023/11/02/world/asia/china-communist-party-xi-women.html.
48. Yun Zhou, "Toward a Feminist Reproblematization of China's Low Birth Rate," *Georgetown Journal of International Affairs* (2023), https://gjia.georgetown.edu/2023/01/06/toward-a-feminist-re-problematization-of-chinas-low-birth-rate/.
49. Li and Li, "The COVID-19 Pandemic's Impact on the Chinese Economy."
50. Xinmei Liu, "No Job, No Marriage, No Kid: China's Workers and the Curse of 35," *New York Times*, June 28, 2023, https://www.nytimes.com/2023/06/28/business/china-jobs-age-discrimination-35.html?searchResultPosition=1.
51. Cho, "Korea's Low Birth Rate Issue and Policy Directions," 8.
52. *President Yoon's Government Policies for Enhancing Child-Rearing*, Korea Institute of Child Care and Education (October 2022).
53. "Time Spent in Paid and Unpaid Work, by Sex."
54. Choe Sang-Hun, "South Korea's Plan to Rank Towns by Fertility Rate Backfires," *New York Times*, December 30, 2016), https://www.nytimes.com/2016/12/30/world/asia/south-korea-fertility-birth-map.html.
55. Sam Hyun Yoo and Tomáš Sobotka, "Ultra-Low Fertility in South Korea: The Role of the Tempo Effect," *Demographic Research* 38, no. 22 (2018): 554.
56. Yoo and Sobotka, "Ultra-Low Fertility in South Korea," 566–67; David Grubb, Jae-Kap Lee, and Peter Tergeist, *Addressing Labour Market Duality in Korea* (Paris: OECD, 2007).
57. Cho, "Korea's Low Birth Rate Issue and Policy Directions," 7.
58. Yoo and Sobotka, "Ultra-Low Fertility in South Korea," 550.
59. Susan Greenhalgh, "Shifts in China's Population Policy, 1984–1986: Views from the Central, Provincial, and Local Levels," *Population and Development Review* 12, no. 3 (1986): 495.
60. Tai-Hwan Kwon, "The National Family Planning Program and Fertility Transition in South Korea," in *Population Policies and Programs in East Asia*, ed. Andrew Mason, East-West Center Occasional Papers: Population and Health Series (Honolulu: East-West Center, 2001), 46.
61. Kwon, "The National Family Planning Program and Fertility Transition in South Korea," 45.
62. Kwon, "The National Family Planning Program and Fertility Transition in South Korea," 58.
63. Jae-Mo Yang, "Family Planning Program in Korea," *Yonsei Medical Journal* 18, no. 1 (1977), 64–74.
64. Andrea den Boer and Valerie Hudson, "Patrilineality, Son Preference, and Sex Selection in South Korea and Vietnam," *Population and Development Review* 43, no. 1 (2017), 119–47: 121.
65. den Boer and Hudson, "Patrilineality, Son Preference, and Sex Selection in South Korea and Vietnam," 128.
66. While female infanticide has been a practice historically, it is now highly uncommon.
67. den Boer and Hudson, "Patrilineality, Son Preference, and Sex Selection in South Korea and Vietnam," 128.
68. den Boer and Hudson, "Patrilineality, Son Preference, and Sex Selection in South Korea and Vietnam," 128.
69. Korean Women's Association United KWAU, *NGO Shadow Report: Republic of Korea*, KWAU (Seoul, South Korea, 2011), 25, https://www2.ohchr.org/english/bodies/cedaw/docs/ngos/KWAU_RepublicKorea49.pdf.
70. The representative's full name is Saito Renho, but she is popularly known by her given name and only Renho is used in the meeting minutes.
71. Budget Committee, *197th Diet*, No. 1, House of Councilors (2018).
72. "Anti-Immigrant Party Opposing COVID Measures Wins Diet Seat," *Asahi Shimbun* (July 13, 2022), https://www.asahi.com/ajw/articles/14668905.
73. Min-ho Jung, "Why Korean Conservatives Are More Open to Immigration than Liberals," *The Korea Times*, February 13, 2024, https://www.koreatimes.co.kr/www/nation/2024/03/113_368726.html.
74. Erin Aeran Chung, "Creating Hierarchies of Noncitizens: Race, Gender, and Visa Categories in South Korea," *Journal of Ethnic and Migration Studies* 46, no. 12 (2020): 2502.
75. Chung, "Creating Hierarchies of Noncitizens," 2504.
76. Chung, "Creating Hierarchies of Noncitizens," 2504.

77. Chung, "Creating Hierarchies of Noncitizens," 2503.
78. Yoonkyung Lee, "Migration, Migrants, and Contested Ethno-Nationalism in Korea," *Critical Asian Studies* 41, no. 3 (2009): 363.
79. Lee, "Migration, Migrants, and Contested Ethno-Nationalism in Korea," 364.
80. Chung, "Creating Hierarchies of Noncitizens," 2502.
81. Haye-ah Lee, "Yoon Says S. Korea Needs Immigrant Policies Fit for Global Pivotal State," *Yonhap News Agency* (May 17, 2023), https://en.yna.co.kr/view/AEN20230517007000315.
82. Lee Hsien Loong, "Q9: On Managing Immigration (and Encouraging Babies)," interview by Steve Forbes, *Forbes Global CEO Conference 2019*, 2019, https://www.youtube.com/watch?v=wg16xR33P4A.
83. Loong, interview.
84. Laavanya Kathiravelu and Junjia Ye, "Jurong West, Singapore," in *Diversities Old And New: Migration and Socio-Spatial Patterns in New York, Singapore and Johannesburg*, ed. Steven Vertovec (Basingstoke: Palgrave Macmillan, 2015), 48.
85. Kathiravelu and Ye, "Jurong West, Singapore," 49.
86. Kathiravelu and Ye, "Jurong West, Singapore," 49.
87. Sim Kang Heong, "What Exactly Is the Singaporean Core—and Why This Matters for Locals and Foreign Workers," *DollarsAndSense.sg* (September 10, 2020), https://dollarsandsense.sg/exactly-singaporean-core-matters-locals-foreign-workers/.
88. Loh Chee Kong, "Two-Thirds S'porean Core in Workforce a Firm Target," *Today Online* (August 21, 2015), https://www.todayonline.com/singapore/two-thirds-sporean-core-all-sectors-firm-target.
89. Singapore Department of Statistics, *Key Findings: Census of Population 2020 Statistical Release 1*, 15.
90. Hye-Kyung Lee, "International Marriage and the State in South Korea: Focusing on Governmental Policy," *Citizenship Studies* 12, no. 1 (2008): 109–10, https://www.tandfonline.com/doi/full/10.1080/13621020701794240.
91. Lee, "International Marriage and the State in South Korea," 110–12.
92. Hae Yeon Choo, *Decentering Citizenship: Gender, Labor, and Migrant Rights in South Korea* (Stanford, CA: Stanford University Press, 2016), 2–3.
93. Lee, "Migration, Migrants, and Contested Ethno-Nationalism in Korea," 371, citing Jungmi Hwang, *A Study on Multinationality and Multiculturality of Korean Society* (Seoul: Korea Women's Development Institute, 2007) [in Korean].
94. Lee, "International Marriage and the State in South Korea," 112.
95. Chung, "Creating Hierarchies of Noncitizens," 2508.
96. Erin Aeran Chung, "How South Korean Demographics Are Affecting Immigration and Social Change," in *Demographics and the Future of South Korea*, ed. Chung Min Lee and Kathryn Botto (Carnegie Endowment for International Peace, 2021), https://carnegieendowment.org/2021/06/29/how-south-korean-demographics-are-affecting-immigration-and-social-change-pub-84819.
97. "Some Duped into Sterilization Surgery under Eugenics Law, Parliament Report Says," *Japan Times* (June 20, 2023), https://www.japantimes.co.jp/news/2023/06/20/national/sterilization-report/.
98. Steven Boroweic, "South Korea Turns to Migrant Labor to Fuel Growth," *Nikkei Asia* (October 17, 2023), https://asia.nikkei.com/Spotlight/Asia-Insight/South-Korea-turns-to-migrant-labor-to-fuel-growth.

Conclusion

1. *World Population Prospects 2024: Summary of Results*, United Nations Department of Economic and Social Affairs, Population Division (New York, 2024).
2. UNFPA, *8 Billion Lives, Infinite Possibilities: The Case for Rights and Choices*, UNFPA (New York, 2023), 78.
3. UNFPA, *8 Billion Lives, Infinite Possibilities: The Case for Rights and Choices*, 73.
4. The Economist, "Canada's Trudeau Trap: How the World's Most Reasonable Country Grew Sick of Centre-Left Liberalism," October 19, 2024, https://www.economist.com/leaders/2024/10/17/canadas-trudeau-trap (accessed November 11, 2025).
5. For a brief critical summary of this line of argument, see Brian Duignan, "Replacement Theory," *Encyclopaedia Britannica*, November 19, 2024, https://www.britannica.com/topic/

replacement-theory. For a more detailed discussion, see Richard Alba, *The Great Demographic Illusion: Majority, Minority, and the Expanding American Mainstream* (Princeton, NJ: Princeton University Press, 2020), https://doi.org/10.1515/9780691202112.

6. One of the classics on this subject is Myron Weiner, *Sons of the Soil: Migration and Ethnic Conflict in India* (Princeton, NJ: Princeton University Press, 2015).
7. UN, *World Population Prospects, 2024 Revision* (UNDESA, New York, 2024).
8. William H. Frey, "The US Will Become 'Minority White' in 2045, Census Projects" (September 10, 2018), https://www.brookings.edu/articles/the-us-will-become-minority-white-in-2045-census-projects/.
9. Associated Press, "Racist Abuse Targets 3 English Players Who Missed Penalty Kicks," *VOA News* (July 11, 2021), https://www.voanews.com/a/europe_racist-abuse-targets-3-english-players-who-missed-penalty-kicks/6208140.html.

Index

For the benefit of digital users, indexed terms that span two pages (e.g., 52–53) may, on occasion, appear on only one of those pages.